A HISTORY OF
EAST AND CENTRAL AFRICA

To the Late Nineteenth Century

A HISTORY OF
EAST AND CENTRAL AFRICA

To the Late Nineteenth Century

◆

BASIL DAVIDSON

ANCHOR BOOKS

DOUBLEDAY & COMPANY, INC.

Garden City, New York

1969

FOREWORD

This book was initially composed with students of history in the countries of East and Central Africa in mind. But the new version for Anchor Books will, I hope, prove of use to American readers interested in the historical growth and value of African civilisation.

Though concentrating on East and Central Africa, I have also touched on the history of peripheral lands to the north, west and south: historically, all these lands and peoples belong to the same over-all development. Only with a broad regional approach can one appreciate the full resonance and variety, and, at the same time, underlying unity and interplay of these many cultures and societies. In point of time, I have begun "at the beginning," and carried the record of development and change down to the eve of colonial times and of the emergence of modern nations. All this is primarily the history of the Africans, although other peoples enter the story now and then.

For a long time it was argued outside Africa, and sometimes even inside the continent, that Africans have no history of their own, or none that is worthy of respect. This approach was reflected in textbooks which claimed to teach African history but seldom taught more, in fact, than the history of the Europeans in Africa. Africa's new independence has called for a fresh approach to the study and appreciation of the past; and this is now made possible by advances in scholarly understanding during recent years. In line with such advances, this book attempts to trace the growth and expansion of indigenous civilisation in East and Central Africa, and, at least in significant and simple outline, to show something of the rich historical heritage of Africa's nations of today.

Many people, over the years, have helped me in the study of African history. But for help in the preparation of this book I wish especially to thank Professor B. A. Ogot of the University College of Nairobi for advice at many points; Mr. J. E. F. Mhina, lately of St. Andrew's College, Minaki, for textual criticism; Mr. Neville Chittick, Director of the British Institute of History and Archaeology in East Africa; Dr. G. S. P. Freeman-Grenville of the University of York, Dr. I. N. Kimambo of University College, Dar es Salaam, Mr. Harry Langworthy and Professor J. D. Omer-Cooper of the University of Zambia, and Professor Merrick Posnansky, lately of the University College of Makerere and now of the University of Ghana, for reading the typescript and making valuable criticisms.

BASIL DAVIDSON

ACKNOWLEDGEMENTS

The following sources have been consulted in the preparation of the maps:

D. Abraham, *Historians in Tropical Africa* (Salisbury, 1962) for maps 31 and 32; E. C. Canning for map 9; A. D. Combe for map 10; B. Davidson, *Lost Cities of Africa* (Atlantic Monthly Press) for map 26; B. M. Fagan, *Southern Africa* (Thames & Hudson, 1965) for maps 2, 13, and 33; J. Kirkman, *Men and Monuments on the East African Coast* (Lutterworth, 1964) for map 18; H. S. Lewis, *Journal of African History* (Vol. I, 1966) for map 8; M. G. Marwick, *Sorcery in its Social Setting* (Manchester University Press, 1965) for map 30; J. Middleton and J. Campbell, *Zanzibar* (Institute of Race Relations, 1965) for map 20; R. Oliver for map 3; R. Oliver and G. Mathew, *History of East Africa,* Vol. I (Oxford University Press, 1963) for maps 23 and 24; J. D. Omer-Cooper, *The Zulu Aftermath* (Longmans, 1966) for maps 22, 29, 35 and 36; Professor M. Posnansky, *East African Geography Review* (Vol. I, 1963) for maps 12 and 25; and for map 6 from Prelude to *East African History* (Oxford University Press, 1966); J. E. Sutton, *Azania* (Vol. I, 1966) for map 7; J. Vansina, *Kingdoms of the Savannah* (Wisconsin University Press, 1966) for maps 27, 28 and 34; E. B. Worthington, *Science in the Development of Africa* (C. C. T. A.) for map 5.

I am especially grateful to the following for their help in the preparation of maps for this book: Professor H. Deschamps for map 16; Dr. G. S. P. Freeman-Grenville for maps 14 and 17; Professor M. Posnansky for map 11.

The publishers wish to make acknowledgement to the following for permission to reproduce copyright material: The Clarendon Press, Oxford, for extracts from *Swahili Poetry* by L. Harries, and for an extract from *Heroic Reci-*

tations of the Bahima of Ankole by H. F. Morris, and J. W. T. Allen for an extract from *The Story of Mbega* by R. Allen published in *Tanganyika Notes and Records,* October 1936.

CONTENTS

LIST OF MAPS

I

Introduction

The study of African history has reached an exciting point of growth. Although fewer than a score of years old as a systematic discipline concerned with remote as well as recent times, it can now claim to have become a window on the whole wide world of the African past. If the window is still a narrow one, many devoted scholars are at work enlarging it. Already the view is far wider and longer than ever before, and the history of the Africans has acquired a depth of definition unknown to any earlier generation.

This book offers the picture of the East and Central African past as it stands today. Not all the important details are yet in place, nor will be for many years, while some of those now there may have to be redrawn as knowledge grows more precise. But the general outline already comes firmly through the work of historians, archaeologists and others who labour in the field of historical reconstruction. It is a picture that seems well worth having, even in its present incomplete condition.

East and Central Africa fit well together for the convenience of historical study. They belong, as does indeed the whole broad "middle belt" of Africa from the Indian Ocean to the Atlantic, to the same large processes of cultural growth. In many ways they have developed separately, divided by the skylines of enormous distance. But they have also developed together in certain other ways crucial to them both. Without the gold-mining enterprise of Central Africa, for example, rich coastal cities such as Kilwa could never have achieved their ancient wealth and power. Without cities such as Kilwa, the miners and ivory hunters of the interior would have had a different story. East and Central not only fit well together for the purposes of study: in fundamental ways, they cannot really be studied apart.

I have divided these countries into three regions: respectively the East African Interior (essentially Kenya, Tanzania, and Uganda); Central Africa (essentially Malawi, Zambia, and Zimbabwe (which is at present Rhodesia); and the East African Coast and Islands, for long the scene of cultural developments not present elsewhere.

Three chronological divisions may also be convenient:

1. The Period of Establishment: or the transition from Late Stone Age times through the development of an Early Iron Age until about AD 1000.

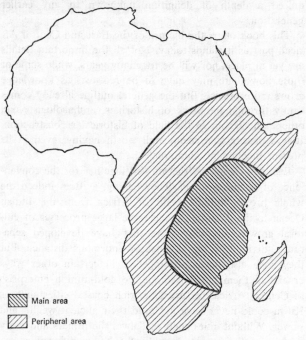

Main area

Peripheral area

1. East and Central Africa:
the areas considered in this book

2. The Period of Expansion, from about AD 1000 until soon after 1800: the centuries of a Mature Iron Age which saw the growth and evolution of all the direct ancestors of the peoples who inhabit East and Central Africa today, with the exception of Indian and European groups.

3. The Period of Crisis, after about 1820 through the colonial period to the present stage of cultural transition from traditional forms of society to the systems of the modern world. Only the early part of this third period is discussed in these pages.

At the same time it needs to be observed that everything we know about the African past confirms that African development has run in an unbroken line from its most distant origins until the present. The Africans are the children of their own past in just the same sense as all other major groupings of humankind, so that even those intrusions or interruptions which have seemed most traumatic and significant of change, such as the colonial period, were in truth no more than episodes or stages in a long continuity of growth. And if it is necessarily the important dates, the big events, the conquering kings or the wise rulers who set the scene for us and tell the drama, one needs always to have in mind the wider scene, the life of every day, the small events and the men and women who are not remembered. To this end I have tried to show the chronology of this history, as far as may be possible in a short book, within the living fabric of its time.

1. THE CRADLE OF MANKIND

All histories have to begin somewhere. But with Africa it is not so easy to know where to begin. For here we have no pleasantly decisive starting points such as the rise of the empire of the Franks or the Norman Conquest of Anglo-Saxon Britain or the coming of the *Mayflower*. Thanks largely to the contributions of archaeology, vital to the study of a past with few or no written records, the history of Africa shades away vaguely into prehistory, while pre-history in any practical sense has no beginning at all. This, however, has an advantage. It makes one look at modern times as the product of what they really are, the outcome of a very distant past.

Most of this book covers some eight and a half centuries. These years after about AD 1000 were the centrally forma-tive centuries of an Iron Age which began in these regions about two thousand years ago and continued, with some exceptions, until the late nineteenth century. They are the period whose understanding is vital to any real grasp of African problems today. They are the centuries of deep indigenous growth. They saw the emergence, reinforce-ment and maturity of a host of peoples and their ways of life.

But where did these peoples come from, who were their ancestors, what were their origins? In prelude to what follows, these are questions that call for at least a brief and summary answer.

The earliest evidence of man's existence comes at pres-ent from the hills of north-western Tanzania. Here, if not elsewhere as well, the earliest direct ancestors of man, of *homo sapiens,* first evolved after countless centuries of natural selection among earlier creatures who were not yet men, but who were also very different from the apes. They evolved through the timeless time of the Early Stone Age when Africa, on present evidence, stood in the forefront of human development.

One authoritative view of all this, though not the only one, is that of Dr. Louis Leakey, who has devoted a lifetime to the study of fossils in East Africa. Dr. Leakey thinks that Darwin was undoubtedly justified in declaring, nearly a century ago, that man had first appeared in Africa. "Now we have found evidence," writes Dr. Leakey, "to show that Darwin was right, and that it was the African continent which saw the emergence of the basic stock which eventually gave rise to the apes, as well as to Man as we know him today." This basic stock consisted of the order of primates, the original family from which men, apes, monkeys, tarsiers and lemurs eventually descended. It emerged more than thirty million years ago in the geological age known as the Oligocene.

But Dr. Leakey awards Africa two other "firsts." He believes that "it was in Africa that the main branch which was to end up as Man broke away from those branches which led to the apes." This is said to have occurred when the family of creatures known as the Hominidae became separated in their evolution from the super-family of the Hominoidae during the Middle or Upper (that is, Later) Miocene, more than twelve million years ago.

But, again, "it was in Africa that true Man separated from his Man-like (but since vanished) cousins, the australopithecines or 'near-men' of two million years ago."[1] When this occurred, there were in existence several different kinds of Hominidae, and it was out of natural selection among these, or among some of these, that *homo sapiens* eventually took shape fewer than 50,000 years ago. By 10,000 years ago all the other members of the family had vanished from the scene, and *homo sapiens* remained the sole survivor.

If Dr. Leakey and others who agree with him are right, then Africa has been the cradle of mankind. Here it was,

[1] L. S. B. Leakey, "The Evolution of Man in the African Continent," *Tarikh* 3 of 1966.

in some words of Posnansky on the subject, "that Man domesticated himself. Selection was no longer a natural process but depended more on Man's ability to transmit ideas, his adaptation to different environments, and on his success as a hunter, using and developing the techniques of making his tools and co-operating with others of his group." All this needed the development of language; and use of language gave another push to progress. From the Early to Middle Stone Age, the brain-size of *homo* seems to have more than doubled. "Much of this evolution took place in Africa and Africa was in some respects the center of the Stone Age."[2]

When *homo sapiens* at last appears upon the African scene, some tens of thousands of years ago, he rapidly develops new communities in many regions of the continent. These communities still live by hunting, but they also have stone tools which are good enough for felling trees and digging up roots. The economy somewhat widens. Man is still a very rare creature, numbered in tens of thousands rather than millions, but his small communities are now beginning to multiply at a faster rate than before. It would also seem that by this period—a Middle Stone Age which modern anthropologists bring down to about 10,000 years ago—there were already present in Africa (and no doubt elsewhere) most of the basic racial stocks, and principal physical variations such as skin-color, from which later "racial diversities" took their rise.

Farming appears in the valley of the Nile about 6500 years ago, develops across Saharan plains which, at that time, are fairly well watered, and emerges to the southward somewhat later. Crops such as dry rice (*oryza glaberrima*) and finger millet begin to be cultivated, maybe as much as four thousand years ago, by early farmers in areas as widely separated as the grassland country of West Africa and the highlands of modern Ethiopia. With these advances, the tiny populations of Middle Stone Age times

---

[2] M. Posnansky, *Prelude to East African History,* 1966, pp. 33–34.

continue to grow larger: even primitive farming greatly helps the food supply. By two thousand years ago there may be as many as four million people in Africa. They have spread, moreover, to every habitable part of the continent. Then and later they make many galleries of rock pictures; in Tanzania alone, there are so far known more than a thousand sites of this Stone Age art.

But in East and Central Africa, as in the rest of Africa south of the Sudanese grasslands, the important "point of change"—of the beginning of transition from the Late Stone Age to new and larger forms of economy and culture—came largely with the development of iron-working technology. Farming cultures in these sub-equatorial areas —in distinction from the Sudan, North Africa, and Middle Asia—seem to have grown with the spread of iron-headed tools. Reasons for this may have included the great sparseness of population, the difficulty of clearing forestland and scrub, and other circumstances upon which the experts are not yet agreed. However that may be, the Iron Age which began in these central-southern and eastern regions rather fewer than two thousand years ago was also and above all the period which saw the development of agriculture, when the peoples of this area were able increasingly to master their environment. Thus it is from about two thousand years ago, or somewhat less, that there began the complex and continuing process of growth and spread which gave them, as the centuries passed, their history of diversification into many hundred ethnic groups, each distinguished by its own language, customs, loyalties and homeland. From a few millions the Africans multiplied to many millions. From primitive beginnings they evolved a civilisation—more exactly, a range of related civilisations— which continued to develop and unfold until the European colonial period, and which, even today, give the Africans their own distinctive attitudes to life. Hence the study of modern Africa has to begin with the study of the Early Iron Age.

2. EARLY IRON AGE
DEVELOPMENTS

Several widely spread types of old pottery have proved useful in explaining where the Iron Age began in Central and East Africa. Of these, the most significant are called "channelled" and "dimple-based," because of the ways in which they were decorated. These types have been found together with signs of iron-making. Such signs are often little clay tubes which early iron-makers used, like others who came after them, so as to connect the "nose" of a pair of bellows to a simple kind of blast furnace for smelting the mineral-bearing rock.

Many sites in eastern Africa have yielded bits of dimple-based pottery or of types related to it, while channelled pottery has been found at sites in Central Africa. This evidence suggests that early Iron Age farming peoples lived in a wide belt of territory running from modern Uganda and Kenya southward through the Eastern Congo, Tanzania, Zambia, Malawi to the lands beyond the Zambezi as far as South Africa.

The Carbon-14 method has provided valuable clues as to approximately when the Iron Age began in East and Central Africa.[1] The oldest Iron Age dates so far obtained

[1] As Carbon-14 dates are of great value to early African history, for which we have few or no written records, it is important to understand the limits of their accuracy. A useful definition of these limits has been lately offered by Professor Thurstan Shaw of the University of Ibadan, Nigeria. Always approximate, these dates are expressed for example as "AD 1000 *plus or minus* 100 years." This means, in fact, that "there are two chances out of three that the actual date lies between AD 900 and AD 1100—but there is still one chance in three that it lies outside these limits. However, it also means that the odds are 20 to one on the actual date lying beween AD 800 and AD 1200, and only one in 20 that it lies outside these limits; while there are only three chances in 1000 that it lies outside the limits AD 700–1300." (*Tarikh,* number 3, 1967).

in Africa south of the Sahara come from central Nigeria, and show that some of the people there had begun to make iron about 2400 years ago. Elsewhere, the Iron Age seems to have begun a little later. The oldest relevant date so far obtained for Central and East Africa is for a vanished settlement at Machili in western Zambia, and suggests that an early Iron Age people lived here about 1900 years ago.

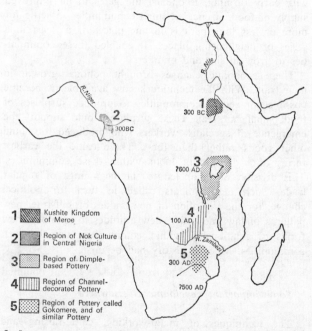

1 Kushite Kingdom of Meroe

2 Region of Nok Culture in Central Nigeria

3 Region of Dimple-based Pottery

4 Region of Channel-decorated Pottery

5 Region of Pottery called Gokomere, and of similar Pottery

2. Important iron-working regions in ancient Africa, with approximate dates at which local peoples began working iron there

Other Carbon-14 dates suggest that the working of iron began at about the same time in neighboring countries. It spread gradually. By about AD 300 several groups of people were making iron in different parts of Central Africa; in northern South Africa by about AD 700; and in some parts of East Africa also by about AD 700 and even, here and there, perhaps considerably earlier.[2] By AD 1000 the knowledge of iron-making was wide-spread throughout the greater part of tropical and sub-tropical Africa.

This Early Iron Age has to be seen as a process of action and reaction. With better hunting and fishing, and with early farming, it opened the gates to an improved supply of food. It enabled small communities to settle for more or less long periods in one place, or at least in a series of neighboring places. It enabled these communities to grow in size and number.

These economic changes brought political growth in their train. With the techniques now available, it became possible for settled communities to produce surpluses of food, small but real. These surpluses could support the emergence of specialist workers who produced tools and other goods rather than food. There came the earliest forms of a division of labor within these communities. This division of labor led to the beginnings of regular trade. Such developments called in turn for political change, for the invention of new modes of self-rule, new patterns of law and order, new attitudes to territory, new forms of relationship within communities and between communities. Modern history had begun.

Some important developments elsewhere

The techniques of metal-working, cattle-raising and food-growing were clearly very useful to peoples of the Early Iron Age. But where did these techniques come from? Or were they invented on the spot?

Historians are not yet agreed about the answers to these

---

[2] The early chronology of Iron Age sites in much of Africa is still a matter for wide research. But recent finds in Kenya suggest that Iron Age techniques were in use there at about the same time as in Central Africa. See p. 34 below.

questions. But something can be said about them from existing knowledge. One probable answer is that the understanding of these vital techniques was first brought into Central and East Africa from West and North Africa, and then was further developed and modified. This is therefore the place to note the importance of other civilisations which had influence on the Early Iron Age in Africa. Foremost among these was the majestic civilisation of Ancient Egypt.

The origins of Egypt go back about 10,000 years, when, because of changes in climate, the level of the Nile began to fall. As its waters went down, small clumps of fertile land appeared; by about 9000 years ago enough land had emerged for nearby Stone Age Africans to go and live on it. Here it was, in the delta of the Nile and along its banks, that early farming first appeared in Africa about 6500 years ago. Out of the development of farming there grew the splendor of Ancient Egypt, no doubt the greatest civilisation of the distant past, flourishing most brilliantly after about 3200 BC when the first of the long line of Pharaohs appeared on the scene.

The people of Ancient Egypt had deep influence on neighbors in North Africa, Western Asia, and Europe. They were pioneers of early science. They excelled in the arts of building and writing. They became powerful in peace and war. Yet it seems they had little influence on most of the peoples of the rest of Africa. Partly, no doubt, this was because Egypt was cut off from most of the rest of Africa by the harsh deserts of the Sahara, and partly because of the great distances which separated Egypt from the tropical lands to the southward and southwestward.

But in one area of Africa, south of Egypt, the civilisation of the Pharaohs had much influence—in the land along the banks of the Middle Nile, in what was afterwards called Nubia and is now the northern part of the Republic of Sudan. This land was rich in gold and other desirable things. Its peoples formed an important early civilisation, known to us as that of Kerma, in about 1700 BC. Then the Egyptians began to conquer and colonise it, building forts and temples there, and founding trading cities. Nubia became a province of Egypt.

Among the Nubians after 1000 BC the strongest were those of the land of Kush. These Kushites began to build a state of their own in about 800 BC, with their capital at Napata on the river Nile. After 750 BC the Kushite kings who ruled from Napata were strong enough to reverse the tide of conquest. They marched northward with their armies and conquered Egypt. For nearly a century until about 650 BC, Kush became a world power.

But while the Kushite state of Napata was Egyptian in many of its beliefs and customs, the Kushites were not Egyptians. They were the descendants of Sudanese-Saharan populations who had long inhabited the regions near the Middle Nile, and they now began to develop their own civilisation in ways that would be culturally different in custom and belief from that of Egypt. This trend was especially strong among the people of the southern part of Kush that is now in the neighborhood of the modern city of Khartum. Here the leading centre of that time was called Meroe, about one hundred miles north of Khartum. Meroe became a leading capital of Kush—perhaps its only capital, but opinions still differ on this—in the sixth or fifth century BC. Here the Meroitic Kushites built a large and imposing city with stone temples, palaces, and dwellings.

A new African civilisation had come into existence. It was based mainly on farming along the banks of the Nile, but also on long-distance trade; among the peoples with whom the Kushites of Meroe traded were the Romans, Arabians, Indians, and many Africans to the west and south of them. It is possible that in somewhat later Meroitic times they also had indirect contacts with China, then under the Han Dynasty of rulers.

Their advances in civilisation included an alphabet of their own, which they appear to have invented soon after about 300 BC.[3] Subsequently they developed a large iron industry, using handicraft methods. Some historians believe that it was partly from Kushite Meroe that the knowledge of iron-working spread southward into the rest of Africa. This civilisation of Meroe prospered until about AD 200. Then it began to decline, and vanished in about AD 350, nearly a thousand years after the foundation of Meroe.

One other civilisation which is important in ancient African history should be mentioned here: Axum. Among the African peoples with whom the Kushites traded were a group of early Ethiopians who lived near the southern shores of the Red Sea. They had begun to be successful traders, in this area, after about 500 BC, learning much from their Arabian neighbors on the other side of the Red Sea, a people called the Sabaeans, some of whom had settled in northern Ethiopia. Out of this mixture of Sabaeans and Ethiopians there emerged another civilisation, whose people were Ethiopians, but who worshipped Sabaean gods and wrote in the Sabaean script.

As time went by, this civilisation became more and more Ethiopian. Like Kushite Meroe, it flourished on trade. Its main port on the Red Sea was Adulis, which became an important maritime trading center. Towards AD 100 these northern Ethiopians made their capital at Axum, in the

---

[3] This Kushite alphabet, and the Kushite script in which it was written, may reasonably be placed among the outstanding cultural achievements of ancient Africa. They were used for a wide range of purposes, such as grave memorials and temple records. By 1967, even though the archaeological excavation of Meroitic Kush remained at an early stage, several hundred inscriptions in the Kushite alphabet and script had been collected by the experts. But because the language of Meroitic Kush is a dead one, the experts cannot yet fully read these old written records. They can make a little use of them, however, because there are several Kushite inscriptions which are "doubled" with Egyptian hieroglyphic translations: since the latter can be understood, the sounds of the Kushite letters in these "doubled" inscriptions can also be read. These give us the names of Kushite kings, queens, and notables, as well as a few Kushite words. Otherwise the deciphering of Kushite script remains one of the as yet unsolved problems of ancient African history.

hills to the south of the coast. Here they formed a strong state. Some of their temples and tall monuments of stone may still be seen at Axum.

In about AD 320[4] the reigning king of Axum, Ezana, was strong enough to invade the land of the Kushites, and to ravage Meroe and other towns. Soon afterwards he was converted to Christianity. Axum flourished for another four centuries, and became the parent of later Ethiopian civilisation.[5]

Both Meroe and Axum were ancient civilisations which belong to the background of developments in tropical Africa. Just how much influence they had on other African peoples remains unknown; but it was perhaps varied and continuous over a long period. It seems likely that their traders went southward to the northern parts of the Congo, Uganda and Kenya. In ways that we cannot now see, they may have helped the peoples of tropical Africa to evolve new methods of life, notably in farming and in metal-working.

But this does not mean that tropical Africans failed to invent new technologies for themselves. Even if the techniques of farming and metal-working came initially from the north, from such ancient African civilisations as Meroe and Axum, this knowledge had to be adapted before it could be useful, because the land and climate of tropical Africa were different from those of the north. Progress, then as now, was a mixture of the borrowing of new ideas and of the repeated adapting of these new ideas to local conditions.

Who were these early Africans who borrowed and adapted and invented new ways of life? To answer this question, we must return for a moment to the Stone Age.

We have seen that East Africa's early ancestors of mankind, more than two million years ago, had large jaws

[4] This date is questioned by some historians; at the moment, however, most authorities accept it.

[5] See Chapter 5, *Ethiopia*.

and heavy brows. The descendants of these and other types of hominid spread gradually across the world during the Early Stone Age, evolving in the process different shapes and sizes of body and appearance, different skin colors, kinds of faces, types of hair.

Little is known about how all this happened. But what we do know is that the ancestors of most of the different races of modern Man had come into existence before the end of the Middle Stone Age. Of course these races went on changing in appearance as they mingled together and intermarried. Yet the main differences among the major ones—the so-called "black," "white," or "yellow" races—evidently go far back into the Stone Age.

Several different types of Africans were living in central and eastern Africa when the Iron Age began there. One of these peoples seems to have been a type of "tall hunter," but this type has long since disappeared. Another was a type of "short hunter" who were the ancestors of peoples such as the Bushmen and the Twa (Pygmies), who still survive in a few places. Other ancestors of modern East Africans, though not of Central Africans, were another fairly tall people who may be called "North-east Africans" and who were partly related, in distant times, to Western Asians. It is from them that the Cushitic group of languages has descended.[6] Present also, in the north, were the ancestors of many modern East African peoples in the shape of populations who spoke one or other branch of the Central Sudanic and Eastern Sudanic language groups.[7] In Central Africa, meanwhile, there were the ancestors of all the many peoples who now speak one or other of the Bantu languages.

While these groups mingled with one another as the centuries passed, in certain ways they remained distinct. The most obvious differences are those of language, though

---

[6] Not to be confused with the Kushite peoples of the Middle Nile, though it is possible that the Kushites spoke one or other of the Cushitic languages.

[7] Formerly, and sometimes still, called Nilotes and Nilo-Hamites.

bodily and other differences have also continued to exist.
A few groups who speak Cushitic languages still flourish
in the north-east: these include the Somali and the Galla.
Others, in Tanzania, may include the Iraqw of Mbulu, and
Mbugu of Shambalai.

A few peoples who now number no more than a few
thousands have kept to Stone Age ways of life. Among
these are the Twa of the forests of the Congo Basin, the
Hadzapi of Lake Eyasi, and the Sandawe about seventy
miles south of Eyasi. The Hadzapi, whom their neighbors
sometimes call Tindega, Kindiga or Kangeju, do not cultivate and keep no cattle. The only animals they have are
hunting dogs. In recent times the Sandawe have taken to
farming, but formerly they lived like the Hadzapi by fishing, hunting and gathering wild fruits and food plants.

But the direct ancestors of most of the modern peoples
of East and Central Africa were the Sudanic speakers and
the Bantu. From Sudanic speakers have developed many
of the modern peoples of northern Uganda and north-
western Kenya, while Bantu speakers were the ancestors
of nearly all the modern populations of the whole of Central Africa, as well as of the central and southern regions
of East Africa. While Sudanic peoples seem to have led
the way in cattle raising, the Bantu appear to have been
mainly responsible for the spread of farming and metal-
working, although in this respect no clear distinctions can
be drawn and all these techniques were in the course of
time practised by many peoples of both groups.

Their movements reflected their different ways of life.
Sudanic (Nilotic) language peoples, Professor B. A. Ogot
tells us, seem "initially to have moved into areas which
more or less resembled the original hot flat lands of the
Sudan, where their cradleland appears to have been. Unlike the East African Bantu speakers, whose economy on
the whole was based on a forest environment, and who
therefore preferred to settle in high-rainfall areas where
they practised hoe-agriculture, the Nilotes preferred the

short grassland or savannah woodland areas suited to a mixed economy of seed culture and pastoral activities."[8]

Sudanic speakers probably began coming southward into the northerly parts of East Africa more than a thousand years ago, giving rise to peoples such as the Kalenjin of Kenya; while Bantu speakers, as we shall now see, had begun spreading through central and southern Africa, and into parts of East Africa, several centuries earlier.

The Bantu: Growth and spread

Who were the Bantu of long ago, and where did they come from? When did they spread across middle and southern Africa? These questions deserve some attention because of the numerical predominance of the Bantu and their occupation of great regions during the last two thousand years.

In the beginning, of course, the Bantu were among the descendants of Stone Age populations, just like all other ethnic groups of African peoples. Though hypotheses on earliest Bantu origins vary, it seems to have been in the grassland country of the south-eastern Congo Basin that, between about AD Zero and 500, they first began to increase steadily in numbers, to split up into different peoples, and to form "daughter languages" from their original mother language.

They continued to multiply and spread, as the map shows, in later centuries. As they did so, they divided into many separate peoples. Each developed its own language, but all these languages are called by the general name of "Bantu" because they are related to one another. Bantu simply means "people"; it is the plural of *muntu,* a person. The root of the word, *ntu,* is found in all the many languages they speak.

By AD 500 there were many communities of Bantu-

[8] B. A. Ogot, *History of the Southern Luo, East African Publishing House,* 1967, p. 37.

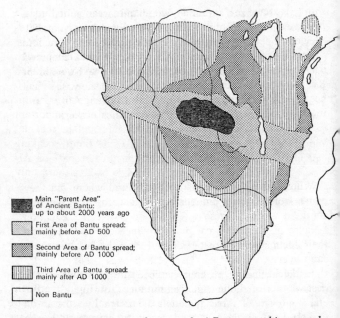

Main "Parent Area"
of Ancient Bantu:
up to about 2000 years ago

First Area of Bantu spread:
mainly before AD 500

Second Area of Bantu spread:
mainly before AD 1000

Third Area of Bantu spread:
mainly after AD 1000

Non Bantu

3. Supposed stages in the spread of Bantu-speaking peoples

language people in Central and East Africa. They lived in
small farming villages, mined and smelted and worked several minerals, notably copper and iron, raising cattle as
well as growing millet and several other crops. They steadily increased their numbers. As they grew more numerous,
they sent off junior clans and families to find new land in
the plains and woodlands to the north-east, south, and
west. The map gives a general view of the way they spread,
and when it is believed on present evidence that they did so.

So the situation of the East and Central African populations in the Early Iron Age, around AD 500–1000, was
as follows: Here and there a few Stone Age peoples were
still living as in ancient times, hunting and gathering wild
plants for food. In the northerly lands, mainly to the north

of Lake Nyanza (Victoria), there were groups of Sudanic (Nilotic) and Cushitic speakers who lived mainly by herding cattle. Elsewhere, and growing rapidly in numbers, there were village communities of Bantu-speaking peoples who tilled the soil as well as raising cattle, and were skilled as metalsmiths.

History has long since done much to change all this. But the general picture remains unaltered in two important ways. Sudanic and Cushitic speakers are still in the majority to the north of Lake Nyanza, while Bantu-speaking people have everywhere occupied the greater part of Africa to the south of it, being ousted here and there only by groups of Europeans who arrived in the late nineteenth and early twentieth centuries.

Climate, soil, tsetse fly

A good deal of progress has been lately made in understanding the ecological circumstances of human growth and spread in these regions: the natural factors which promoted specific forms of expansion, discouraged other forms, and generally framed the possibilities that were open to man. The natural conditions of East and Central Africa are alike in several important ways. These are mainly tropical countries, most of them at much the same height above sea-level. But they also differ much among themselves. Some are hotter and drier than others; some have dense forest, while others have open plains.

During the last two thousand years, there appears to have been little fundamental change in the natural conditions of East and Central Africa—in the annual amount of rainfall, the intensity of heat, the fertility, or lack of fertility, of the soil, and the presence of pests such as the tsetse fly and the malarial mosquito.[9] Many of the forests are smaller than they used to be; and, as we shall see, new

[9] But tsetse fly has spread much more widely in Tanzania, Uganda and Zambia since the last years of the nineteenth century.

crops have come into Africa during this time. But the basic conditions of today are essentially much the same as those of two thousand years ago.

Much of the whole area has always been short of rainfall. As the map shows, large parts of it can expect less than thirty inches of rain in most years, and some parts even less. This lack of rain has limited the possibilities of farming. Here and there the rainfall is so scanty that wide areas of half-desert have come into existence: in the regions bordering on the Sahara, in parts of North-eastern Africa, in the Masai plains of northern Tanzania, in the south-western part of Zambia.

Over much of the area, too, the soils are poor in fertility. They become exhausted by three or four crops, and are easily swept away by storms of rain or flooded rivers.

Adapting themselves to this dryness and poor soil, African stock-breeders such as the Masai long ago adopted a nomadic way of life. It was the only possible way of feeding their cattle.

Many food-growing farmers have had to solve the same kind of problems. Thus the Bemba of north-eastern Zambia, for example, know that they can cultivate a farm for three or four years, but then they must leave the land to lie fallow for perhaps as many as fifteen years. So they move from one farm to another, shifting their villages when all the land around them has been used and must be left fallow. In the absence of artificial fertilisers and other modern scientific methods, no other kind of farming could be successful.

Elsewhere there is more rainfall and better soil. In contrast with the dry Masai plain, for example, the highland countries of the Kikuyu and their neighbors in Kenya, and of the Ganda and their neighbors in Uganda, often receive ten times as much rain annually. Still other peoples have faced the problem of floods that cover their land every year. About half the homeland of the Dinka and the Nuer, in the southern Sudan, goes under water during the rainy season. To meet this problem, the Dinka and the

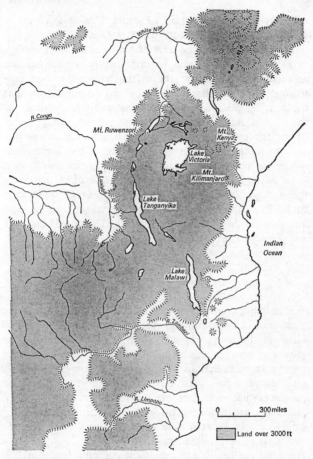

4. East and Central Africa: main physical features

Nuer have worked out a specific seasonal pattern of life.
During the flood time they take refuge in cattle camps
raised on little "islands" in their waterlogged plains. When
the floods recede they drive their cattle to the freshened
pastures and cultivate millet. Another example of the same

problem is that of the Lozi of western Zambia, much of whose land also goes under water once a year.

All the way down the hills of the Western Rift Valley, as far as Lake Kivu and beyond, natural conditions are especially favorable for the raising of cattle. Not surprisingly, the peoples of these upland countries, such as western Uganda, Ruanda, and Burundi are famous for their herds. But elsewhere, as the map shows, the presence of the tsetse fly has made it difficult, or even impossible, to raise cattle. Carrier of various forms of trypanosomiasis —often called *nagana* in cattle, or sleeping sickness in man —the tsetse fly has existed in some parts of Africa since the earliest times of human presence here. Today it is found in dangerous density over about two-fifths of East and Central Africa, but worst of all in parts of Tanzania and Zambia.

More and better supplies of food

If animal domestication was of critical importance to the great transition from Stone Age hunting to settlement and farming, the spread of cattle was no less crucial to the growth of human population. Types of African cattle were present in north-eastern Africa in ancient times. Gradually men drove them southward through those parts of the continent that were free, or fairly free, of the tsetse fly. Humpless cattle, long-horned or short-horned, were being raised in north-eastern Africa—and in far western Africa— as long as five thousand years ago during the Late Stone Age. But the breeds of cattle most common today in East and Central Africa, the humped Zebu and Sanga types, became common only much later, after about AD 700, when East and Central African peoples had already entered, or were entering, their Early Iron Age. These two breeds, Zebu and Sanga, have been of central importance to the growth and welfare of the populations of East and Central Africa.

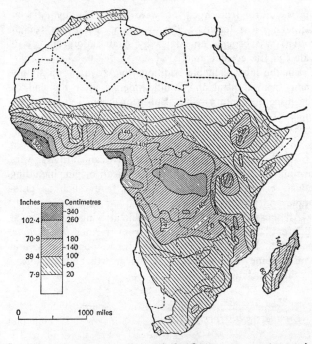

Inches | Centimetres
— 340
102·4 | 260
— 180
70·9 | 140
— 100
39·4 | 60
— 20
7·9

0   1000 miles

5. Africa: mean annual rainfall (figures in centimetres)

Early farmers also cultivated several food crops native to Africa, including sorghum, millet and several roots. After about AD 300 this rather limited range of food was improved by the addition of the valuable type of banana (plantain) which is especially popular in Uganda, but also well-known elsewhere. This banana belongs to the species *musa paradisiaca,* which appears to be native not to Africa but to South-east Asia. It was possibly brought to Africa by Indonesian sailors who first came to the shores of East Africa after about AD 300. It is also possible that these Indonesians brought new types of yam as well. Other Asian food plants, including the sugar-cane and citrus fruits, were carried to Africa across the Indian Ocean during the Early Iron Age, and were taken over by African farmers. After about AD 700 a type of Asian rice (*oryza sativa*) was brought to Africa by Arab sailors and cultivated in the coastal areas.

But the most valuable additions to African food supply came from Central and South America after the end of the fifteenth century, when European crews returned with types of food previously unknown. Europeans introduced these plants to West Africa, and gradually they spread from farm to farm into Central and East Africa. After about AD 1600, many Central and East African farmers were beginning to cultivate crops of American origin, including maize, cassava, sweet potatoes, and fruits such as pineapple and pawpaw.

All these crops of foreign origin, arriving in Africa at different times and spreading from farmer to farmer, helped to build the strength of African populations, and thus became leading factors in the growth and expansion of these societies.

Contacts with foreign lands

Africans were little helped in their progress by the inventions and skills of people in other continents, for they were largely cut off from the rest of the world. But while this isolation was often a major factor in deciding the course of African development, and should be kept in mind, a number of African peoples were by no means without contact with foreign lands.

As the preceding section has shown, Africans were able to make use of foreign contacts to import new food plants. But the value of these contacts was not only in farming; it was also in trade. From about 500 BC there grew up around the Indian Ocean a network of trading communities which embraced many coastal peoples.

At first the ships sailed along the coasts of Arabia and India and north-eastern Africa, and all these countries be-

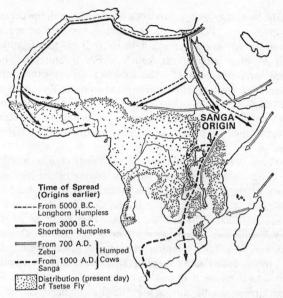

6. *Early movements of different kinds of cattle*

gan exchanging goods with one another. Then Arab and Indian sailors learned how to improve their sails and ships, and how to find their way even when out of sight of land. They took over sailing inventions, such as the magnetic compass, which the Chinese had first discovered; and, becoming bolder, began to take advantage of the force of the seasonal monsoons of the Indian Ocean. The winter monsoon, which blows night and day for several months from the north-east to the south-west, enabled the sailors of western India to reach Arabia and Africa. On the summer monsoon, blowing the other way, they could sail home again. More and more ships made these journeys. The East African coast became part of a wide circuit of trade in which many Asian countries were included. This was to have far-reaching consequences for Africa.

Foreign contacts reached African shores during the

Early Iron Age, before AD 1000, from three main centers of civilisation. First of all, probably in the first or second centuries BC, there came a few ships from the Egyptian and Arabian ports of the Red Sea. For a long time they were rare. But gradually the Red Sea sailors came more often, and pressed further down the coast. By about AD 100 they were coming every year, though still few in numbers, to little trading settlements as far south as Tanzania. Mostly their captains and crews were from southern Arabia.

There is one excellent reason for being sure of all this. In about AD 120 a Greek merchant of one of the Egyptian ports of the Red Sea, possibly Berenice, wrote a guide to the ports and markets of the Indian Ocean trade, including those of East Africa. This book, the *Periplus of the Erythraean Sea* (*Guide to the North-West Indian Ocean*), has survived. It has interesting details which explain the sea routes followed by these early traders: how they sailed out into the Indian Ocean from the ports of the Red Sea and turned southward along the East Coast as far as Rhapta, a port which has long since vanished but was probably on the coast of Tanzania. The *Periplus* relates how the merchants of the Red Sea used to send Arab trading agents who settled among the coastal Africans, married African women, and learned African languages. It describes what the traders bought from coastal Africans —ivory, tortoise shell, and other products such as rhinoceros horn—and what they sold them in exchange: glassware and metal tools from Arabia, and cotton stuffs from India.

Another important influence came from South-east Asia after about AD 300, when sailors arrived from Java and Sumatra, and began to visit the Coast and settle in the island of Madagascar. They brought useful things, among them bananas of a better kind than any that Africans then had. Indonesians also introduced a new type of canoe, with outriggers, that was especially good for work on the seacoast. These outrigger canoes, *ngalawas,* became popular along the Coast; many are still being made even today. Another thing possibly brought by the Indonesians were xylophones, instruments since developed by African musicians into many types, among them amadinda, marimba and zeze.[10]

There were further contacts with Arabia and India after about AD 700. By this time Muslim merchants from Arabia had settled in the seaports of India, Ceylon, South-east Asia and southern China, linking the whole area into the flourishing circuit of the Indian Ocean trade. Now they came more frequently to East Africa. They founded new settlements, drawing East Africa more closely into the Indian Ocean trade, and, indirectly by way of East African ports, the peoples of Central Africa as well. It was at this time that the gold and ivory of inland Africa began to find markets in foreign countries as far as China.

Early social development

Little can be said with any certainty about social systems at the end of the Early Iron Age. Yet it is clear from available evidence that some of them had reached, through the changes brought about by early settlement, farming and metal-using, a point of complexity which contained, if still in embryo, all the essential forms of mature expansion in later times. Well before AD 1000, for example, there were polities in these regions that could claim considerable achievements. A few examples will illustrate this.

By about AD 300 it is known from the work of archaeologists that the first settlements were in being at the famous southern site afterwards called Great Zimbabwe. These settlements were those of early farmers and cattle-raisers who lived in clay-and-thatch huts and knew how to smelt iron. They were few in number and weak in organisation, compared with later times, but they had al-

---

[10] Several scholars doubt whether these xylophones were in fact of non-African origin.

ready entered on the path of social development which was
to lead, a thousand years later, to the famous empire of
the Mwanamutapa.

Further north, in the copper-rich area of the Katanga,
another Iron Age people had established an important
early civilisation by about AD 700. They lived around Lake
Kisale and mined copper. They were skilful in the making
of copper ornaments, and enjoyed some trade with neighbors. Their everyday life had become sufficiently complicated for them to need chiefs; and these chiefs were
buried in special graves with a quantity of copper goods
and other marks of respect.

At about the same time, strong little Iron Age settlements also appeared on either side of the Zambezi river.
These likewise had a much more complicated social organisation than the Stone Age families who still hunted in
their neighborhood.

By about AD 900, some of these Iron Age settlements
had developed into early states, some of which had chiefs.
One of these was described by the Arab geographer, al-
Mas'udi, who travelled down the East Coast in AD 916.
In his book completed in Cairo in AD 943, *The Meadows
of Gold and Mines of Gems,* he relates that he took ship
at Sohar, in the south Arabian land of Oman, and sailed
across the Indian Ocean until he came to the East Coast.
He says that he went as far south as the island of Kanbalu.
We do not know exactly where Kanbalu was, but perhaps
it was Pemba or Zanzibar. Here, he wrote, the climate of
the mainland "is warm and its soil is fertile." And it was
in this region, perhaps around the mouths of the Zambezi
river, "that the Zanj have built their capital." ("Zanj" was,
and occasionally still is, a familiar Arab word for Africans.) These Zanj, al-Mas'udi found, had built a big state,
ruled by a king who had other kings under his command
and a large army. The people, al-Mas'udi says, chose their
supreme king in order that they should be governed justly.
"But once the king becomes a tyrant, and stops ruling
justly, they kill him and refuse to allow his descendants

to inherit the throne. They do this, they say, because in ceasing to rule justly the king has ceased to be the son of the Supreme Lord, that is to say the God of Heaven and Earth. They call this Supreme Lord by the name of Mkalanjalu. . . ."

In this description there may already be glimpsed a great deal, at least in outline, about subsequent state organisation in these regions. The method of choosing a king has usually been by electing one from a number of royal candidates. Many of these kings, in the eyes of their peoples, have had a sacral nature as spokesman of God or the great ancestral spirits. All have been liable to dethronement if they failed badly in their duties. Thus the roots of state organisation were already planted by AD 1000.

Such states must often have taken shape under the influence of long distance trade. Al-Mas'udi lifts the veil on this side of things as well. He tells of a large ivory trade between the people of the state he described and the merchants of the Indian Ocean. "Tusks from their country go generally to Oman. From Oman they are sent to India and China. That is the way they go. And if it were not for this, ivory would be very easy to buy in the Muslim countries (that is, in Arabia and Egypt). But in China the kings and their military or civilian officers need ivory for their carrying-chairs, and they use only ivory for this purpose . . ." By the tenth century, in short, the ivory of East Africa was being used as far afield as the court of the emperor of China.

Looked at from another angle, al-Mas'udi's description of this "kingdom of the Zanj" also does something to lessen the apparent cultural distance between ancient Africa and other parts of the world, including Europe. In explaining that the Zanj could dethrone an unworthy king, al-Mas'udi showed in 943 that they made a clear distinction between the man and the office, the king and the kingship. Now it was precisely this distinction that was insisted on, three hundred years later, by the leaders of English society when they forced their King John to sign

Magna Carta in 1215. The central point about this "great charter," often cited as the foundation of English liberties, was that it restated the right of the English people—in practice, of course, their leading nobles—to harass their king and even drive him off the throne whenever, in al-Mas'udi's words about the Zanj, he "ceased to govern justly."

Afro-European parallels will become numerous as more knowledge comes to hand, and full-scale comparative history grows possible. Already it is luminously clear that while the Africans undoubtedly developed differently from the Europeans, they also developed according to a social logic that was essentially the same. If there is much that is strange and hard for us to understand about the development of the Africans, we should remember that the strangeness and obscurity come from our ignorance of Africans and their history rather than from any African "inferiority" or natural inability. This is a point we shall come back to in Chapter 22.

II

Growth and Expansion after AD 1000

This section contains five chapters on the period between about AD 1000 and 1500. These were centuries of steady growth and expansion from Early Iron Age foundations. The first two of these chapters are concerned with the countries which have now become Kenya, Tanzania, Uganda, Zambia, Malawi, and their immediate neighbors. Then follow two short chapters on certain large developments in North Africa and Western Asia that are necessary to an understanding of later events in Africa, especially along the Coast. Chapter 7 takes up the history of the Coast and Islands, treating it separately because, with the rise of the Indian Ocean trade and the coming of Islam, the coastal cultures became greatly differentiated from their neighbors of the Interior.

This diversification was never so complete as to mean complete separation, if only because it was from the peoples of the Interior that the peoples of the Coast had to obtain their trading commodities, notably ivory and gold. Yet much of the Interior remained outside the Indian Ocean trading network, while Islam did not penetrate inland from the Coast until later times. Throughout this period the links between the coastal peoples of what are now Somalia, Kenya, Tanzania and Mozambique were always closer, and even much closer, than the links between these peoples and their inland neighbors.

A brief note on sources may be useful. Those for the Coast and Islands include a fair number of documentary records made at first- or secondhand by Arab travellers and writers before 1500. Archaeological investigation has lately supplemented these at several crucial points of early foreign influence, such as the Lamu archipelago,[1] Gedi,

---

[1] The small near-shore islands of Lamu, Pate and Manda, all of them important in the history of the Coast.

and Kilwa. After 1500, there is an increasing quantity of European memoirs and reports of varying quality.

Written records for the Interior are altogether lacking until the sixteenth century, unless we bring al-Mas'udi's brief report of the mid-tenth century and a few other similar fragments under this heading. For a long time after that, moreover, the bulk of European reports bear on the Interior only to the extent of Portuguese penetration along the Zambezi valley and at a few other points. But the Iron Age archaeology of the Interior is now fairly well understood, at least in outline, for Kenya, Tanzania, Uganda, Zambia and Zimbabwe (Rhodesia), although that of Malawi only began to be investigated in the late 1960s while that of Mozambique continues as an almost complete blank.

Some good progress has meanwhile been made in another direction: the collection and interpretation of oral tradition, although here too there remain serious gaps. In spite of such gaps, the historical memories of a number of non-literate peoples have already made a useful contribution. A good example is Ogot's research into the traditions of the Luo of eastern Uganda and western Kenya. Until lately it was often said that peoples such as these could yield no worthwhile historical memories because they had never formed centralized states, and so lacked the tradition-remembering customs associated with kings and lines of kings. Ogot has shown otherwise. By patient collection and interpretation of many "clan memories" he has been able to form a picture of Luo migration and settlement as far back as about 1500.

For times earlier than 1500 oral traditions have yielded, not surprisingly, very little. Those of the early kingdoms of Uganda make a partial exception, while royal or chiefly traditions after 1500 have repeatedly helped to explain the origins and development of many states: those of the southern Congo grasslands, those of the metal-exporting peoples between the Zambezi and the Limpopo, those of seventeenth century Zambia, and others.

Even at this relatively early stage of historical reconstruction, it becomes possible with these materials to sketch the movement and emergence of peoples undoubtedly ancestral to those of today.

3. EAST AFRICA: THE INTERIOR
1000–1500

Background to the peopling of Kenya

Little but imprecise archaeological indications are as yet
available about the inhabitants of Kenya during the first
millennium AD. Late Stone Age populations, whether of
"short hunter" or Cushitic stock, were evidently joined by
others who, presumably though as yet by no means certainly, were the distant ancestors of later Bantu-speaking
peoples; and these "Bantu ancestors" are the people who
are generally believed to have introduced the earliest iron-
using cultures.

Yet this can be no more than an hypothesis. It is an
hypothesis, moreover, somewhat weakened by the latest
archaeological work in Kenya. This points to the probable
existence of iron-using cultures in east-central Kenya by
the third century AD,[1] a considerably earlier date than historians have hitherto envisaged in their estimates of
"Bantu-spread" into eastern Africa. If this new evidence is
found to be confirmed, then the earliest iron-using cultures
of Kenya are substantially no later than those of Zambia
and Rhodesia, and may well be related to them. Generally,
this latest evidence suggests a wide extension of similar
iron-using cultures through much of East and Central Africa well before AD 500. It remains to be confirmed that
the peoples who formed them were in fact the ancestors
of later Bantu-speaking groups.

Surviving "folk memory" has little to help us here. Central Kenya traditions speak of five peoples who lived there
before the rise and expansion of its present inhabitants.
These are remembered as the Mwoko and Njuwe, Gumba,

[1] R. C. Soper, "Kwale: An Early Iron Age Site in South-Eastern
Kenya," *Azania* 1967, p. 3.

Athi and Dorobo; all but the last have long since disappeared. In many places, too, there are small saucer-shaped dips in hillsides. These were certainly made by men, and are known as Sirikwa holes; probably they are the places where men lived or kept their cattle, and were possibly dug out by the ancestors of the Kalenjin, who were Sudanic speakers. In other places there are many signs of stone terraces for farming on hillsides, and artificial water channels and ponds; these, it is suggested, were mainly the work of early Bantu populations.

From about AD 1000 the inhabitants, by then mainly Sudanic and Bantu speakers, grew in numbers as they mastered the lands in which they lived, and became the ancestors of all the different African peoples of Kenya today. But they were undoubtedly joined, from time to time, by groups of related peoples who came from outside Kenya. Such movements have given rise to many traditions, of which the most important should be noted. They manifestly contain a core of truth about the distant past, though it must be remembered that they seldom refer to the movement of more than small numbers of incoming people. These newcomers moved into a land that was not much different in appearance from today, except that the forests were bigger, and was peopled by hunters, farmers, and breeders of cattle. Here the newcomers mixed with the more ancient inhabitants, and new cultures gradually evolved and spread.

Of the oldest traditions of such movement, the most important include one that is connected with Shungwaya, an area that evidently lay between the Tana and Juba rivers in north-eastern Kenya and south-eastern Somalia. Shungwaya seems to have been the homeland of coastal peoples whom we know as the Pokomo, Kilindi, Swahili and their neighbors. This explains why the coast of southern Somalia—the northern Banadir Coast—became peopled with the Swahili and their relatives, the Somali arriving here only at a later time.

In Shungwaya a number of Bantu peoples grew in num-

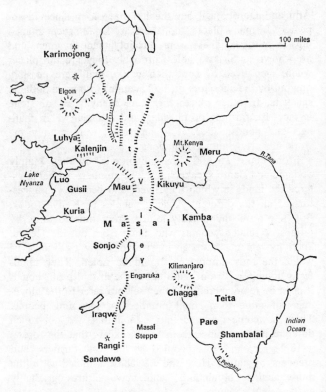

7. Location of some peoples of East Africa

bers and began sending out groups in search of new land. A second reason for movement out of Shungwaya may have been the arrival from the north of groups of Galla who were also searching for new land.

It is also possible that Shungwaya was the first homeland of some of the early ancestors of the peoples of Central Kenya, notably the Kikuyu, Kamba and Chuku. Like the Pokomo along the Coast, some of these Central Kenyan peoples evolved a form of self-rule which had a gov-

erning council called by a similar name. From the root
-ama, such councils were called *ki-ama, nj-ama,* or *nz-ama*
according to local variations of speech.

But this evidence for movement out of Shungwaya into
Central Kenya, even if more than mythical, can refer only
to small groups. The main point to note is that the Bantu
speakers of Central Kenya—the Kikuyu, Kamba and their
neighbors—were well established in their present countries
by AD 1500, while most of their ancestors must have been
living there for many centuries before that time. Their
strong establishment in these lands has been calculated,
though very roughly, by counting the number of groups
of age-grades which are remembered in their traditions.[2]

Sudanic speakers, represented mainly by the ancestors
of the Kalenjin, had likewise begun to grow in numbers
and expand across new territory before AD 1500. This expansion, at least after 1600, is especially associated with
the growth of one of their branches, the Nandi. In about
1500 and after there also began entering Kenya, from the
north, a number of different groups who included the
ancestors of the Luo, Baluyia and Masai, most of whom
arrived from southern Sudan and southern Ethiopia. By
1500 or earlier there were present in Kenya, and growing
steadily in numbers, the direct ancestors of nearly all its
present ethnic groups.

[2] An age-grade, a group of boys or men who were all born within
a few years, is part of a system of self-rule among many African
peoples. Each age-grade has certain duties to perform on behalf of
the community, which it must fulfill over a fixed number of years.
Among the Nandi, for example, each age-grade provided the warriors of that people for a period of fifteen years. Then they retired,
and another age-grade took over. A complete set of age-grades might
cover a period of about one hundred years: the whole lifetime, in
short, of a very long-lived man.

Somali and Galla developments

The Somali are cattle-raising people who have lived in the inland country of the Horn of Africa since very ancient times, and belong to the ancient Cushitic language group. Their distant ancestors were known to the Egyptians who visited them in ships going down the Red Sea, in the second millennium BC, to a country the Egyptians called Punt. Punt was probably on both sides of the lower end of the Red Sea, in what is now northern Somalia and southern Arabia.

Much later we probably catch a glimpse of the Somali in a Chinese description of the ninth century AD. It is unlikely that the Chinese of those days ever visited the Horn of Africa, but they had information about foreign countries from Indian Ocean merchants. This Chinese description, written in AD 863, says that the people of Bo-ba-li (that is, of Berbera or northern Somalia) did not eat grain but only meat, and "often stick a needle into the veins of cattle and draw blood which they drink mixed with milk." Some cattle-raising peoples of the Horn of Africa, in northern Kenya and Uganda, still use mixed milk and cattle blood as part of their diet.

In northern Somalia new Muslim states came into existence during the twelfth century. These prospered on trade with inland peoples but clashed increasingly with the Ethiopians. In the sixteenth century their great leader, Ahmad of Adel, led an army into Ethiopia and all but conquered that country. By this time the Somali were also spreading towards the Coast. Gradually they occupied the coastal towns, inhabited previously by Bantu people related to the Swahili, but did not establish full control over them until about AD 1700. After that the history of the northern coast is that of the Somali.

Historians disagree on where exactly the Galla lived in ancient times. Some think they occupied most of the east-

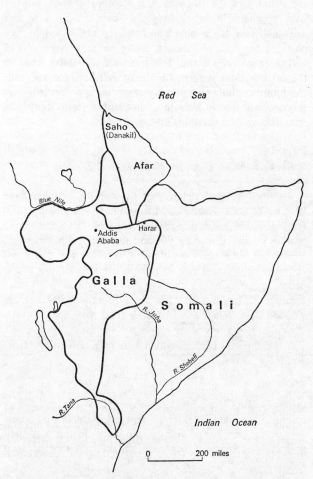

8. *Main areas where the Galla, Somali, Afar and Saho peoples live today*

ern country of the Horn of Africa, others that they came
from southern Ethiopia. Like the Somali, they were and
are a cattle-raising people who have repeatedly sought new
pastures for their herds. In doing so they have spread
across much of central Ethiopia and Somalia, and, as
the old traditions suggest, they may well have clashed with
the Bantu of Shungwaya many centuries ago. But it is certain that they have long lived in north-eastern Kenya, in
Somalia, and in parts of Ethiopia.

Background to Uganda: Farmers and herders

The well-watered uplands of the countries which have
become Uganda, Ruanda and Burundi, saw a broadly similar growth of local population with the development of
new ways of community life and methods of government.

Most of these early populations were farmers and herd-
ers who had moved out of the parent area of the Bantu
people, possibly in the south-eastern Congo, during earlier
centuries.[3] They prospered in good country that was more
wooded than today. Most of their food they got by growing millet and a few other crops. Among these, by AD 1000,
was the type of banana which had originally come from
South-east Asia.

For a long time these farmers lived in small family or
clan villages, each running its own affairs and remaining
fairly isolated from its neighbors. But gradually they
found they could benefit from appointing chiefs who would
rule over a number of villages and clans; in this way their
political development began to differ from that of their
Bantu neighbors in Kenya.

The reasons for this difference are not entirely clear,
but seem mainly to have been the result of geography. In
Kenya the Kikuyu and Kamba, for example, lived in
broken country, rich in woodlands, where the grouping

[3] See map on page 18 (Bantu spread).

of several villages under a chief could give no obvious advantage over other methods of self-rule. West of Lake Victoria the country was more open, less wooded, and the people had more cattle. No doubt it was partly the need to solve cattle problems, such as the dividing up of pastures, which led to the growth of chiefly authority.[4]

At first, in any case, these chiefs in Uganda were men of little power, each with authority over a few people. But the grouping of villages continued as cattle-raising people from northern Uganda increasingly took the lead. Chiefs became stronger. After about AD 1300 a line of rulers known as the Abatembuzi are said to have had a great influence in northern Uganda, and to have continued to be powerful until the coming of the Luo after 1450. At the same time, in southern Uganda around AD 1300, there emerged other lines of kings belonging to the Hima people. Who these kings were is variously described in the traditions. One set of traditions, those of Bunyoro, speak of three early dynasties: the Gabu, the Ranzi, and the Chwezi, of whom the last were particularly successful. Another set of traditions, those of Buganda, place great emphasis on a legendary hero called Kintu, who is said to have come from beyond Mount Elgon in the north-east and to have united the Ganda. Whatever truth may lie behind these confused memories of distant times, there is little doubt about the historical importance of the line of kings who are remembered as the Chwezi.

The Chwezi rulers and the foundation of kingdoms

Remarkable tales are still told about the Chwezi kings and chiefs. Sometimes the traditions even speak of them as gods. "They wandered," it is said, "without fear or difficulty to places where no man had ever been before. And you could not look them in the face, because their eyes

[4] See also *Ntemi Chiefs* and *Trade and Chiefs* in this Chapter.

were so bright that it hurt your own eyes to look at them, for it was like looking at the sun."

Legends apart, there is no doubt that these Chwezi kings really did exist. They were almost certainly of Hima origin, and they left more than legends behind them; they also left a number of imposingly large earthworks within which

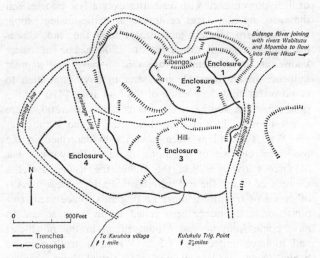

9. *The old Chwezi capital at Kibengo, showing how trenches were dug to make four enclosures, the innermost of which contained the royal residence*

they had their royal dwellings and kept their huge herds of cattle. As many as eighteen of these Chwezi sites are known in western Uganda. Several are very large, notably at Bigo on the south bank of the Katonga river, and at Kibengo in the district of Mubende.

The Chwezi dynasty ruled in southern Uganda between about AD 1350 and 1500. Under it there developed new ways of government which were to be used in later kingdoms of Uganda. Two among these Chwezi rulers are especially remembered for their power and wisdom. One of these was Ndahura, whose capital was at Kibengo in the district of Mubende. He is said to have ruled the whole of southern Uganda from Lake Albert in the west to the slopes of Mount Elgon in the east, around AD 1400, when the Chwezi system was at its height. The other was Wamara, who probably ruled around 1450. By this time the empire was smaller. Yet Wamara's capital in the district of Bwera, at Bigo, had protective trenches, surrounding the royal herds, which enclosed a circular area more than two and a half miles wide from west to east. They can still be seen today. Archaeologists conclude that Bigo was occupied by the Chwezi until about 1500. Then history took another turn.

Coming of the Luo and the Bito kings

Towards 1500 another group of cattle-raising people began moving in from the north. These were the ancestors of the Luo of today. In the course of time they spread far across eastern Africa and gave rise to many peoples, including, in northern Uganda, the Acholi, Lango and Alur.[5]

Their first homeland or dispersal area lay somewhere in the grassland country of the southern Sudan and northwestern Uganda. At some time between about AD 1300 and 1400 they began to send off groups in search of new pastures. Some of these groups went north: under the leadership of two legendary heroes, who are remembered as Nyikango and Dimo, they crossed the Nile and settled at a place called Wipac, in the grassland country now known as the Bahr al-Ghazal. Here, after a while, a further split occurred: one group moved on north-eastward and, after AD 1500, founded the kingdom of the Shilluk, while a second group became the Anuak who live in the Sudan on the south-western borders of Ethiopia.

[5] Apart from the Madi and Lugbara, all the peoples of northern Uganda are of Luo origin.

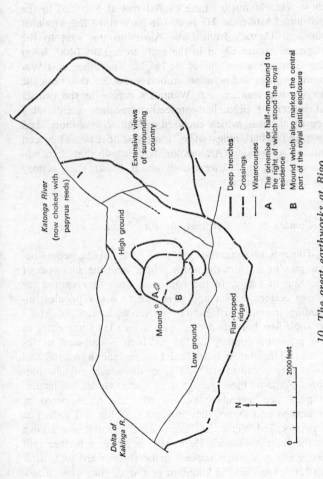

10. The great earthworks at Bigo

Katonga River
(now choked with papyrus reeds)

Extensive views
of surrounding country

High ground

Mound

A

B

Low ground

Flat-topped
ridge

Delta of
Kakinga R.

N

0   2000 feet

Deep trenches

Crossings

Watercourses

A   The oriembe or half-moon mound to
     the right of which stood the royal
     residence

B   Mound which also marked the central
     part of the royal cattle enclosure

A third group of ancestors of the Luo moved south-ward. They it was who gave a new turn to the history of southern Uganda, and afterwards of western Kenya. This southward-moving group went at first to an area called Puhungo, near Lake Albert, where, in the course of time, they split once again into several groups. One of these, under a leader called Nyipir, moved west and conquered the lands of the Lendu, Okebo and Madi peoples, all of whom, like the Luo, were and are cattle-raising folk. Another group continued to the south, under Labongo, and invaded the Hima kingdom of the Chwezi rulers, from there spreading gradually into neighboring lands. Some of their descendants moved eastward towards Kenya around 1500, and became the ancestors of the Padhola and of the Kenya Luo.

This coming of the Luo set the stage, though by means that are not yet fully understood, for many changes. The last Chwezi king and his followers retreated to the south, and vanished from the scene. New Luo or partly Luo rulers, the Bito, took their place. They too formed an empire with its center in Bunyoro: the empire of Kitara, the main headquarters of which were at the old Chwezi royal settlement, probably in what is now Mubende District. The history of Bunyoro-Kitara, and of neighboring lands such as Buganda, will be taken up in the next section and in Chapter 14.

Peoples such as the Luo, who were nomadic, often invaded the pastures of other peoples. Sometimes they succeeded in this; at other times they were thrown back, and had to move on. But it generally would be wrong to think of any of these migrations as being made by large numbers of people. The true picture is more often one of small or very small numbers of warriors, tried and toughened by long experience on their wanderings, who invade a new area, defeat its inhabitants in a few battles, and settle down in peace, intermarrying with the local inhabitants and gradually giving rise to a new people. Sometimes this new

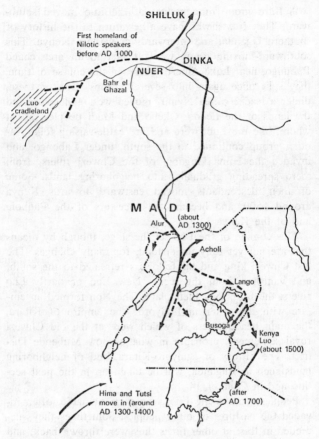

11. Luo migrations into Uganda, Kenya and Tanzania,
whose modern frontiers are shown

people would take the language of the local inhabitants; sometimes it would keep that of the newcomers.

It would therefore be mistaken to regard the Luo invasion of the Chwezi empire as being the work of a single large army. On the contrary, small groups of Luo warriors will have come from the north, infiltrated gradually into the pastures of the Hima, settled down and intermarried with Hima people, and prepared the way for the overthrow of the Chwezi line of kings. This overthrow was probably violent, but none of the details are known. There is one tradition, however, which casts a valuable light on what may have happened. It says that the Chwezi kings and chiefs became unpopular because they wanted too much of the country's wealth. They lost prestige. People saw that they were only human beings like anyone else, and not the children of the gods. By the end of Wamara's reign, that is, the times were ripe for change; and in making this change Luo influence played a leading part.

New Kingdoms: Buganda, Ruanda, and others

The historical importance of the Chwezi rulers and their political system lay in their elaboration of new laws and customs for the government of a kingdom considerably larger than any that had existed before in this region. These laws and customs were taken over by their Bito successors, who were careful to claim the Chwezi as their own lineal ancestors, and thus legitimate themselves in the eyes of ordinary people.

Bito took over the royal symbols of the Chwezi: their drums and ceremonial copper spears, their bearded crowns topped with cones of copper, their ornaments made from the skins of the colobus monkey, and their manner of building palaces from finely woven reeds. Even more significantly, they copied certain aspects of Chwezi organisation, such as the method of ruling districts through subchiefs, and the practice of drafting all the young men of the empire into the army. In many ways the Bito kings were true successors of the Chwezi.

There were comparable results elsewhere. South of Bunyoro another group of Hima rulers, called the Hinda, set up other kingdoms of much the same kind after about

AD 1500. One of these, including part of Ankole, was ruled by a famed leader called Ruhinda whose country lay on either side of the Kagera river which now divides Uganda from Tanzania.

The population of these kingdoms consisted principally of cattle-raisers and tillers of the soil, with the cattle-raisers in control, a division that made other changes possible. The Hinda cattle-raisers, for example, used to farm out their beasts to the cultivators of the soil, each of whom would keep a few Hinda cattle in exchange for Hinda protection against raiders or other perils. The extra manure enabled them to grow more bananas, and, as the food supply improved, the population increased. This hand-in-hand expansion of food and population took place over much of the Interior in this period.

Other kingdoms were formed in southern Uganda. Among these was Buganda which seems to have taken shape, according to the traditions, at about the same time the Chwezi were ruling Bunyoro, and which was probably included within the Chwezi dominions. After 1500 Buganda for a time became part of the Bito empire of Kitara, as is indicated by the tradition that the founder of its present line of kings, Kimera, was a Bito. Buddu also acquired a new line of rulers. So did Bugungu. Other areas, like Kitakwenda and Kiyaka, were ruled by offshoots of the Bito royal line.

Farther south, in Ruanda and Burundi, similar developments took place as cattle-raising peoples such as the Tutsi established their rule over cultivators of the soil such as the Hutu.

By AD 1500 or soon after, in short, many peoples of the western highlands, from Lake Albert in the north to Lake Kivu in the south, had worked out new political systems which were all much alike. These kingdoms were dominated by a number of cattle-raising peoples who were stronger, in warfare, than the sedentary farming peoples.

There were various reasons for this, but the most important lay in differing social organisation. The soil-cultivating farmers lived mainly in small family groups, each of which could call on very few men for its defence. The cattle people were so organised that each group could call on the men of many families. In time it came to be accepted that the cattle-raisers, who provided the kings and chiefs, were the warriors in each kingdom, while the soil-cultivators were the workers. In these kingdoms there accordingly developed, as we shall see, a two-way system of rights and duties. The soil-cultivators had to work for the cattle people as well as for themselves, but the cattle people had to defend the soil-cultivators if the kingdom was attacked.[6]

In one form or another, these western kingdoms continued until the twentieth century.

Background to Tanzania: Early changes

In very early times, just as in Kenya and Uganda, the inland country of Tanzania was occupied by scattered families of Stone Age people who lived in caves or grass shelters, and obtained their food by hunting, fishing, and gathering wild plants. There were also a number of the group which may be called North-east Africans, who had cattle and practised a little primitive farming. A few of the descendants of these early Cushitic speakers still live there.

Then, at least twelve centuries ago, the knowledge of metal-working and improved methods of farming appeared in the land as a result—or so it appears on existing evidence —of the arrival and expansion of the Bantu peoples. These Bantu groups were few in numbers, and had arrived after stages of migration from their early homelands in Central Africa. Gradually they wrought great changes, leading the area out of the Stone Age into the Iron Age, with the

[6] For a more detailed discussion of this and other systems of self-rule, see Chapter 12 on rights and duties, and Chapter 22 on social history.

consequent beginnings of village life and agriculture. Many villages appeared. The stone ruins of their hut foundations are scattered all over Tanzania.

These early villages governed themselves on family lines. They were so small that authority could be exercised by the heads of two or three families. But here, too, farming

12. (a) *The Chwezi Kingdom in the reign of Ndahura during the early fifteenth century*

provided more food, and, as villages increased in size, a growing division of labor. At a stage of development that was reached probably around AD 1300, some of the peoples of northern Tanzania, south of Lake Nyanza, began to appoint chiefs to rule over groups of villages. In this they followed the same path as the farmers of Uganda but not, as we have seen, of the farmers of Central Kenya. Some traditions indicate that the first inland Tanzanians to appoint chiefs, or to accept the rule of chiefs provided by their neighbors, were the Nyamwezi and Sukuma south of Lake Nyanza. They adopted a type of rule by purely local chiefs that appears to have resembled the system in Uganda before the rise of kingdoms there. This or similar methods of self-rule also appeared in other parts of Tan-

12. (b) Uganda Kingdoms in the late fifteenth century

zania. By 1500 it had spread to the northern end of Lake Malawi.

The role of ntemi chiefs

By 1500 most of the peoples of western Tanzania were ruled by chiefs. These chieftainships resembled each other in many ways: each consisted of a small group of villages ruled by a single chief whom the villagers appointed. Such chiefs were known as *ntemi* or *mtemi*, a word which comes from the Bantu verb *ku-tema*, meaning "to cut"; the *ntemi* chief, in other words, was the man appointed to "cut discussion" so as to reach judgments in legal cases and decisions on political questions. The system gradually spread from people to people, over about two centuries, and across a thousand miles of inland Tanzania between the Nyamwezi-Sukuma country in the north and the shores of Lake Malawi. It was adopted in the south by the Hehe, Bena and Sangu: by the Pangwa, Kinga, and Nyakyusa: by the Ngonde, Safwa, and many others.

Each *ntemi* chief or king was held in the respect due to a man whose position enjoyed the special blessing and power of God and the ancestors. Each was the holder of special symbols such as sacred spears, and maintained a royal fire from which all the fires of his little chiefdom or kingdom were supposed to be kindled. Whenever an *ntemi* chief died, he was buried with special ceremonies and expressions of sorrow by his people.

These many little states did not unite. Each remained on its own, speaking its own language, revering its own ancestors, thinking of itself as separate and different from its neighbors. There was plenty of land for all of them, and the problem of settling disputes between neighboring states can seldom have arisen.

Historians have so far suggested a number of different reasons why chiefs were accepted by peoples who had previously managed without them, or had managed only with the very limited chieftainship of family headmen. High on the list of these reasons stands the religious need of each separate people to make regular contact in a spiritual sense with ancestors who, they believed, were in turn the channel of communication with divine power. This religious need gave rise to rituals and ceremonies generally presided over by senior family heads, or by heads of important family groupings; and these representative men, it is supposed on fairly good evidence, gradually came to be recognised as also possessing political power. "The religious needs of the community," in other words, "were at the heart of political evolution."[7] Then, depending on the local geography and the everyday problems to be faced, there followed a number of political developments which made chiefs more powerful. Apart from the always important religious role of chiefs (see also Chapter 17, *The Chiefs Grow Stronger*), one may detect four main reasons for these developments:

1. The first reason, working always for political change, lay in the steady growth of population as improved techniques enlarged the available food supply. Villages outgrew the authority of family headmen. Here and there, although by no means everywhere, chiefs took their place, often no doubt as war-leaders when expanding peoples clashed with each other in rivalry for land or cattle.

2. The spread of cattle-raising. Nearly all these peoples with *ntemi* chiefs say, in their traditions, that the idea was brought to them by cattle-raising folk who came to live among them. We may guess that the spread of cattle-raising brought new problems to people who were cultivators of the soil: how to divide broad pastures, how to make the best use of manure, how to combine agriculture with the keeping of cattle. These problems required a new kind of authority to settle them.

3. The expansion of iron-working. Skills in making iron-tipped tools and spears were increasingly prized as these populations grew in number. Among some of them, as for example among the people of the Pare Mountains, families of metalsmiths tended to become families of chiefs as well.

4. The spread of local trade between one people and its neighbors, and of long-distance trade between the peoples of the Interior, whether in East or Central Africa, and those of the Coast and Islands, is a fourth factor which

[7] I. N. Kimambo, *The Political History of the Pare People to 1900*, 1967.

seems to have worked steadily towards an expansion in the power of chiefs.

The link between trade and chiefs

The political influence of trade, making for a steady increase of "power at the center," appears also to have become increasingly important after about 1300. Here the evidence stands on somewhat firmer ground. Its general explanation almost certainly lies in the fact that trade, and especially long-distance trade, called for new types of economic organization which, in turn, required stronger authority "at the center" than any that had existed before. There came the need for appointed men who could take important trading decisions on behalf of their community. As elsewhere, new forms of economic power led onward to new forms of political power.

There is the interesting example of the consequences of the ivory trade of the Interior of Tanzania. When coastal merchants began asking for ivory in exchange for cottons and other manufactured goods from India and Arabia, it was not only necessary for the peoples of the Interior to find and kill elephants. This they had done, in any case, for many centuries. Now they had to face new problems. They had to organise safe transport of their tusks to the distant Coast, often hundreds of miles away. They had to bargain with their coastal trading partners. All this demanded new forms of leadership.

What generally happened is suggested by the case of the Nyamwezi of western Tanzania. After about 1700 these people became leaders in the long-distance ivory trade of the Interior. Even before this time they had *ntemi* chiefs of their own, and it may be that this was one of the factors in their trading success. But now, increasingly, their system of chieftainship became directly connected with the ivory business.

Several Nyamwezi customs show this link between chief-tainship and the long-distance trade. They often chose their chiefs from bold leaders of the trading caravans. After 1700, too, they made an interesting change in the head-dress of their chiefs. Until then they had decorated this headdress with the horns of the *impala.* Now they added the *kibangwa,* part of a giant shell-fish which lives in the coastal waters of East Africa, no doubt as a sign of their achievement in running the difficult caravan trade across hundreds of miles of hills and plains.

For the Nyamwezi, success in the caravan trade went hand-in-hand with having chiefs who could organize it. Other peoples, in different ways and in other places, found the same kind of advantage in chieftainship.

The link between trade and chiefs went further than this. Once they were appointed, chiefs tended to become traders, and often worked to augment their power so as to increase their trading wealth. Thus the growth and expan-sion of trade aided the growth and expansion of states. As we shall see, this was especially true in Central Africa among the Shona and Malawi peoples. Among the latter, for example, one tusk of every elephant killed in a chief's territory had to be given to the chief. So he was interested in enlarging his territory, because the bigger it grew the more ivory he received.

It would be wrong, however, to think of these chiefs simply as enterprising men who profited from their posi-tions in order to enrich themselves at the expense of their people. Bad chiefs undoubtedly did this, and often faced revolt by those who had appointed or accepted them. But the general rule was otherwise. In such systems as these, lacking any regular "income distribution" by wages, money taxes, or other means such as we have today, a leading part of every chief's duty was to ensure the circulation of wealth. A chief was expected to collect wealth, whether by tribute or by taxation-in-kind, but he was also expected to distribute it among the various sections of his people.

For all these reasons, with trade and self-defence among

the most important, the little village groups of early times grew into small states; and the small states gradually expanded to include many villages.

Big settlements appeared as the years went by. Among the largest of these known to history was Engaruka. This group of stone-built villages lay on the eastern slopes of Mount Ngorongoro, south of Lake Natron. It was probably destroyed by raiders such as the Masai, and has long been ruined and deserted. But a visitor may still see the hut foundations of a settlement three miles long, where thousands of people once lived, dwelling on many terraces of stone huts along the broad hillside above the floor of the Rift Valley. These ruins form an impressive monument to the work and skill of the inland peoples of the past.

South of the Rufiji: the Makua, Yao, and others

Further south in Tanzania, through the inland country between the Rufiji and Ruvuma rivers, and southward again across the Ruvuma in what is now northern Mozambique, changing ways were scarcely felt during this period of history. Groups such as the Makonde and Makua continued to live in much the same way as they had in the distant past, fishing, hunting, growing a little food, and dwelling in small villages.

Trading caravans from Kilwa crossed this country on their way to and from Lake Malawi and beyond, where they bought ivory from the Chewa and other Malawi people, and gold from the people of Mwanamutapa across the Zambezi. It is not known when these Kilwa caravans first made the journey to Malawi, though they were certainly rare before the sixteenth century. Their passing seems in any case to have had little effect upon the peoples of this southern country, none of whom entered the caravan trade during this period.

Late in the sixteenth century this country was much ravaged by a wandering horde of nomads of several ethnic origins, whom history knows as the Zimba. What it was like in 1616 was described by a Portuguese traveller, Gaspar Bocarro, who travelled in that year from Tete on the Zambezi to Kilwa.[8] He met a few small chiefs on the way, but passed through much uninhabited territory. Later the Yao moved into this area and became important traders like the Nyamwezi farther north.

Beyond the Makua and the Yao, in middle and southern Mozambique, were other groups who belonged to the large Nguni branch of the Bantu language-family, including the Swazi, and, southward again, the Ngoni (Mtetwa, Ndwandwe, Zulu, and others) of modern Zululand and Natal. These southern Bantu peoples did not impinge on East or Central African history until the nineteenth century. Then the Ngoni moved up from the south with dramatic results to be discussed in later chapters.

[8] The relevant Portuguese memoir of Bocarro's journey is translated in G. S. P. Freeman-Grenville, *The East African Coast: Select Documents*, 1962 p. 165.

4. CENTRAL AFRICA 1000–1500

Chapter 2 has described how Early Iron Age peoples of Bantu origin established themselves before AD 1000 in many parts of Central Africa: in the southern Congo, in the grassland plains to the south of Katanga and Lake Tanganyika, and in the lands beyond the Zambezi river. By AD 1000, there were groups of farmers and metalworkers in all the countries now called Congo, Angola, Zambia, Malawi, Zimbabwe, Mozambique, and South Africa. These groups, as in East Africa, were few and consisted mainly of village peoples. For the most part each small village will have governed itself, although here and there a few large states such as the one described by al-Mas'udi had begun to emerge. But after AD 1000, again as in East Africa, these lands became the scene of steady growth of peoples who evolved new forms of community life.

From the Indian Ocean to the Atlantic

Central Africa's present populations, like those of East Africa, derive from ancient ancestral stocks of diverse origin. But in spite of local differences, early Central Africans had much in common. With a few exceptions, such as the Bushmen, they were nearly all Bantu people who had become farmers, cattle-raisers and metalsmiths, who lived in small groups which gradually grew into larger groups, and who evolved very similar states. These states developed for the same basic reasons as in East Africa. As populations grew larger, they needed more effective government than the family heads could provide. They required men of authority who could settle disputes on matters such as the division of pastures or land for cultivation. Where they engaged in long-distance trade, as among the copper producers of Katanga after about AD 700, or at the southern Zambian settlement of Ingombe Ilede near where the Kafue joins the Zambezi, they also found that chiefs could be useful in handling trade problems.

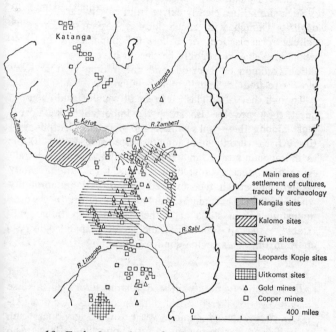

13. *Early Iron Age cultures in Central Africa*

Like the *ntemi* rulers in Tanzania, the chiefs and kings of these early Central African systems were revered as men whose positions gave them spiritual as well as political and economic authority. Indeed, it was the belief in their spiritual force that often gave these Bantu kings their other powers. Their spiritual efficacy was celebrated in ritual and by the possession of royal regalia such as sacred spears.

At the ninth-century site of Ingombe Ilede, for example, archaeologists have found that some of the ancient burials, presumably those of members of a ruling family, were distinguished by gold and other ornaments not present in other and presumably more humble graves nearby. The same differences in the graves of "nobles" and "commoners" have been found at other Iron Age sites.

Such similarities clearly derive from closely parallel ways of life. Though with much local variation, whether of culture, organisation, or belief, the populations of this whole area may reasonably be said to have forged a civilisation common to them all, and one, moreover, that was closely related to that of their neighbors.

Though they often clashed in small wars of raid or conquest, these peoples also conserved important links. Foremost among these links within and between Central and East Africa were those of long-distance trade. By AD 1000, as the accounts of Arab writers repeatedly show, Central African producers of gold and ivory were sending their goods eastward to the south-east coast: to the ports of what afterwards became Mozambique. In return, they were importing cotton stuffs and other goods from India and Arabia. After AD 1000 this trade greatly expanded, especially in the lands to the south of the Zambezi.

Background to Zambia: the Kalomo Culture

The population of Zambia was certainly very sparse in AD 1000, and was to remain so for a long time afterwards. It consisted of several groups of Iron Age Bantu farmers, ancestors of the Tonga and other peoples, and of scattered families of Stone Age Bushman hunters. Gradually, as time went by, the Bantu farmers increased in numbers and spread across the country, while the Bushman hunters dwindled or were absorbed by the Bantu.

Various early iron-using cultures, notably that of Kalomo, have been lately identified by archaeologists. They all appear to have taken their rise during the first five centuries of the first millennium AD, and to have been formed initially by peoples who came from elsewhere, and probably from the Congo grasslands. "Remains of the villages occupied by these settlers," a recent summary of the evidence has noted, "have been found widely distributed in Rhodesia and Zambia and in parts of Botswana and the Transvaal. They are marked by a common ceramic tradition and appear to be both contemporary with, and successive to, sites of the ceramic stone-using communities. Metallurgy first appears in association with this widespread type of pottery, iron being found in all areas while the distribution of copper and gold follows that of the mineral deposits."[1]

These farmers tilled the soil with hoes which had iron blades, but they do not seem to have had any iron cutting tools. They also had wooden sticks weighted with stones which they used in their gardens, or for grubbing up edible roots. They made pottery by hand, without a wheel, and their best huts were built of sticks plastered with *daga* clay and thatched with grass. They had some trade with their neighbors of the Zambezi valley, and even imported *conus* shells from the Coast, using them for personal ornaments.

The main food crop was sorghum. Domestic animals included cattle, sheep and goats, and also tame dogs. With iron-pointed spears they hunted for buffalo, zebra, eland, kudu, water buck, warthog, bushpig, and other animals, bones of which have been found in the ruins of their villages.

People like these occupied the Batoka plateau and the Gwembe valley, in southern Zambia, until about 1300.

[1] D. W. Phillipson, "Early Iron-Using Peoples of Southern Africa," paper read at Lusaka History Conference July 1968; cf. also *ibid.* "The Early Iron Age in Zambia—Regional Variants and Some Tentative Conclusions," *Jnl. of African History,* 2 of 1968; and B. M. Fagan, "The Later Iron Age in Southern Africa," Lusaka History Conference, July 1968.

Then they were followed, as populations grew in size and needed more land, by new ancestors of the Tonga, Ila, and other Bantu farming peoples. There were steady improvements in farming life, and a slow but continued growth of population. Not until about 1650 was there to be any serious interruption in this story. Then the ancestors of peoples such as the Bemba and Lozi appeared on the scene, migrating from the Congo grasslands, and brought large changes in their wake.

Background to Malawi: Ancestors and chiefs

The picture of Malawi in AD 1000 and after differs little in its general lines from that of Zambia. Small groups of Bantu farmers had long been coming into the lands near the Lake, settling down alongside Stone Age peoples who had occupied the country in much earlier times.[2] Gradually they increased in numbers. Here too the idea of being governed by chiefs appeared as populations increased and the problems of everyday life grew more complicated. The idea of chiefs seems to have come into northern Malawi with the small groups who came from Tanzania, who already had chiefs of their own. *Ntemi* chiefs were ruling in parts of northern Malawi by 1500.

Around 1300, another and stronger grouping of peoples took shape. These were the Malawi, from whom the modern Republic takes its name. They became one of the most powerful peoples of Central Africa, and were united for a short time, after 1600, in an imperial system or confederacy.[3]

The Malawi were not a single people but a grouping of closely related peoples of whom all but one, the Nsenga, speak the same Bantu language, Nyanja, the "language of the lake." They included the Chikunda, Chewa, Chipeta,

---

[2] The beginnings of the Early Iron Age in Malawi have yet to be securely dated.

[3] See Chapter 17.

Zimba, Mbo, Ntumba, Manganya, Nyanga, Nyasa, and Nsenga. They occupied central and southern Malawi, eastern Zambia, and north-western Mozambique.

Like their northern neighbors, most of the Malawi say that the ancestors of their first chiefs came from the north, not from the area of western Tanzania but from that of Katanga in the country of the Luba.[4] This should not be taken to mean that all their ancestors came from somewhere outside their present country. The truth is rather that small bands arrived from Lubaland around 1300, bringing chiefs and new ideas about community life and government. They intermarried with the local peoples, both Bantu farmers and Stone Age hunters; and this mingling gradually gave rise to a new people, so that we can think of the Malawi as emerging around 1400 or a little earlier.

This mingling of newcomers and old inhabitants, and the consequent if gradual formation of a new people, can be traced to some extent in Malawi traditions. Thus it has been the Phili clan, among the Chewa, who provided the men who became chiefs and wielded political power, while the Banda clan provided those who performed religious duties, such as rain-making and other ceremonies which, it was believed, helped to ensure good harvests. Behind this division in Chewa society, we can glimpse the distant arrival of people with chiefs and their gradual unification with another people, already living in the land, whose ancestors were believed to represent the spirits of the Earth.

By 1500 there were several dynasties of chiefs among the Malawi, each named after the first chief of his line. Among these were the chieftainships of Karonga, Undi, Nkanda, Mwase and others. These chieftainships did not yet form a single union or confederation, but generally kept on good terms with each other. They were active and successful in the long-distance ivory trade with the Coast, working together for this and other purposes against their

[4] See Chapter 16, *The Luba-Lunda States.*

rivals or enemies, including the Portuguese who arrived here in the middle and late sixteenth century.

Other peoples of modern Malawi, notably the Yao, belong to a different line of development. They look southward for their early ancestors, being descended from peoples who took shape, during Early Iron Age times, in the country to the south and south-east of the Lake. They too increased in numbers and occupied more land, but the big expansion of the Yao came only after 1700. Others again, such as the Lake Tonga[5] and the Ngoni, reached Malawi only in later times.[6]

South of the Zambezi: Zimbabwe and the long-distance trade

Related peoples who raised cattle, grew a little food, and could make simple tools and weapons of iron, were settled south of the Zambezi river, just as others like them were settled north of it, soon after the beginning of the first millennium AD. They were evidently all of much the same ethnic stock and culture, and are identified today by the "type sites" at which archaeologists have found their traces. Of these sites the two of most importance, as guides to the nature of these early cultures, are those at Gokomere and Ziwa. Both have yielded fragments of pottery bearing a "channel" decoration about the rim. This pottery is generally agreed to mark the beginning of the Iron Age in these regions, and appears to be related, even if distantly, to the "dimple-based" pottery of Uganda and the "Kwale ware" lately unearthed in eastern Kenya.

These peoples were few in number. Towards AD 900, however, the same improvement in ways of life occurred to the south of the Zambezi as among their neighbors to the north of the river. The main group who carried out

[5] Not to be confused with the Zambian Tonga, a different people with the same name.
[6] See Chapter 17.

this development were probably ancestors of the Shona, known as the Leopard's Kopje people after the place, near Khami not far from Bulawayo, where archaeologists first came upon the evidence of their settlements.

The Leopard's Kopje people lived much in the same way as those of the Kalomo culture,[7] to whom they were perhaps related, building huts of sticks plastered with mud and thatched with straw, making iron arrowheads and hoe blades, keeping several sorts of domestic animals, and gathering wild fruits, seeds and vegetables. The animals they hunted included buffalo, impala, zebra, duiker and other sorts of buck. They built their villages in river valleys as well as along the ridges of hills, and as with other Early Iron Age clusters further north, their dead were usually buried in a crouched position.

Settlements of these "Leopard's Kopje people" are known to have existed in many parts of what is now Rhodesia, and for a long time after AD 900. Traces of such settlements have also been found to the south, in the valley of the Limpopo river, and beyond it in the northern part of modern South Africa. A further cultural change occurred in about AD 1100. The people then living at what afterwards became the large stone-built settlement of Great Zimbabwe[8] began building in stone for the first time, instead of in mud-and-thatch. This change was probably associated with the arrival on the scene of another group of the early ancestors of the Shona-speaking group of Bantu who now occupy much of the country.

These Shona were to play a great part in Central African history. Like the Malawi, they took shape from different but closely related groups who all spoke variations of the same Bantu language, and some of whose distant an-

[7] See p. 60.

[8] This word *zimbabwe* is of Shona origin, and means the dwelling of a chief. There were many zimbabwes in Rhodesia and western Mozambique. The famous one near modern Fort Victoria is usually called Great Zimbabwe because its stone buildings are the largest that are known, and because it was a capital of the Rozwi kings of the Karanga in later times. See Chapter 18.

cestors had come from the most ancient homeland of the Bantu, perhaps in the region of Katanga and northern Zambia. The earliest stone buildings which the archaeologists have dated, at Great Zimbabwe, to around 1100, were possibly their work. Yet it seems that other Shona groups went on moving southward over the Zambezi for many years afterwards, mingling with the Leopard's Kopje and other peoples whom they found. After 1400 these Shona built the wide empire of the Mwanamutapa.

They may also have had some early links with the Malawi whose expansion similarly dates from around 1400. The word *mambo,* which the Shona used for king, is not of Shona origin but belongs to the group of languages spoken by the Malawi. Yet the Shona differed from the Malawi in important ways. They spoke, and speak, a different Bantu language, and they trace descent patrilineally while the Malawi traced it matrilineally.

The political development of the Shona, much more than that of the earlier peoples with whom they mingled, was closely linked to the growth of long-distance trade in ivory and gold, for it was during the period after 1100 that this trade with the ports of the Coast became really important for these inland peoples. The Shona, it is true, were not the first group to engage in this trade; the Leopard's Kopje people and their neighbors had already long been doing so. Even after the rise to power of the Shona, it is possible that the Leopard's Kopje people continued to do the work of mining and smelting. But steady expansion of the trade after 1100, with the Coast becoming ever more closely linked to the trading world of Asia, brought political changes. It encouraged the appointment of chiefs, for reasons already discussed; and it was for early Shona chiefs who were also traders that the first stone buildings at Zimbabwe were probably erected.

As many as 7000 ancient mine workings, mainly for gold, have been found in these lands between the Zambezi and the Limpopo rivers. Some of these were opened before AD 1000; nearly all of them before AD 1500. Very few of the near-surface deposits of gold-bearing ore in this area were found by Europeans; almost all were first located and exploited by African miners of the past.

These miners were skilled in the techniques of finding gold-bearing rock, in digging for it to a depth of as much as eighty feet, in crushing the ore by hand methods, in smelting it in primitive blast furnaces made of anthill earth, and in pouring the gold into little moulds of clay. These produced gold ingots, which were used to make various ornaments for local use, or were sold to the coastal merchants. Large quantities of gold were exported between AD 1000 and 1500, most of it to India. In exchange, the chiefs of the mining people imported Indian cottons, brassware and beads, and a little foreign pottery and Chinese porcelain.

Soon after 1400 the history of these lands took another decisive turn. Shona-speaking people known as the Karanga, who lived in the western part, began organising themselves into a strong state. They became renowned for their military strength, their skills, and their trading wealth. This development, and the empire of the Mwanamutapa which the Karanga built after 1425, will be discussed on present evidence in Chapter 18.

South of the Limpopo: Growth of Sotho and Ngoni

We should look briefly at the early history of the peoples of South Africa, for they too belong to the same broad pattern of Early Iron Age development.

The most ancient surviving peoples south of the Limpopo are the Khoikhoi, whom Europeans have called Hottentots and Bushmen. While the former were cattle-keeping people in ancient times, the Bushmen remained hunters and food-gatherers as in the Late Stone Age. Both lived in small and scattered communities all over the habitable land of South Africa, down to and including the Cape of Good Hope. In ancient times the cattle-keeping Khoikhoi (Nama and others, or Hottentots in European usage) tended to exclude the Bushmen from some of their hunting lands, and were in turn enslaved or driven out by Europeans after the Dutch began expanding from the Cape of Good Hope in the late seventeenth century. Groups of Bushmen are still in existence in the Kalahari, while the Nama and their cattle-keeping relations took refuge in what is now South West Africa, where they were much harassed and reduced in members by German colonial wars after 1885.

Bantu farming and metal-working people entered the northern part of South Africa, coming from Central Africa, around AD 700. They settled at first in the country along the south bank of the Limpopo river and in the Zoutpansberg mountains. They were very like the Gokomere and Leopard's Kopje peoples of the north, and probably were relatives of those Central Africans. They too increased in numbers as they improved their supplies of food and strengthened their social organisation, and as lesser groups were sent off southward in search of new land. In this way there was formed the large group of southern Bantu peoples, the Sotho- and Nguni-speaking Bantu. By AD 1652, when the Dutch made their first settlement at the Cape of Good Hope, these southern Bantu were living all the way down the eastern part of South Africa as far as the southern coast. Later Ngoni migrations and other matters involving these groups will be taken up in Chapter 20.

These southern Bantu developed a civilisation that was different in its details from the civilisation of the Bantu of Central and East Africa, but was basically the same in ideas about rule by chiefs who possessed spiritual power, in ways of community life such as the respect paid to ancestors, and in customs for keeping law and order.

Those who lived in the northern part of South Africa also used stone for their settlements, just as in Zimbabwe. Even as late as 1820 a European traveller, the missionary Robert Moffat, described their ruined towns as showing "signs of immense labour and perseverance, every fence being composed of stones, averaging five or six feet high, raised apparently without either mortar . . . Everything is circular, from the inner fences which surround each house to the walls which sometimes encompass the town . . ." Towns like these flourished by 1500.[9]

Mapungubwe

One other important Iron Age culture may be mentioned. In about 1100 there appeared a number of new settlements on hilltops along the south bank of the Limpopo, in what is now the northern Transvaal. Ruins of more than thirty have been found. Of these the most important is on a hilltop known as Mapungubwe, the "hill of jackals." These settlements were offshoots of the same culture as the one that appeared at Great Zimbabwe in about 1100. They were Bantu settlements; probably their people were related to the Shona.

In the fifteenth century this Mapungubwe Culture was ruled by strong chiefs. These chiefs were not part of the empire of Mwanamutapa which the Karanga built after 1400, but they and their peoples followed the same way of life. They had skilled metalsmiths who worked beautifully in gold, and traded in gold, ivory and copper with the coastal people of Mozambique. Like the Shona rulers of Mwanamutapa and the somewhat later kingdom of Urozwi, the Mapungubwe chiefs were buried with ornaments of precious metal.

Other Bantu peoples meanwhile occupied the lands to the southwest, modern Botswana, and fertile regions of South West Africa beyond the Kalahari.

Little is known of the history of inland Mozambique before 1500, but certainly it underwent many of the same developments. When the Portuguese first reached that coast, and settled after 1500 in a few places such as Mozambique Island, they began trying to capture the gold

[9] For the reasons for their decline, see Chapter 20.

trade of the inland country, but they found their way
barred by several small kingdoms. Of these the most important were Manyika and Uteve along the inland frontiers
of Mozambique. Both became part of the early empire of
the Mwanamutapa after about 1450.

Western Congo and Angola

It remains to sketch the development of those Bantu
peoples who live in the Western Congo and Angola, and
are the western neighbors and relatives of the Bantu of
Central Africa. They it was who carried Iron Age skills
and customs along the western lands of the Congo river
and to the shores of the South Atlantic Ocean.

By at least 800 there were Bantu farming groups in
most parts of the wooded grasslands which lie, in a broad
belt, between the lakeland country west of Tanzania and
the lower Congo river. This savannah belt, like the grasslands of Zambia and Zimbabwe, provided a home for many
groups who practised a simple kind of hoe cultivation,
like their neighbours in Central and East Africa, and made
tools and spears of iron. In all this they resembled the
Kalomo and Leopard's Kopje folk.

Around 1300 they began to develop into small states
governed by chiefs. This development seems to have taken
place in three separate places. One of these was around
the Katanga lakes Kisale and Upemba.[10] Here the Luba
and the Songye states first appeared. A second center of
development—it could also be called a dispersal area for
political ideas—lay in the more wooded country to the
north-east: this was the home of the Bolia people. A third
center was possibly the area round Stanley Pool, on the
Congo river not far from the modern capital of Kinshasa.

After 1500 these developments led to the emergence of
bigger states in the eastern Congo grasslands. These were

[10] Where, of course, small copper-producing states had existed in
much earlier times: see page 28.

the states of the Luba and Lunda peoples who were to be of much importance for Zambia as well. Larger states in the western grasslands developed at about the same time, one of the most successful being that of the Kongo people. This took shape along both banks of the Congo river, before it enters the Atlantic Ocean, and in northern Angola; these areas are where the Kongo still live today.

At some time not long before 1400 a son of the chief of the little Kongo chiefdom of Bungu (near the modern town of Boma) moved south over the Congo with a band of followers. They settled in the country of northern Angola, where they conquered the local people, who were Bantu like themselves, and gradually built a kingdom of their own. They made their capital at a place called Mbanza not far from the south bank of the Congo; later, after the coming of the Portuguese and the introduction of Christianity, Mbanza's name was to be changed to Saint Salvador.

Having conquered the local people, the Ambundu and Ambwela, the Kongo took care to get on to good terms with them. Here we have a good example of Bantu political customs. The first recorded king of the Kongo ruled in about 1400. His name was Nimi a Lukeni, and his title was *ntinu*. The traditions say that *ntinu* Nimi married the daughter of a local family or clan which was believed to possess the spiritual guardianship of the land; its chief had the title of *mani,* which meant Lord of the Earth, or Earth Priest. He accepted the overlordship of Nimi; and, to prove the good will of the Kongo people, Nimi married his daughter. Afterwards Nimi also took the title of *mani.* So the Kongo and the local inhabitants gradually became one people ruled by chiefs with religious as well as political powers. Because this kind of mingling and unifying often occurred, many peoples have two sorts of traditions: one which comes from the ancestors of those who arrived in a new country and settled in it, and the other from the ancestors of the peoples whom they found there, and with whom they intermarried.[11] Often these two sorts of traditions have become so intertwined that it is hard or impossible to tell exactly which is which.

By 1450 the *mani*-Kongo ruled over most of the northern part of Angola and some of the riverside country on the north bank of the Congo. The area was divided into provinces—Mpemba, Nsundi, Mbamba, and Soyo to begin with, and others later—ruled over by lesser chiefs or governors who accepted the *mani*-Kongo's overlordship.

In 1500 the Kongo kingdom consisted of six main provinces, those just mentioned together with Mpangu and Mbata. Each governor also had the title of *mani*. Under him he had district chiefs, and under these were village headmen. Officials at the king's court of Mbanza included the *mani lumbu*, in charge of the palace: the *mani vangu vangu*, who was the senior judge; and various others, such as the *mfutila* and the *mani samba*, who looked after trade and tax questions.

South of Kongo there was a smaller kingdom formed by the Mbundu people and called Ndongo. Its ruler had the title of *ngola*. When the Portuguese arrived, after 1500, they mistook the title of the king for the name of the country, and called it Angola.

Portuguese mariners landed at the mouth of the Congo river in 1483 and opened a new chapter in the history of these western kingdoms, to be described in Chapter 19.

---

[11] We have noted the same thing among the Malawi on page 63 of this Chapter. The Phili clan, which has political duties, looks back to one line of tradition, that of the incoming line of the Malawi ancestors from the north; while the Banda clan, which has religious duties, looks back to another line of tradition, that of the peoples already living in the country.

5. NORTHERN CHANGES—
1: EGYPT, PERSIA, INDIA, ETHIOPIA, SUDAN

While tropical Africans were developing in their Early Iron Age, during the first millennium AD, far-reaching changes were going on elsewhere. Ancient civilisations and empires declined and fell; others rose in their place. In Egypt the grandeur of the Pharaohs vanished from the scene. Meroe of the Kushites likewise disappeared in AD 320, and was followed after AD 550 by a Christian civilisation in the northern Sudan. A new empire was formed in Persia, new states took shape in India, and the foundations of modern Ethiopia were laid on the distant stones of Axum.

Because many of these developments were important for the later history of Africa, especially of the Coast and Islands, I have included this short chapter, and the following one which deals with the rise and growth of Islam, as essential background to subsequent events.

Egypt, Persia, India

The Egypt of the Pharaohs produced a remarkable civilisation at least as early as 3200 BC. Famous for the arts of peace, and powerful in war, the Land of the Nile flourished for two thousand years. But by 1000 BC, the power of the Pharaohs had much declined. Foreign invasions followed from many sides. Princes of the Libyans of North Africa[1] ruled parts of Egypt in the tenth century BC. The kings of Kush (in the northern Sudan) marched their armies into Egypt during the eighth century BC and ruled there for a

[1] Mainly, that is, of the coastal and desert parts of Libya to the immediate west of Egypt.

hundred years. In the seventh century Egypt was invaded
by the Assyrians, in the sixth century by the Persians, and
in the fourth century by the Greeks under Alexander of
Macedon. Greek kings and queens then ruled Egypt for
nearly three centuries. After the Greeks came the Romans.

All this submerged Pharaonic civilisation. Yet Egypt remained rich and influential. Under its Greek rulers, after
325 BC, Egyptian trade flourished with the lands of the
Red Sea and the northern Indian Ocean. This was the
period when Greek and Indian merchants began to form
the wide circuit of trade of the Indian Ocean which the
Arabs later carried to completion. It has been noted that it
was a Greek merchant of Egypt who wrote the first description of the East African Coast, the *Periplus of the Erythraean Sea,* in about AD 120.[2] For about five centuries, first
under Greek rule and then under Roman, the ships of
Egypt dominated the trade of the Red Sea and the coastal
waters of Arabia and North-east Africa.

This domination declined for a number of reasons. One
was the emergence of a new empire in Persia under the
Sassanids, who broke away from the overlordship of Rome.
By the time of King Bahram V (AD 420–39), the Persian
navy was strong enough to control the ocean trade along
the coasts of Arabia, Persia and western India, seriously
weakening commercial links between Egypt and East Africa. The Sassanid empire continued until Muslim Arabs
overwhelmed its armies in AD 643.

Another set of events that were to have some importance
for Africa occurred at this time in India. After about AD
300 there was founded the famous empire of the Gupta
rulers in the north, introducing a period of progress in
many fields of Indian life. The foreign trade of Indian
states began to grow, and the demand for African products
increased. When Muslim Arab sailors and merchants took
over the Indian Ocean trading circuit after about AD 700,

[2] See Chapter 2.

they found many Indian partners. Trade with East and Central Africa steadily expanded.

Later Events: Sudan and Egypt

The ancient kingdom of Kush, in the Northern Sudan, declined after about AD 200. Nomad peoples from the half-desert lands to east and west of the Nile, among them the Noba and the Blemmye, began to move into its fertile pastures along the Nile, and settle there.

In about AD 320 the cities of Meroitic Kush were ravaged by an invasion of the king of Axum in Ethiopia. These cities never recovered. But the Axumites appear to have made no effort to remain in Kush. They took their invading armies back to their own country, leaving the Noba and the Blemmye largely in control. These peoples were nomadic cattle-raisers who had moved into the good farming lands along the Meroitic Nile and begun to change their way of life, as many others had done before them. Such slender evidence as we have suggests that they had reached some kind of understanding with the urban Kush-ites, and were living more or less peacefully alongside them. But now, with the collapse of the Meroitic system, these farmers or at any rate some of them evidently min-gled with the Kushites and themselves began living in towns. Out of this came a new variant of Nubian civilisa-tion, non-literate and cruder than that of Kush and yet distinguished by some aspects of its own, such as flamboy-ant jewellery. This variant was known to the archaeologists of the early twentieth century, who first uncovered it, as "X Group." This "X Group" mingling then gave rise to something very different.

Christian monks from Alexandria set out to convert the old lands of Kush around the middle of the sixth century. Here they found three small kingdoms which clearly re-flected, if at a much lower level of general culture, the old divisions of the Kushite empire in Nubia. In the north, with its capital near Wadi Halfa, was Nobatia; in the middle, with its capital near Dongola, lay Makuria; while far to the south, with its capital at Soba on the Blue Nile not far from modern Khartum, was Alodia. By AD 600 all the leading people of these three kingdoms had accepted Christianity.

This new Christian civilisation of inner Africa endured for more than six centuries, and made progress that was often brilliant in its cultural achievement. Monasteries and churches flourished, and handsome towns. Books were written in Nubian, using a Greek script, as well as in Greek. Artists decorated churches with excellent paintings. In AD 950 an Egyptian traveller, Ibn Selim al-Aswani, described the city of Soba, capital of Alodia, as having "fine buildings, spacious houses, churches with much gold, and gardens."

Nubian Christianity reached its zenith in the tenth and eleventh centuries, strong in its social structure and its faith. Relations with the Muslim Arabs who had ruled Egypt since the seventh century were generally good, and there was much trade between them. But they came to blows in the twelfth century, and eventually the Egyptians prevailed. Even so, the southernmost kingdom, Alodia, was able to conserve much of its Christian culture until the late fifteenth century and the rise on the Middle Nile, around 1500, of a new line of African Muslim rulers known as the Fung, who made their capital at Sennar on the Blue Nile.

Egyptian conquest of the northern Nubian kingdom was associated with the rise of the Ayyubids, a new line of rulers in Cairo who were of Turkish origin. Their coming was among the consequences of the rise of the Seljuk Turks in Western Asia after AD 1000. These bold horsemen, whose leaders were Sunnite Muslims, swept out of their Turkish lands and conquered the Muslim countries to the south. In 1055 they took Bagdad, in 1076 Damascus. In Egypt the rule of the Shi'ite kings of the Fatimid line was gravely threatened. Then in 1096 a new danger appeared on the scene from Western Europe: the Crusaders, who strove to win back from Muslim hands the Holy Places at Jerusalem.

Egypt came under the rule of the Seljuk Turkish leaders. In 1171 the greatest of them, Salah ad-Din Yusuf ibn Ayub, whom the Crusaders knew as Saladin, ousted the last weak Fatimid ruler and took power, beginning the Ayyubid dynasty in Egypt.

But in 1250 the Ayyubids were displaced by another line of rulers called the Mamluks. These were leaders among the soldiers whom the Ayyubids had recruited, mainly from the slave markets of Western Asia, to fight the Crusaders and other enemies. The Mamluks proved to be strong rulers. They defended Egypt against many perils, holding off invaders from Asia and expelling the Crusaders from the footholds these had gained. The foremost of these Mamluk rulers were Sultan Baybars (1260–77) and Sultan Kala'un (1279–90). Through all this time, as the next chapter will show, Egypt prospered. There was steady growth of trade with many lands including the coastal areas of East Africa.

In 1517 the Mamluks were in turn displaced by Ottoman Turkish viceroys who remained in power until late in the nineteenth century. In 1820 their viceroy in Egypt, Muhamad Ali, invaded the Sudan and opened a direct contact between Egypt and the Interior lands of East Africa that were to become the southern Sudan and Uganda.

Ethiopia

The foundations of Ethiopia, as briefly noted in Chapter 2, were laid before the Christian era began. After several centuries of successful growth, the Ethiopians who were living in the northern part of the country were strong enough to found the state of Axum in about AD 100. Axum flourished on long-distance trade, with its main port at Adulis on the Red Sea. Merchants of many countries came there, as did Christian missionaries from the lands of the Eastern Roman Empire. Soon after AD 300 the king of Axum accepted Christianity.

By about 350 Axum had become the strongest state in the southern area of the Red Sea and North-east Africa. Its trading caravans moved far into the inland country in search of gold, ivory and other goods. They may have gone as far as northern Kenya and Uganda.

After 700 Axum declined in the struggle against pagan peoples in the south and west and against Muslims in the north and east. Little is known about the long years of trouble that followed. But this was the period in which modern Ethiopia first took shape.

After 1100 a new line of rulers, known as the Zagwe, grew strong in the mountain country to the south of Axum. These were the men who rescued early Ethiopia from destruction by its enemies and rivals. Tough warriors, always in the field at the head of their soldiers, the Zagwe kings gradually extended their power. One of them, King Lalibela, is also remembered because of a remarkable palace and several churches which he caused to be hewn in solid rock at a place called Roha.

Meanwhile, new states ruled by Muslims came into existence along the shores of north-eastern Ethiopia and what is now northern Somalia.[3] Following the inland trade routes from Zeila, these states dealt in ivory, gold and slaves. These they got in exchange for cotton goods and other manufactures from the pagan peoples who lived to the south of Ethiopia, among whom the traders of Axum had once carried on their business.

Not long before 1300 the Christian kings of Ethiopia, now of the Solomonic line (so named because of their legendary claim to have descended from King Solomon and the Queen of Sheba), began to move against these Muslim states. Small raiding wars continued through the fourteenth century. Soon after 1400 the Muslims began

[3] See also Chapter 3, *Somali and Galla.*

to fight back, objecting to the taxes which the Ethiopians demanded they should pay.

In 1415 the Ethiopians defeated Ifat, whose capital was at Zeila. Northern Ifat became an Ethiopian province, but its rulers escaped and built another Muslim state further east, Adel. A hundred years later, Adel declared war on Ethiopia in the name of Islam, and, under the lead of a forceful ruler, Ahmad Gran, invaded the eastern lands of the Ethiopian empire. Adel won many successes in these wars, partly because it had firearms, which were now used in Ethiopia for the first time. Only the help of a Portuguese military expedition, which also had firearms and came to Ethiopia at the last moment at the request of the Ethiopian emperor, saved the country from Muslim conquest.

Not for another three centuries was Ethiopia again invaded. Safe in its mountains, the Christian empire avoided the fate that overcame the Christians of Nubia, and Ethiopia today can rightly claim to be the oldest surviving Christian state in the world.

Comparably great changes had meanwhile been in course in other parts of the continent, notably in the west. Here, too, the simple systems of Early Iron Age times had developed into powerful states and empires; and here, too, the influence of long-distance trade had had a fructifying effect. Expansive centres of cultural growth took shape in Ghana, Mali, Songhay, Kanem-Bornu, Benin and elsewhere. Meanwhile to the north-west of the Sahara the Almoravid Berbers, and then their Almohad successors, had expanded the Muslim colonisation of Spain and built a lavish and often brilliant civilisation there. Comparative dates are indicated in the Time Charts at the end of this book.

Influences for East and Central Africa

This brief sketch of changes in the outside world may be enough to illustrate the rich and various nature of East

and Central Africa's contact with foreign lands. By direct
contact through sailors who came to the Coast, and by
indirect contact through trade with parts of the Interior,
many Africans were influenced, from time to time and in
differing ways, by a wide range of civilisations.

Egypt, Persia, Arabia, Ethiopia, Sudan, India and some
Asian lands still further away, all had their part in this.
But it was along the Coast, and among the Islands, that
this contact was much the strongest. After the rise of Islam
the people of these areas were drawn increasingly within
the Islamic community.

6. NORTHERN CHANGES—2: RISE AND GROWTH OF ISLAM

On July 16, AD 622, the man who was to become the Prophet Muhammad, revered by millions, journeyed with three companions from Mecca to Medina. From this journey or *Hijra* there flowed the world religion of Islam. Within a hundred years its soldiers, teachers and merchants had carried their faith all the way across North Africa and south-western Europe, and, in the East, as far as Malaysia and China.

Rise of Islam

Muhammad preached against the old pagan beliefs of Arabia. He wished to make the Arabs a "people of the Book," as were the Jews and the Christians, and for this purpose he composed the Koran which, Muslims believe, was dictated to him by God. Many listened and were moved by his call to a new way of life. So great was the success of the Muslims, a mere handful though they were at first, that within twenty-two years of the *Hijra* the men of the new religion, taking to the sword, had brought wide areas of Arabia, Syria and Egypt within their control.

Having done that, they went still farther afield. Their expeditions swept far to the west and east. By 670 one of their foremost generals, 'Uqba ibn Nafi, had established Muslim Arab rule over most of northern Libya and Tunisia. Thirteen years later the horsemen of these victorious armies had come within sight of the waters of the Atlantic along the north Moroccan coast. In 711 another of their generals, Tariq, sailed across the narrow Mediterranean straits at the head of an army, and burst into Christian Spain, carrying all before him and laying the foundations

of a brilliant Muslim civilisation. Only in 732 were the
northward expeditions of the Muslims turned back by
Christian knights at the battle of Poitiers in central France.

These successes were repeated in the East. In 643 the
armies of Islam scattered those of Sassanid Persia, and
pushed eastward. Henceforth it was to be the Muslims,
whether Arab, Persian or Indian, who would dominate
the commercial life of the countries along the northern
shores of the Indian Ocean. By the eighth century there
were Arab and other Muslim trading settlements as far
distant as the Chinese port of Canton. A wide network of
Indian Ocean commerce was knit together by the ties of
Islam.

Soon after this the beliefs of Islam began to be accepted
by a few of the trading peoples of the Coast and Islands
of Africa. Here too, Muslim civilisation began to put down
firm roots that were to grow and flower across many years.

The Great Age of Islam

To understand why the peoples of the Coast and Islands
entered on a period of many-sided achievement with the
acceptance of Islam, it is necessary to reflect a little on
the nature of Muslim civilisation.

It may be said to have gone through three main periods.
During the first, from 622 until about 800, the Arabs made
their many conquests, settled in new lands, and built up
their power and wealth. The second period, which has
been called the Great Age of Islam, lasted from about 850
until about 1300. In these four centuries the peoples of
the Muslim world, reaching from south-western Europe to
the middle of Asia and beyond, lit the lamps of learning,
art, and science in a host of splendid cities. They were in
the vanguard of world progress. Then after about 1300,
a third period opened with the rise of soldier kings and
a gradual cultural decline and stagnation. There were considerable achievements after 1300, but the historical glory

of Muslim civilisation belongs mainly to the Great Age before that time, when every important city had its scholars and scientists, poets, historians, geographers, architects, teachers of religion, who rescued, from forgotten libraries, the scholarship of the Ancient World of the Mediterranean that had vanished when nomad peoples from northern Europe overthrew the Roman empire. They translated into Arabic the books of Ancient Greek thinkers such as Aristotle and Euclid. They studied these books and wrote others of their own. They founded great libraries. They built fine mosques. They composed much poetry. Learned men travelled up and down the world, and described what they saw. Many of their writings, such as those of al-Mas'udi, are of value for the history of many lands, including much of Africa.

It would be wrong, however, to think that the Muslims were always at peace among themselves, or united under a single government. On the contrary, the early unity of the Muslim Arabs under Muhammad soon gave way to conflicts. The first of these arose not long after the Prophet's death, when 'Ali, who had married Fatima, the Prophet's daughter, became the fourth Caliph. Mu'awiya, the governor of the Muslim province of Syria, broke away from the Caliph in 657 and set up a new dynasty, the Ummayads. Out of this there came the principal division of loyalties within Islam between the Sunnites, who accepted Mu'awiya and his Ummayad successors, and the Shi'ites who did not.

Other conflicts had a geographical basis. New states emerged in North Africa and in Spain, as also in western Asia, known to history by the names of their various lines of rulers. After the ninth century much of western Asia was ruled or deeply influenced by a Muslim state ruled by the Abbasids, whose capital was Bagdad in Iraq. After the tenth century the greater part of Egypt, Libya and Tunisia was ruled by the Fatimids. Southern Spain knew a period of high civilisation under the Ummayads of the West, then under the Almoravids (1061–1147), and afterwards under the Almohads (1147–1289).

Within the wide boundaries of the Muslim community, the *Dar al-Islam*,[1] there were also differences of belief and custom. Both in Asia and Africa the new religion became mingled with the old religions of those lands. Some Muslims remained strictly loyal to the early teachings of Muhammad, while others adapted them to earlier ideas. One of the most important of these adaptations was Sufism. Another, of a different kind, was the Karidjite brotherhood which became important in north-western Africa.

A further development within Islam should be noted here. The Prophet had taught the need for equality among all who accepted his inspired message. It was this message that lay at the core of much of Islam's early success. In this respect the teachings of the Prophet were of a revolutionary kind. He opened a vision of life in which the poor and humble should be able to share in the blessings of this world along with the rich and powerful.

But these teachings about equality and social justice were defeated by the political realities of the times. As early as the reign of the Caliph Umar (634–44, or years 13–24 of the Muslim Era) it had to be recognised that there were political and social differences among Muslims. Some were rich and others poor: what was more important, a few people were growing richer while most were not.

By the beginning of the ninth century, or about the year 185 of the Muslim Era, these differences had grown very sharp. A Muslim writer of those days, Ibn Faqih, described the scene. There were, he said, four main ranks of people in the Muslim states: "the ruler, whom merit has placed in the first rank: then the vizier (chief governor or prime minister), who is distinguished by wisdom and

---

[1] Muslims divided the world into two areas: the *Dar al-Islam,* the Area or Home of Islam where Muslims ruled, and the *Dar al-Harb,* the Area of War which Muslims were supposed to conquer on behalf of their Faith. Christians, of course, had much the same idea.

power: then the high-placed people, whose wealth has carried them upwards: and then the middle classes who are linked to these three other ranks by their education." As for the remainder of mankind, who were of course the majority, Ibn Faqih dismissed them as "mere scum who understand nothing but food and sleep." By this time, in other words, the grand vision of the Rightly-Guided Caliphate, the rule of equality and social justice within the Dar al-Islam, had almost vanished from the scene of practical affairs. Yet it remained alive in the minds of men. Again and again, in later centuries, Muslim reformers and revolutionaries were to try to renew this vision and make it a reality.[2]

The Unity of Islam

This worldwide civilisation was increasingly joined by the peoples of the Coast and Islands of Africa after about 900: in a period, that is, when Islam was approaching the peak of its historical achievement. As Muslims, they shared in a great culture; and men of learning and religion could find a welcome in the cities they founded. Distant though they were from the centers of Muslim civilisation, these peoples reproduced along the Coast a little of the comfort and luxury of Cairo and Bagdad.

They were able to do so because of the underlying unity of all Muslims. There were indeed many divisions within Islam: of political loyalty, of religious custom, of social organisation. Yet all Muslims continued to feel themselves members of a single great community and tended to unite against all non-Muslims, whether these were Christian, Buddhist, or of other beliefs.

[2] Those who wish to read further in the political history of Islam might begin with G. E. von Grunebaum, *Medieval Islam,* 1946, and then go straight to the greatest of all Arabic historical works, *The Muqaddimah* of Ibn Khaldun, trans. F. Rosenthal, 3 vols. 1967 (2nd edn.), especially vol. 1.

This fundamental unity was especially important in two ways: in the development of thought and science, and in the development of trade. What united the Muslims, in these ways, proved more important than the conflicts which divided them. The former meant that Muslim scholars could pass freely from one Muslim country to another, always hopeful that they would find hospitality, help, and companionship. And many of them did travel widely. We have noted that the geographer, al-Mas'udi (born about AD 890, died about 956), sailed down the East African coast as far as Tanzania. The spirit of such men was well expressed by another famous scholar, the historian al-Biruni (973–c.1050). "It is our duty," he wrote, "to proceed in our work from what is near to what is distant, from what is known to what is less known, to gather the traditions from those who have reported them, to correct them as much as possible and to leave the rest as it is, in order to make our work help everyone who seeks truth and loves wisdom."

Ibn Battuta, a Moroccan, was another celebrated traveller of the fourteenth century who was acquainted with East Africa. As a young man he set out from Morocco upon a journey to India and China, visiting on his way the coasts of Somalia, Kenya and Tanzania. In 1331 he went as far south as Kilwa, which he praised as a beautiful city. Towards the end of his life, in 1351, he made another long journey across the Sahara to the empire of Mali and other lands of West Africa.

This worldwide fellowship of the learned led to the writing of countless books and the foundation of countless schools for the teaching of religion, philosophy, and other subjects. When they joined Islam, the peoples of the Coast and Islands were linking themselves to a great network not only of trade but also of scholarship.

Throughout the Great Age of Islam, and for long afterwards, there were two major areas of Muslim trade: one centering on the markets of North and West Africa and

Spain, and the other on those of the Indian Ocean. Joining the two was the rich city of Cairo.

Trading towns and ports were linked by travelling merchants. In the western area they travelled by camel across the Sahara, carrying with them goods which they bartered to West Africans for gold, ivory, and other African products. In the eastern area they sailed across the Indian Ocean to Africa and India, Ceylon, South-east Asia, and China. In Cairo one could buy gold from West Africa, silk from China, ivory from East Africa, cotton goods from India, fine swords from Syria, and a variety of other things from all over the Muslim world and its fringes.

7. THE COAST AND ISLANDS
1000-1500

At the beginning of this period there were only a few small trading settlements along the Coast between the Horn of Africa and southern Mozambique, and on some of the Islands. Then came a steady growth of civilisation as Asian traders sailed back and forth across the Indian Ocean, and linked the Coast and Islands ever more closely to the whole network of seagoing commerce. Villages grew into small towns, and small towns into stone-built cities. By 1400 there were no fewer than thirty-seven towns, some of them wealthy and well-known.

The Coming of Islam

Villages of fishing and farming folk came into existence along the coral shores of East Africa more than two thousand years ago. But the earliest regular settlements of any size that are known to archaeologists were founded only in about 700 or a little later. These include a small settlement at Unguju Ukuu on Zanzibar, and others, which had stone buildings even in this early period, at Manda on Manda Island. At Unguju Ukuu the inhabitants lived in simple huts made of clay plastered on a framework of poles stuck in the ground, a method of hut-building used by many Africans. The people of Unguju Ukuu were already in touch with sea-traders from the north, for pottery from the countries round the Persian Gulf has been found there. As yet, however, none of them seems to have been Muslim; in any case no mosque sites of this early period have yet been found.

Towards 900 this situation changed in two important ways. First, as the Great Age of Islam got into its stride, more ships and merchants came from Arabia and India in quest of gold and ivory, tortoise shell, and other products. It was at this time that the villages began to grow into small towns. Traders came ashore and stayed for longer periods, or settled here permanently. Secondly, Islam won its first firm footholds among the coastal peoples, to begin with, mostly on islands such as Manda, Pemba, and Zanzibar.

Out of this mingling of local Africans and Muslim visitors from Arabia and India, there came the civilisation of the Swahili, a Muslim civilisation that was also African.[1] By 1000 there were many Muslims in these growing towns, especially on Zanzibar and Pemba, and in the towns of the Banadir Coast. In 1100 the first stone mosques were built. Some of the towns were now growing into city-states. A few of them, notably Kilwa, eventually became strong enough to exercise control over several smaller ones, though none ever achieved power in the inland country beyond a dozen or twenty miles from their walls. Often they quarrelled over the sharing of trade and taxes. But all belonged to the same culture and drew their strength from trade. And the same language, kiSwahili, was spoken in all of them, though with varying dialects, while their leading citizens usually knew Arabic.

Early Muslim traders: The Daybuli

Most of the people of these towns were ancestors of the Swahili of today. They were an East African people of the Bantu language group. But there was a constant arrival of traders and settlers from across the seas, mainly from Oman and the Persian Gulf, who married local women and founded new families. So this culture, partly because it was Muslim and partly because of this continuing migration of Arab settlers whose influence was

[1] See Chapter 10, *The Civilization of the Swahili.*

much greater than their numbers, became significantly different from that of the inland peoples.

In determining who these settlers were, where they came from, and when, historians face a difficulty, for the evidence of archaeology seldom agrees with that of the traditions. The archaeological evidence shows that Islam had no important footholds along the Coast, or among the Islands, until about 900. But local traditions tell a different tale. Several Swahili histories have come down to us from earlier times. Six of them are important. One of these is from Mogadishu on the Banadir Coast; four are from Kenya (Pate, Lamu, Mombasa, Vumba); while one, in some ways the most valuable of all, is from Kilwa in Tanzania. They suggest that Islam had been accepted long before AD 900. The *History of Pate*, for example, claims that a group of Syrian Muslims founded thirty-five towns along the Coast in AD 696, while the *History of Lamu* states that a Muslim city was founded on that island at about the same date.

Faced with this conflict of evidence, modern historians have given a clear preference to that of archaeology. Most of the Swahili histories seem first to have been written—as distinct from being orally recited—within the past hundred years; much that they have to tell about events in the distant past is unlikely to be exact. The correct conclusion seems to be that Muslim traders, and perhaps a few settlers, did indeed begin coming down the Coast after about AD 650, but that they had little cultural influence on the coastal peoples until several centuries later.

This opinion is supported by the history of the rest of the Indian Ocean seaboard. One tradition common to much of the Coast, for example, is that the earliest Arab settlers of this period were the "Daybuli." It is suggested that these were in truth people from Daybul, an ancient seaport in north-western India which Muslim Arabs had captured in AD 711. From that time, Daybul developed as a chief base for Muslim Arab commerce in the Indian Ocean. Its merchants and captains increasingly dominated the trade with the Persian Gulf, with other Arab seaports such as Siraf in southern Arabia, and with the trading settlements of the Swahili Coast. These were the enterprising pioneers who now brought prosperity to the coastal trade, and whose descendants, mingling with the Swahili, helped to develop the coastal villages into towns, and the towns into city-states.

The "Daybuli" are thought to have begun arriving in about 750 or soon after, and to have been joined later by other newcomers from Arabia, Persia, and India. They were evidently few in number, but they and their new ideas about trade and town-life seem generally to have been welcomed by the peoples of the Coast and Islands. The cities they helped to build were increasingly Muslim in their religion. Their peoples thought of themselves, more and more, as part of the *umma,* of the wide family of Islam; and these worldwide connections became a source of pride for them.

But this should not be interpreted to mean that the coastal cities were Arab or Indian. In their great majority they undoubtedly were African; even the rulers with Arabic-sounding names were the sons of local people. This was therefore an *African* Muslim civilisation. Islam became naturalised here just as it did in North Africa among the Berbers, and in the Western Sudan among the Mandinka, Songhay and other African populations. These cities were not Arab or Indian colonies, but African city-states which retained strong Arab and Indian links through trade and culture.

So strong was the Muslim accent in this new civilisation, however, that for long it was thought to be Arab and not African. It may be worth noting, therefore, that what happened here was comparable to what happened in Anglo-Saxon England after the Norman invasion of 1066. After that Norman conquest from France, many French ideas and customs were introduced to the Anglo-Saxons. Kings and noblemen spoke French to one another. Great cathedrals were built in styles influenced by those of Normandy. The civilisation of the Anglo-Saxons was greatly modified. Yet this civilisation became not French but English, a blending and mingling of French with Anglo-Saxon. Much the same happened along the East African Coast and Islands. A new civilisation sprang to life. And the Swahili language, for example, developed with the adoption of many Arabic words and usages, just as the language of the Anglo-Saxons in England developed, with the use of many French words, into the parent of the English that we speak today.

Zanzibar and Pemba

Swahili language repeatedly evolved with the adoption of Arabic words. The name of Zanzibar, one of the most important centers of the Daybuli period, is a good example of this change of language. Its old Swahili name was Unguja. But the Arab newcomers called the East Coast Zanj-Bar, "the coast of the Zanj" or Africans. And because Unguja was one of their most frequent places of call, the island began to be known as Zanzibar.

There are other examples. Some of the newcomers to Unguja, or Zanzibar, must have come from the Persian Gulf. This is confirmed by an interesting piece of evidence. In Persia the Muslims went on reckoning time by months and years based on the changes of the sun, and not of the moon. They celebrated the first day of the solar year by the feast of *Nauruz*. This festival was also kept in Unguja after it had become Zanzibar, and even today is called the feast of *Nairuzi*. It is the same with the words *sheha* and *diwani*, old Zanzibar titles for governing officials, which are of Persian origin. It should be noted, however, that almost all these words of Persian origin probably reached the East Coast through travellers or settlers whose own language was not Persian, but Arabic, for the Arabic dialect spoken round the Persian Gulf had in its time likewise absorbed a number of Persian words.

Zanzibar and Pemba were among the first Muslim settlements of any size. Most of these settlements were on small islands such as Tumbatu or along the seashore at such places as Kizimkazi on Zanzibar, or Mkumbuu on Pemba. They had to be skilfully placed for defence against enemies on land and raiders from the sea. The earliest piece of writing known in East Africa comes from Kizimkazi. This is an inscription on a wall which states that the Shaikh al-Sayid Abi Amran ordered the building of a mosque on the first day of the month of Dhul-Qada in the year 500 of the Muslim Era: that is, on July 27, AD 1107.

As the towns grew in strength, they became increasingly Swahili. Their trade expanded, and their rulers and merchants were able to live comfortable lives, building good stone houses, buying Chinese and Persian cups and saucers for their tableware as the decoration of their dwellings, and dressing in coloured cottons imported from India. Not everyone, of course, shared in this prosperity; here, as elsewhere in the world, the good of the few had to be built at the cost of the many. The kings and merchants forced the local farmers and fishermen to work for them and seized from the local farmers the land they needed for coconut or other plantations. This is no doubt why the Hadimu farmers of Zanzibar have remembered the people they call the "Daybuli" as cruel masters.

Yet Swahili civilisation continued to expand, as many ruins on Zanzibar and Pemba, and at other places along the Coast, amply prove. These ruins confirm that several prosperous towns came into existence during the Daybuli period between about 900 and 1200.

Links with distant lands

This early period of the founding of stone towns, and the establishment of Islam, was followed by another and still more successful epoch of growth and expansion, beginning in about 1200 and continuing until the Portuguese ravages shortly after 1500.

During these three fruitful centuries the ancient civilisation of the Coast and Islands reached the peak of its achievement. Member-states of the wide Muslim world, these cities grew rich and powerful. Their kings and leading merchants lived in palaces of stone, often finely decorated with windows and niches of carved coral that were filled with splendid plates and vases from Persia and China.

All this reflected a commercial expansion across the Indian Ocean, for which there is plenty of written evidence from several foreign countries. In about 1250, for example, an inspector of customs in southern China wrote a book[2] in which he described how the ships of the northwest Indian kingdom of Gujerat sailed every year to East Africa, to the "land of the Zanj," with supplies of cotton cloth and other goods. A century earlier the outstanding medieval geographer, al-Idrisi, had also published useful though secondhand information about the Coast and Islands. He says that one of East Africa's most valued exports was iron, and that there were many iron mines there. So highly was this metal prized in India, for its good quality, that traders from as far away as Java and Sumatra found it worthwhile to come every year in order to buy it for sale to Indian markets. This book, completed in 1154 but often using earlier sources, contains the first mention of Malindi and Mombasa.[3]

Gradually East African sailors began to engage in the ocean commerce. They had long been skilled in sailing along their own shores; now they ventured further. Thus the Swahili *History of Pate*[4] recounts that Sultan Omar, who ruled in about 1350, "was extremely fond of money

[2] Chao Ju-kua, *Chu Fan-chi* (*Record of Foreign Peoples*): Eng. trans. Hirth and Rockhill, St. Petersburg, 1911.

[3] al-Idris, *Kitab Nuzhat al-Mushtaq Fi'khtiraq al Afaq*, Palermo, Sicily, 1154. (Various partial translations in English: notably, for the East African sections, by S. Maqbul Ahmad, Leiden, 1960.)

[4] Reprinted in English translation in G. S. P. Freeman-Grenville, *The East African Coast; Select Documents*, 1962, p. 241.

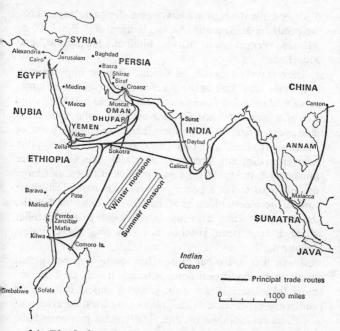

14. The Indian Ocean and its trade in about AD 1200

and of trade, and caused men to make voyages in ships, and sent them to India and traded there; and he had great good luck in making money." Pate is said in this *History* to have been the strongest city-state along the seaboard, and to have dominated the others as far south as Kilwa. Other Swahili histories disagree and apparently with good reason; but Pate was certainly an important commercial center at this time.

Of the ships they used, the biggest were like the *jahazis*[5] of today. True, Africans also sailed on Indian ships bound for the Far East. In 1515 a Portuguese who was living in the seaport of Malacca, not far from modern Singapore

[5] *Jahazi* is from the Hindustani word for a ship.

described the foreign traders whom he met there. They included, he said, many Arabs, Indians and Persians, as well as "people from Kilwa, Malindi, Mogadishu, and Mombasa."

They travelled as far as China. Chinese imperial records state that ambassadors arrived from "Ma-lin," presumably Malindi on the Kenya seaboard, in 1415 with the gift of a giraffe for the Chinese emperor, who, two years later, sent a fleet to carry them home and make visits of exploration. This, and one other expedition a few years later, are the only occasions on which the Chinese are known to have visited the Coast in ancient times. But large quantities of Chinese porcelain were imported to all these towns, the oldest piece of which, lately found at Manda, dates to the T'ang Dynasty (AD 618–906). Any stroller along East African beaches can still pick up countless fragments.

There was one other reason for coastal prosperity that needs to be mentioned here, although it will be discussed more fully later. This was the growing importance of gold and ivory production in the inland countries, especially of the Zambezi-Limpopo plateau. Throughout this period the gold of the Interior, especially of the area that was to become the empire of the Mwanamutapa, was bought by all the peoples of the Indian Ocean seaboard, and by more distant foreigners, while the gold trade became especially valuable for the cities of the south-eastern coast, above all for Kilwa. Without it they could never have attracted so much foreign trade. Together with ivory, gold was the most useful of all the products that the Swahili could obtain for sale abroad.

The Shirazi

The second period of expansion, after 1200, is linked by some traditions along the Coast, especially in Tanzania and Zanzibar, with newcomers called the Shirazi.

The *History of Kilwa,* written in Arabic in about 1520, describes the coming of the Shirazi as follows: "Historians have said that the first man to come to Kilwa came in the following way. There arrived a ship in which there were people who claimed to have come from Shiraz in the land of the Persians. It is said that there were seven ships.

"The first stopped at Mandakha (almost certainly on Manda island); the second at Shauga; the third at a town called Yanbu; the fourth at Mombasa; the fifth at the Green Island (Pemba); the sixth at the land of Kilwa; and the seventh at Hazuan. They say that all the captains of the first six ships were brothers, and that the one who went to the town of Hazuan was their father . . ."

In this case tradition is again in conflict with other evidence. But it appears to have at least a core of truth. In the case of the Shirazi, historians now believe that newcomers from the north did indeed come down the Coast in about 1200, but probably from the towns of the Banadir Coast, north of Kenya, and not from Shiraz in Persia. They may of course have had some Persian ancestors; it is very likely that they did. Nonetheless, the ruling families who afterwards called themselves "the Shirazi" were no doubt merely remembering their distant ancestors, or were perhaps inventing a distinguished foreign ancestry for themselves, a habit by no means limited to Africans.

Kilwa City and its influence

Of the many cities which rose to fame and wealth after 1200, none was more successful than Kilwa. Its history helps to illustrate not only that of the East African coastland in this period, but also of parts of Central Africa as well. For Kilwa won increasing control over the southeastern coast, and here lay the ports which handled the gold and ivory production of the inland countries.

This strong commercial position brought many advances. The first king of the Shirazi period, Ali bin al-

Hasan, began minting coins for the first time. Like those of his successors, these were mainly copper, though a few were also made of silver. They show the name of the king who minted them, but, unfortunately, no dates. Though all are of much the same size, they were of several different values. Other coins of this kind were afterward minted on Zanzibar, and probably also at Mogadishu on the Banadir Coast, though the evidence for this last is not yet conclusive. As well as these coins the trading cities also used a currency of cowries, which they imported in large quantities from the Maldive Islands of the Indian Ocean.

An interesting point about these coins is that more of those minted for King Ali bin al-Hasan have been found at Kisimani, on the island of Mafia, than at Kilwa itself. Long since ruined, Kisimani was a flourishing seaport after 1200. In 1964 the biggest single collection of East African coins ever discovered, including no fewer than 570 of King Ali's, was found in a pot buried against the wall of a ruined mosque there, suggesting that Kisimani in 1200 was as important as Kilwa, and may even have been the capital of the early rulers of Kilwa.

But Kilwa soon outshone Kisimani. Travelling there in 1331 the wandering Ibn Battuta, then on his way to China, was impressed by what he saw. Long afterwards he dictated his memoirs. "Kilwa," he recalled, "is one of the most beautiful and well-constructed towns in the world. The whole of it is elegantly built . . ."[6] Among the buildings that he must have admired was a large palace outside the city walls, now the ruin that the people of Kilwa call Husuni Kubwa, the Big Fortress. The British archaeologist, Neville Chittick, worked there in 1961–65, and uncovered

[6] This sentence can also be read, in the original Arabic, to mean that Kilwa was built "entirely of wood." But we know from the archaeologists that this was not true: Kilwa in 1331 had large stone buildings. If Ibn Battuta really said "built entirely of wood," his memory must have been at fault; after all, he dictated his memoirs nearly thirty years later. But some scholars have suggested that the sentence can also be read as "elegantly built," and I have adopted this reading here.

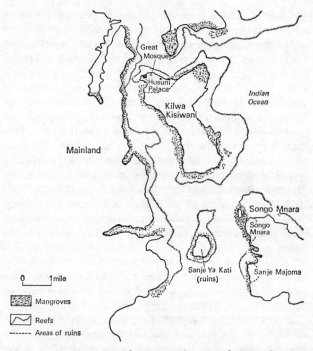

15. Kilwa and its neighboring settlements before the coming of the Portuguese

the ruins of a fine group of buildings with courtyards, good washing arrangements, a large eight-sided bathing pool, and many dozen apartments.[7] The Portuguese were also impressed by Kilwa, as by other coastal cities, when they first arrived. One of them, a merchant called Barbosa, described Kilwa as he saw it soon after 1500. It was, he wrote, a town "with many fine houses of stone and mortar, with many windows after our European fashion, and very well arranged in streets . . . The house doors are of wood,

[7] See P. S. Garlake, *Early Islamic Architecture of the East African Coast,* 1966.

well carved, and with excellent joinery. Around the town
are streams and orchards and fruit gardens . . ."

The same Portuguese wrote of Mombasa that it had
"lofty houses of stone and mortar, well aligned in streets
like Kilwa." It was also "a place of great seagoing trade
with a good harbor, where boats and big ships of many
kinds are always to be found. These ships trade with Sofala," the south-eastern seaport for the gold trade of
Central Africa. "Some of them come from the great (Indian) kingdom of Cambay, from Malindi, and from Zanzibar." Malindi was another city with "many handsome
houses of stone and mortar several storeys high, with many
windows and flat roofs . . . and well laid-out in streets."
Here, too, the Cambay merchants often came "in many
ships with cargoes of goods which they sell for gold and
ivory and beeswax, making great profits and earning much
money . . ."

Zanzibar and Pemba, wrote Barbosa at the beginning
of the sixteenth century, "are very fertile islands, with
plenty of food: rice, millet, and fish, and abundant oranges
and lemons . . . There are people in these islands who live
in great luxury and comfort. They dress in good clothes of
silk and cotton which they buy in Mombasa from the Cambay merchants who live there. Their wives wear many
jewels of gold from Sofala, and silver chains, earrings,
bracelets and rings, and they dress in silk." To this it needs
to be added, however, that there were many people in
Zanzibar and Pemba who lived in no luxury at all, but as
poor farmers and fishermen.

Other towns likewise flourished. Some have long since
declined and today show only by their ruins what they
once were. Among these is Gedi, not far from Malindi.
Gedi was abandoned about 1650 for reasons that are not
yet clearly understood, but it knew a period of comfort
and prosperity after 1400, as its ruins amply prove. Northward there were strong trading towns on the Banadir
Coast, notably Mogadishu. An inscription still surviving
on the principal mosque of Mogadishu says that its minaret

was built in 668 of the Muslim Era (AD 1269). Mogadishu was thus among the first of the cities to change from building in clay-and-wood to building in stone, a sure sign of growing wealth.

Wealth from trade and taxes

The source of this wealth was always trade, not production. The cities certainly grew their own food: we have just seen, for example, how much Barbosa admired the gardens of Kilwa. They grew several grains, and cultivated coconuts, pineapples, and other fruits. They bought meat from the cattle-raisers of the inland country and fish from neighboring villages. But they produced little or nothing of what they sold abroad. They were middlemen, and most of their wealth came from acting as the link between the African producers of the inland country and the Asians. Partly it resulted from their own activities as traders, and partly from the taxes which they gathered from other traders.

An early Portuguese account describes how the kings of Kilwa made every visiting merchant who wanted to sell his goods in Kilwa or Sofala, then under Kilwa's overlordship, pay heavily for the right to do so. He had to declare what goods he was importing and turn over a fixed quantity of them to the customs officers. He also had to pay export taxes on the African goods he bought in exchange for the Asian goods he sold. If he sold his goods at Sofala in exchange for gold, he was then supposed to sail back to Kilwa and pay the king another tax, fifty mitcals of gold on every thousand mitcals' worth of gold he had purchased.[8] There was also an export tax on ivory at Sofala, and again at Kilwa, where the visiting merchant was supposed to pay one tusk in every seven that he bought, or

[8] The *mitcal* was an Arab measurement of value. Generally it may be reckoned as being equal in value to about one-eighth of an ounce of gold.

slightly more than fourteen per cent on his ivory purchases. The gold and ivory thus brought into the royal treasury were used by the king for his own trading activities, or for the upkeep of his government, soldiers, and other expenses.

One may note in passing that a similar system existed in western Africa. There, too, it fell into three distinct parts. There were first of all the West African producers of gold and ivory, who lived far from the places of export, but were visited by merchants from middleman cities, such as Timbuktu and Jenne, situated near the southern "shore" of the Saharan "sea of sand." From these middleman cities the gold and other products were sent across the Sahara, just as in East Africa they were sent across the ocean. All this commerce, whether in West or East Africa, had many political consequences not only for the trading cities but also for the producing peoples. These inland consequences will be discussed later.

→ First Indonesian migrations

⇦ Successive migrations (Indonesian and African)

16. (a) Suggested Indonesian routes to Madagascar and the Comores up to the tenth century AD

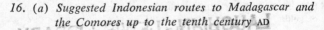

Madagascar and the Comores

The large island of Madagascar was partially settled by Indonesians from Java, Sumatra, and other South-east Asian islands at some time before about AD 500.

Indonesians came in groups over many years, as venturers and traders who conquered and mingled with the Stone Age peoples whom they found. In the course of time, through this process, they ceased to be Indonesians and became a new people, the Malagasy; but their language and some of their customs have retained much that is Indonesian. They took part in the trading network of the Indian Ocean, especially during the Rasikajy period which flourished, in the northern part of Madagascar,

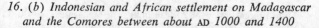

16. (b) Indonesian and African settlement on Madagascar and the Comores between about AD 1000 and 1400

from about the eleventh century AD until the coming of the Portuguese. In the course of time they were joined by settlers from the African mainland, Bantu people who founded new states in the northerly part of the island. Meanwhile the early kingdoms which had been formed in the central part of Madagascar broke down, for reasons that are not yet fully understood; and people lived in hundreds of fortified villages.[9]

The islands of the Comores, groups of small islands along the coast, such as the Kerimbas off Mozambique or the Bajuns off Somalia, have little history of their own. They were used by sea-merchants at least from 850, and their small populations became mingled with newcomers from Arabia, India and the African mainland. Gradually there emerged an island folk of mixed ancestry.

The Portuguese ravages

In 1498 the Portuguese captain Vasco da Gama sailed with three small ships round the southern point of Africa and led the first Europeans into the Indian Ocean. Having voyaged up the Coast, and visited several of its cities, he found at Malindi a pilot named Majid, who took service with da Gama and showed him the way to north-western India. In 1499 da Gama returned to Portugal. His expedition proved to be a turning point in history.

The Portuguese had long been attempting to find a way of outflanking the strong Muslim states of North Africa and Egypt, because they knew that much wealth and trade existed in the African and Asian lands beyond that Muslim barrier. But they could not get there by land, since the Muslims would not let them travel freely through their countries. A few Christian merchants had succeeded in penetrating through North Africa to the Western Sudan.

[9] For a recent review of African links with Madagascar, see R. K. Kent in *Jnl. of African History*, 3 and 4 of 1968, and 1 of 1969.

But the rest of Africa, and the whole of southern and eastern Asia, remained unknown to Europeans.[10]

Thus the Portuguese had for years been trying to sail round Africa, and reach India by sea. They had begun doing this in the 1430s. By 1440 they had gone as far as Senegal in the far west of Africa. In 1472, exploring further, one of their captains reached the coast of modern

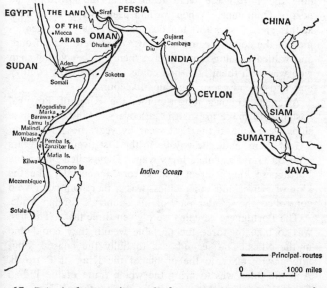

17. Principal countries and places mentioned by Ahmad bin Majid who piloted Vasco da Gama to Calicut in 1498

Nigeria. In 1483 Diogo Cão anchored in the mouth of the Congo river. In 1488 Bartolomeu Diaz sailed as far as the Cape of Good Hope, and a little way beyond. Then in

[10] Much information became available in Europe, however, from the reports of Jewish traders of North Africa who were on good terms with the Arabs, and worked and travelled freely in Muslim lands. See S. D. Goitein, *Studies in Islamic History and Institutions*, Leiden, 1966, espec. Chapters 11 and 17.

1498 da Gama entered the Indian Ocean, and found not only India but also, to his great surprise, the rich cities of the East African coastland, about which Europeans up till then knew nothing.

Da Gama and his sailors were astonished by the wealth and comfort they found there. In a well-known passage of the logbook of his flagship, the *Saint Gabriel,* it is told how the Portuguese were received at the Mozambique port of Quilimane. "When we had been two or three days at this place," says this logbook of 1497–99, "two gentlemen of the country came to see us. They were very proud, and valued nothing that we gave them . . . A young man who was with them . . . had come from a distant country and had already seen big ships like ours."

After da Gama's return home, the King of Portugal hastened to make use of this discovery. Many Portuguese ships were sent to the East, year by year: no fewer than 247 of them made the voyage in the first twenty-five years after da Gama's pioneering voyage. They sailed under the Portuguese king's direct orders, for Manoel III, like the king of Kilwa and other cities, was a merchant-ruler who controlled the greater part of his country's foreign trade.

The Portuguese captains were given three tasks. The first was to take by force the portable wealth they could find in the cities. The second was to bully the coastal kings into paying taxes to the agents of the King of Portugal. And the third was to bring the whole trade of the Indian Ocean, from East Africa to India and southern China, under Portuguese control for the benefit of Manoel III and his business partners.

At this point in time, the Europeans had only two advantages over the Africans of the cities. They were able to attack without warning, and they were trained in a harsher form of warfare than any then known in these countries. Otherwise they had no advantages. Their ships were no bigger, and often were smaller, than those of the Indian Ocean fleets. They had early kinds of guns, but few of these. Their navigating instruments were often inferior to those in use by Indian Ocean shipping. But surprise and ruthlessness served them well.

They brought a new and savage piracy to the Indian Ocean. There had, of course, been quarrels and conflicts before the coming of the Portuguese. One city-state competed with another and sometimes came to blows; but no city-state or other power had any interest in destroying their enemies. It was not their custom or interest to burn and ravage and ruin. Few of the city-states bothered much about building forts or preparing for self-defence, though they nearly always chose a site which could give them natural protection from attack, especially from the mainland. The spirit of the region was neither bitter nor generally dangerous to peace. This spirit was well recorded by a Chinese writer, Chang Hsieh, in 1618. He reminded his readers that they had nothing to fear in meeting foreign peoples so long as they behaved well. "The only things one should be really anxious about," he went on, "are the means of mastery of the waves of the sea, and, worst of all dangers, the minds of men who are thirsty for profit and greedy for gain . . ."

It was not the sort of advice that the voyaging Portuguese, or other Europeans, would have welcomed. The only thing that their captains were anxious about, apart from the waves of the sea, was failure to bring home big profits or capture rich loot. They spared no violence in securing both. They wrecked and looted and burned with a destructiveness previously unknown in Africa.

A German traveller, Hans Mayr, who was with the Portuguese fleet in 1505, described how they behaved at Kilwa and Mombasa, neither of which city was prepared for any such assault. "In Kilwa," he wrote, "there are many strong houses several storeys high. They are built of stone and mortar and plastered with various designs. As soon as the town had been captured [by the Portuguese] without opposition, the Vicar-General and some of the Franciscan priests came ashore, carrying two crosses in procession. They went to the palace, and there the cross was set down and the commander [of the Portuguese] prayed. Then everyone started to plunder the town of all its goods." Two days later, as another Portuguese account explains, they set Kilwa on fire.

They did the same at Mombasa. Mayr, who was there at the time, wrote that "the commander [of the Portuguese] ordered that the town should be sacked, and that each man should carry off to his ship whatever he found. At the end, there was to be a division of the loot. Each man was to be allowed to keep one-twentieth part of what he had found [the rest going to the commander, or for transport to the king in Portugal]. . . .

"Then everyone started to plunder the town and to search the houses, beating open the doors with axes and iron bars. There was a large quantity of cotton cloth for Sofala in the town, for the whole coast gets its cotton cloth from here. So the commander got a good share of the trade of Sofala for himself. A large quantity of rich silk and gold-embroidered cloths were seized, and some carpets. One of these carpets, without equal for its beauty, was sent to the king of Portugal with many other valuable things."

When the people of Mombasa came back to their fire-blackened city, the king of Mombasa wrote afterwards to the king of Malindi, they found "no living thing there, neither man nor woman, young or old, nor child however small: all who had failed to escape had been killed and burned."

In their second aim, that of making the coastal cities pay tax to Portugal, the Portuguese were partly successful for a time. But they largely failed in their third task, which was to bring the Indian Ocean trade under their own control, and use it for their own profit. They could surprise and loot the unsuspecting cities which opposed them, both in Africa and in Asia; but for the long and difficult work of commanding the Indian Ocean trade routes they had neither enough ships nor enough sailors.

They tried hard for more than fifty years, but gradually

they failed. By 1600, as will be seen in Chapters 8 and 9, their power in the Indian Ocean had dwindled to a mere shadow of its former strength. Yet in grossly interfering with the Indian Ocean trade, they had also gone far to wreck the prosperity of all those African and Asian cities and peoples who had built up this trade in earlier times, and had prospered by its benefits.

III

East Africa after 1500

The eight chapters in this section carry the history of East Africa from about 1500 until the late nineteenth century, and provide the background to Kenya, Tanzania and Uganda. Chapters 8 to 11 are concerned with the Coast and Islands, and Chapters 12 to 15 with the Interior.

Up to about 1820 or a little later there was continued growth and expansion from the achievements of earlier centuries. But in some countries, especially in parts of Kenya and Tanzania, large population movements, mainly of cattle-raising nomads, now began to cause serious setbacks and upheavals. Along the seaboard the coming of the Portuguese proved disastrous for the Swahili cities.

A significant change may be noted around the year 1820. There opened at about that time a new period of widening crisis in the political and social life of many peoples—a crisis which, as later pages will show, preceded and was finally crowned by the European colonial penetrations and invasions of the late nineteenth century. Various causes explain this large and tortuous upheaval. Basically perhaps, the root cause lay in the fact that population growth had now begun to pose problems of a kind which Iron Age solutions could no longer settle or even contain, although this basic cause was then complicated by the arrival of new dangers from outside. There came an increase of warfare, increasingly with firearms; a new expansion of raiding for slaves; and, in the end, conquest from Europe.

A few guiding points may be noted here.

As this period advanced, trade between the Coast and the Interior increased and the two areas became less distinctly separate in their culture. Yet the civilisation of the Coast and Islands, notably in its Muslim faith, remained distinct from that of the Interior. What happened along the Coast, at least until 1820, had little direct effect on what happened in the Interior, and the same was true in reverse.

From 1500 onwards, the people of the Coast and Islands were repeatedly faced with foreign invaders or overlords, whether European or Arab, who established themselves at a few strong points. Wherever they were thus attacked, coastal Africans tried to defend themselves by playing off one invader against another. They had some success in this, but generally failed to unite against these threats from outside Africa.

The Interior remained largely free of outside interference until the nineteenth century. Populations continued to grow in size; there was continued political development. New forms of leadership evolved; kingdoms became stronger and more dangerous to their neighbors.

Various kinds of foreign interference increased towards the middle of the nineteenth century, culminating in colonial invasion. This ending of inland Africa's long isolation from the outside world was marked, almost everywhere, by a profound crisis of society.

8. THE COAST AND ISLANDS
1500–1600: A TIME OF RUIN

The Coast and Islands entered on a period of decline and disaster. Those cities that resisted the Portuguese were attacked without warning, looted and burned: Mombasa and Kilwa in 1505, Brava in 1506, Mombasa again in 1529, and others at other times. Some found it possible and preferable to pay tribute, and so escape assault. Kilwa did this in 1502 (and yet was ruthlessly attacked in 1505), while Zanzibar paid tribute in 1503 and was spared destruction. Lamu and Pate gave way without resistance in 1506, though both were to become the scene of bitter fighting in later years. Only the king of Malindi, looking for an ally against Mombasa, welcomed the invaders and was treated as a friend.

Less is known about the fate of other cities. Not all of them were sacked and burned, but all suffered in another way that was to prove still more destructive to their wealth and livelihood. This was the violent Portuguese attempt to seize for themselves the Indian Ocean trade on whose prosperity these cities had always depended.

This went far to wreck the trade of the Indian Ocean, although that, of course, was not the intention of the Portuguese; what the Portuguese wanted was to keep the trade alive but to take its profits for themselves. Once they had got control of the Coast, they applied their own import-taxes on goods coming to the ports they controlled in East Africa. More serious in its effects on the trade, they also declared that every Asian or African ship must have a Portuguese passport before it put to sea. Otherwise they would attack it with their warships, confiscate its goods, and imprison its crew and passengers or sell them into slavery. The idea behind this passport system was to ensure that they knew how many ships sailed, and with what quantity and value of goods, so that they could collect as much as possible in taxes. But the result was different. It simply cut down the number of ships that put to sea, for rather than facing the expense and trouble of getting a passport from the Portuguese, or enduring ruin if they sailed without one and were then stopped by a Portuguese warship, many captains and merchants now preferred to stay at home.

These moves brought a decline in the commerce and therefore in the wealth of the principal cities, as may be seen from the fate of the gold trade. In the years before the Portuguese ravages, Sofala merchants dealt in gold exports from Central Africa to a value that was perhaps nearly one and a half million dollars every year. This trade the Portuguese grabbed for their own benefit. But in doing so they hurt the interests of the coastal traders who went inland for the gold, and offended such inland Africans as they met near the Coast. The trade fell apart in their hands. They could capture the goose which had always laid the golden eggs, but they could not make it go on laying as it had before. By 1600 the annual value of the gold trade through Sofala was down to less than $300,000, or less than a fifth of its value a century earlier.

Many coastal merchants were driven to smuggling so as to escape Portuguese control.[1] Such ventures were often successful, because the Portuguese never had enough ships or soldiers to patrol more than a few places. Yet smuggling could bring no more than partial relief, for it was not only the East African cities that suffered from the Portuguese, but those of southern Arabia, the Persian Gulf, and India as well. All these markets shrank in size.

Throughout this once flourishing network of commerce, there now set in a far-reaching decay which has been repaired only in modern times, and which affected, in one

[1] Some moved from Kilwa to the Comore Islands, while others went to Malindi. There they could hope to carry on their trade under Portuguese licence.

degree or another, every city along the Indian Ocean sea-board.

The Turks: Ali Bey

How much the coastal cities resented their Portuguese overlords may be seen in the revolts which followed the arrival of a Turkish captain, Amir Ali Bey, in 1585 and 1588.

Such experience as the Coast had known with the Turks before Ali Bey's coming was not encouraging or pleasant. After their conquest of Egypt in 1517, the Turks began sending ships and soldiers southward down the Red Sea in quest of loot and profit, very much as the Portuguese were doing elsewhere. By 1547 they had the whole of the Red Sea coast of Arabia under their general control as far as Aden. But there they were stopped, partly because they did not have many ships, and partly because they met op-position from the Portuguese, who wanted maritime and coastal control of the Indian Ocean for themselves.[2] Yet the Turks continued to send occasional galleys on raiding expeditions as far down the Coast as Malindi. Gradually, however, these raids ceased as well.

Then came Amir Ali. He arrived in a single galley from southern Arabia in 1585, but not as a raider. The Turkish aim now was to win allies against the Portuguese. Whether or not Ali Bey was really under the Sultan of Turkey's orders—and probably he was not—he told the peoples of the Coast that he came with the Sultan's promise of aid against Portugal. With this message of encouragement he visited Mogadishu, Brava, Kisimayu, Faza, Pate, Lamu and Kilifi. Responding to it, nearly all the cities northward from Mombasa, and including Mombasa, rose in arms for their freedom. Mombasa asked for a permanent Turkish garri-son. Faza, a city on Pate Island, accepted a Turkish soldier

---

[2] Cf. R. B. Serjeant, *The Portuguese off the South Arabian Coast: Hadrami Chronicles,* Oxford, 1963.

as its ruler. At Mogadishu the king ordered a new set of coins, modelled on those of Turkey, to be struck in his mint. Only Malindi, still loyal to its old alliance with Portugal, stood aside.

But Ali's coming was followed by no aid from the north, while in 1586 he himself sailed back the way he had come, his galley loaded with gifts and loot worth $150,000, leaving the rebellious cities to shift for themselves. In 1587 Malindi asked for punitive action by a Portuguese fleet from Goa, then the Portuguese headquarters in the Indian Ocean. The fleet duly arrived, and the cities made their peace with Portugal as best they could, though still hoping that Turkish aid might come.

Even so, not all of them escaped unhurt. Mombasa was sacked once more by the Portuguese. Faza suffered even worse. The Portuguese not only sacked it, but are said to have killed every living thing they found, men, women and children, even down to the household dogs and parrots. According to local tradition, the men of Faza did not give in easily. This is confirmed by the account of a Portuguese soldier who took part in the battle, and reported that the last remnant of Faza's army, thirty-five men under their king, fought on until the last was killed.

But hopes of Turkish aid were not completely disappointed. Next year, in 1588, Ali Bey returned with five ships and fresh promises of help. Once again the northern cities, save only Malindi, rose in furious revolt against Portuguese overlordship.

At first this revolt carried all before it. One Portuguese garrison after another was destroyed or driven to its ships. Inflamed by the Portuguese massacres of the year before, the northern cities killed every Portuguese they could find. The Pemba people drove out their pro-Portuguese ruler, and killed all the Portuguese in their island. Ali himself attacked Malindi, but without success, and then went on to Mombasa. There, together with his African allies, he prepared to build a fort, knowing that the Portuguese would surely come back.

But he had come too late. Across the Indian Ocean, at their eastern headquarters in Goa, the Portuguese were on their guard. Through spies, they had learned of Ali's preparations for his second expedition; even before his five ships had sailed from the Red Sea on their way to East Africa, twenty Portuguese ships with nine hundred men left Goa for the same destination. Arriving at Mombasa, the Portuguese fleet at once stormed the town and drove its African and Turkish defenders within the walls. But at this point a new power appeared on the scene. Its intervention was brief but grim.

The Zimba and Segeju

This power was a rootless mob of raiders from the south. Seeking a new homeland for themselves, they had moved up through eastern Tanzania from the region of the Lower Zambezi river. The Portuguese called them Zimba, a name they used for all such homeless marauders, though it may be that a few of these raiders had once belonged to the Zimba people of Malawi. But early on their march they took into their ranks many recruits from other peoples, so that they had become a band of no single origin by the time they reached north-eastern Tanzania and eastern Kenya. Like other wandering groups of that kind, they were warriors much feared for their cruelty, and, as time went by, they became increasingly destructive. After they had attacked and captured Kilwa in 1587, they slaughtered many of its four thousand inhabitants. Traditions say that they ate the flesh of their dead enemies as part of a custom which, they believed, would increase their own strength; and this is apparently confirmed by a Portuguese missionary, João dos Santos, who was an eyewitness.

These were the warriors who reached Mombasa by land as the Portuguese, bent on revenge, were attacking it by sea. With this combination against them, Mombasa could not escape disaster. First, the Portuguese from Goa destroyed the Turkish ships in the harbor, landed their own soldiers, and plundered the merchants' houses. Then they withdrew to their ships, leaving the Zimba, with whose chief they had exchanged messages, to run into the town and complete its ruin. Ali Bey himself, and about two hundred of his men, were rescued by the Portuguese from the Zimba; and this was the last that was ever heard of Ali and his promises of Turkish help.

For the Zimba, fate had another trick in store. After helping to wreck Mombasa, they continued up the coast, moving, though they did not know it, to their own destruction. Passing Gedi, which seems not to have suffered from them, they laid siege to Malindi. Its king had no more than thirty Portuguese soldiers to help protect the town. There seemed every chance that it must fall like Kilwa and Mombasa. But things worked out differently.

Unknown to the Zimba, another African people from the inland country, this time from the north, were also on the march in search of a new homeland. These were the Segeju, who came from the cattle-raising country of northeastern Kenya and southern Somalia, and probably moved south because of Galla and other raids on their pasturelands. On their way they attacked several of the towns of the Banadir Coast. Now they reached Malindi and found the Zimba in their path. With the advantage of surprise, the Segeju at once attacked the Zimba in their rear, killing all of them except their chief and about a hundred of his men, who fled away into the bush.

Ruin and survival

For a second time the Portuguese took stiff revenge on the cities which had risen against them in response to Ali Bey's call.

Their soldiers quickly restored their control over Mombasa. Then they went on to Pate, where they reimposed another ally as ruler of its people. Next they moved to

Lamu Island, ravaged Lamu city and its surrounding farm-
land, and seized King Bashir, its ruler, taking him back to
Pate, where they publicly beheaded him, together with
some of the leading men of the cities of Pate.[3] Turning
south again, they next attacked the city of Manda. Its people had fled into the bush, however, so the Portuguese
had to content themselves with cutting down two thousand
coconut palms. Finally, they returned to Pate Island and
forced the peoples of Pate and Siu cities to break open
their town-walls. Not for a long time could the northern
cities recover from these disasters.

Shaken by these stiff revolts of 1585 and 1588, the
Portuguese decided to build a permanent base on the
northern coast, and chose Mombasa Island. For the southern coast they already had a permanent base, with a fort,
on Mozambique Island. Now they began building a much
larger fortification at Mombasa. They had in fact started
work on a small one there as early as 1569, long before
the revolts associated with Ali Bey. But in 1592, spurred
on by this renewed resistance, they placed Mombasa under
the formal rule of their ally, the King of Malindi, who
thenceforth lived at Mombasa and governed it under Portuguese overlordship. A year later, with a military archi-
tect from Italy which was then the foremost country in
military engineering, with masons from Goa, and with labor from Malindi, the Portuguese laid the foundations of
their great castle of Fort Jesus.

Though not completed for many years, Fort Jesus became the center of Portuguese power along the central
and northern parts of the Coast. The "Green Island," of
Pemba, rich in grain, was brought under its overlordship,
and all the coast from Brava in the north to Cape Delgado
in the south was placed under the control of a Portuguese
official whose title was "Captain of the Coast of Malindi
and of the Fortress of Mombasa." This official had his
headquarters at Fort Jesus, where he governed partly di-

[3] Pate Island had three cities, Pate, Faza, and Siu.

rectly, and partly through the king of Malindi, now reduced to the status of a Portuguese puppet.

There was not much that the Swahili could do in their further defence. Several of their cities were ruined; many of their best soldiers were dead. To reinforce control from Mombasa, Portuguese lesser officials were placed at other important points along the coast: at Kilwa, on Mafia Island, and on Zanzibar, Pemba, Pate and Lamu. Efforts were now made to revive the ocean trade along the northern Coast, but with little success. The exports of this section of the seaboard were mainly ivory, ambergris, tortoise shell, beeswax, millet, rice, and some slaves, which were traded for manufactured goods from India, mainly cottons. But the Portuguese never prospered here. Resentment against them was too strong, and efforts to escape their control were too many and successful.

Malindi, now in sad decline from the prosperous times when it had sent ambassadors to the court of China, continued on good terms with the Portuguese until after 1600, and was rewarded by being given a third of all the taxes received at Mombasa. But these friendly relations were disturbed by quarrels over distribution of the money, and, even more, by the rivalry of Mombasa when this city became the principal Portuguese trading center after the foundation of Fort Jesus. Though the king of Malindi, ruling from Mombasa, was supposed to be the main Portuguese ally along the coast, Portuguese captains increasingly turned to their fellow countrymen at Mombasa, and ignored their own king's orders to remain on good terms with Malindi. The execution of policy made in Lisbon, all too often, was left to tough adventurers who came out to the Coast for the loot it could offer them. Primarily interested in enriching themselves quickly, local Portuguese commanders stole and bullied and threatened both friend and foe.

Another important consequence of all these burnings and battles was the gradual depopulation of some of the cities, for people left them in fear or despair. A few dwindled never to recover: among these, after 1600, was Gedi. Others went into a long decline. None of them ever regained the commercial brilliance of the years before the coming of the Portuguese, when they had been members of the wide world of Islam in its greatest age. Now they were cut off from all that, their trade severely damaged, their civic splendor reduced to a mere echo of the past, their daily life in constant danger of upset.

Yet the old prosperity did not altogether vanish, even in cities such as Kilwa which suffered serious damage and lost much of their trade. In 1583 a Dutch traveller called van Linschoten could find Kilwa still a handsome town. Like earlier travellers, he reported that its houses were made of stone as well as wood, and were surrounded by pleasant gardens growing "all sorts of fruits and flowers." Its people "all wear fine white clothes of silk and cotton. Its women have bracelets of gold and precious stones about their necks and arms, and many silver ornaments . . ." But four years later came the disastrous Zimba raid on Kilwa: and not for many years after that did the city regain even a portion of its former strength.

These were also times of decline for the Portuguese. They could not sustain their military effort. Fewer ships and soldiers came from Portugal; when new rivals arrived to fight them on the seas, they proved too weak for the challenge. By 1600 their days of supremacy in the Indian Ocean were almost over.

New rivals: The Dutch and English

The first rivals to follow the Portuguese round the Cape of Good Hope were the Dutch, at that time the strongest trading country in all Europe. They came in the 1580s, eager to milk the wealth of the East as the Portuguese had done before them. Soon they were followed by the English and then by the French. All these had more ships, sailors, money and commercial skill than the Portuguese.

By 1600 the Portuguese were almost too weak to defend themselves against their new rivals. Citizens of a poor and backward country, whose population at home consisted of little more than a million small farmers and a few rich noblemen and merchants, they had made their big effort in the years before 1550. Between 1500 and 1528 as many as 299 Portuguese ships had sailed from Lisbon for East Africa and the Far East, an average of about ten every year. For the years 1529 to 1612 the annual average declined to about six ships, and by 1600 there were often years when none sailed at all. Many of their ships had long become old and unseaworthy, but were neither repaired nor replaced.

If ships were difficult to find, men proved harder still. By 1600 there were probably no more than four hundred Portuguese on the Coast and along the lower and middle reaches of the Zambezi river. They were commanded by a few military officers and noblemen whose main ambition was to enrich themselves by means of loot and conquest so that, retiring after a three-year term of service, for this was the usual term they served oversea, they could live at ease in Portugal during the rest of their lives. This ambition explains why the whole course of Portuguese history in East Africa, from their first coming until modern times, has been one of scandals, corruption and revolt among men who quarrelled for the personal spoils they could hope to gain.

When the Dutch and English appeared on the scene, the Portuguese were increasingly outsailed and outfought. Soon they could do little but cling to their principal forts and trading stations along the shores of the Indian Ocean, and even of these they lost many in India and South-east Asia. If they failed to lose them in East Africa as well, this was largely because the Dutch and English concentrated on the Far East and India, and turned their attention only occasionally to East Africa.

These sharp European rivalries must be seen against a wider background of changes in Europe itself. Now was the time when the strong powers of Europe began their great period of commercial expansion, and laid foundations for their later supremacy in science, trade, mechanical production of goods, and military conquest. Leaders among these powers were the Dutch, the English and the French. Unable to face this competition, the Portuguese were steadily deprived of their military and commercial control of Indian Ocean waters.

9. THE COAST AND ISLANDS 1600–1700: RIVALRIES ON SEA AND LAND

The seventeenth century brought a period of violent competition on sea and land between Europeans struggling for control of the Indian Ocean and its seaboard, and of renewed attempts by the peoples of the Coast and Islands to regain their former independence.

The Portuguese failure

The Portuguese had succeeded in dominating the Coast and Islands, during the previous century, because of their strength in firearms, their ruthlessness, and the chronic lack of unity among the Swahili city-states. But they failed to establish any lasting positions of strength except at Mombasa and along the Mozambique seaboard. Unable to win allies but for a few puppet rulers, they were universally distrusted or feared. All they could do was to settle in their garrisons and trading stations like a blanket of misfortune, ruining much of a civilisation that had been the product of a rich heritage of Muslim culture. How little they gave to the civilisation of the Coast and Islands may be seen in the Swahili language, which even after centuries of Portuguese was to absorb no more than about sixty Portuguese words, such as the names for playing cards. Even the architecture of the Portuguese—confined as it was to a few hated castles—had no influence upon the building styles of the Coast and Islands.

One valuable contribution, however, they did make; although it was scarcely from their own civilisation: they helped to bring new food plants and fruits from the Americas. Among these, as noted in Chapter 2, were maize and

cassava, pineapples and pawpaw, the cashew nut and the
avocado pear. African farmers greatly benefited from these
Brazilian and other American crops. Lesser contributions
by the Portuguese included an improvement in the rigging
of ships and the practice of a wider use of dung as soil
fertiliser.

It should also be noted that this general failure to add
anything to the civilisation of the Coast and Islands was
largely the result of the fact that the majority of people
in Portugal were as much oppressed by their lords and
landowners as were the Africans. What was at fault was
the Portuguese political system, in which a privileged,
grasping, and poorly educated few lived on the poverty
and bondage of the majority of Portuguese. And it was
these grasping few who, for the most part, were unleashed
on Africa, though the Portuguese also made a habit of
getting rid of their criminals by transporting them to Africa.

Their failure was made complete when new rivals entered the battle for the Indian Ocean. But these came not
only from Europe. After 1650 the Arabs of Oman in southern Arabia began to recover their strength. And with these
Omani Arabs the Swahili city-states were at last able to
find useful allies.

Rivalries and shifts of fortune fill the coastal record of
the seventeenth century—and to a lesser extent of the eighteenth as well—with the din and tumult of battles on sea
and land, fought along the whole seaboard from Sofala
in the far south to the towns of the Banadir Coast in the
far north. Cities repeatedly changed hands between one
rival and another. Merchants saw their fortunes engulfed
by fire or carried off by raiders. There was much waste
and destruction.

Yet the political record is misleading if left by itself. It
needs to be understood, because it explains the rise and
fall of different rulers, of one city or another, as these
dangerous years went by. But many escaped ruin. At certain points along the Coast, especially in the north, Swahili
civilisation now began to recover from the ravages of the

sixteenth century, and this recovery led in time to a new flowering of Swahili culture.

Mozambique, Mombasa, Pate

Much of the political history of the Coast and Islands can be followed through this period of confusion by looking at the varying fortunes of Mozambique, Mombasa, and Pate.[1] The first two were the main centers of Portuguese military strength; and so of the general struggle for power; while the third, Pate, became a leader of a new resistance to Portugal after the Omani arrival in 1652.

Mozambique Island had for long been the principal Portuguese base along the southern coast, just as Mombasa would become their principal base along the northern coast after 1592. From Mozambique the Portuguese aimed at three objectives: to provide aid and protection for their ships sailing between Europe and the East; to dominate the southern coast; and to control and help their little settlements of the inland country at Sena and Tete along the Zambezi river, and in the kingdom of the Mwanamutapa (in what is now north-eastern Rhodesia).

Given these tasks, the Portuguese were never in possession of adequate men and supplies even at their main base on Mozambique Island. In 1604, for example, they had only sixty soldiers to man their fort, and a few old rusty cannon. The men were often sick, while the cannon were almost as dangerous to the soldiers who fired them as to those at whom they were fired. Yet the fort was strongly placed for self-defence; and its garrison, feeble though it was, nonetheless held off Dutch assaults in 1604, 1607 and 1608. The third of these all but succeeded. The Dutch admiral fired no fewer than 1250 cannon balls at the stone walls of the fort, and then ordered his men to take them by storm. Happily for the Portuguese, many of the Dutch

[1] Pate: pronounce *Pah-tay*.

soldiers were drunk at the time and failed to climb the walls.

These Dutch defeats had far-reaching consequences which could not be seen at the time. If the Dutch had taken Mozambique Island, they would probably have made it into their main base for the western part of the Indian Ocean, and used it for the same purposes as the Portuguese. Failing to capture it, they looked elsewhere for an African base, and found one in 1652 at the Cape of Good Hope. In this sense, at least, the foundations of modern South Africa were laid in the Dutch failure to capture Mozambique Island.

Dutch attacks helped the peoples of the Coast and Islands by weakening the Portuguese. Another such indirect ally had appeared by about 1620 in the shape of the English. The first English ships to sail the Indian Ocean had come from the East, and not from the Atlantic, in two round-the-world voyages made by Francis Drake in 1577 and Thomas Cavendish in 1586. Not until 1591 did the English send another ship, the *Edward Bonaventure* under James Lancaster, who came round the Cape of Good Hope, and opened an English bid for control of the Indian Ocean. The Portuguese replied by denouncing the English as pirates. By 1620, with more of their ships in these seas, the English had made an alliance with the Dutch: though offensive in nature, its joint fighting force was diplomatically called the "Fleet of Defence."

Later again, in the 1640s, the English East India Company, which, by then, ruled and was robbing part of India, became interested in the possibilities of East African trade. In 1651 they sent a ship from India to Malindi with a trial cargo of rice and calico cotton cloth, which was exchanged for ivory and gold. The same ship was ordered to come back the year after. But this time storms prevented her from reaching the African coast, and the venture was not repeated. India was keeping the English fully occupied.

By 1650 the Portuguese had fallen far behind: while the Dutch seized many of their best bases in South-east Asia, the English thrust them steadily out of India. In 1639 they had been expelled from Japan on the grounds that their missionaries were interfering in Japanese affairs. Meanwhile, in 1622, they had also lost Ormuz in the Persian Gulf. Worse was to follow. In 1650, with the revival of military power among the Omani Arabs, they were driven from their important base of Muscat in southern Arabia.

This general collapse was reflected in the sorry condition of their African settlements. As less gold came from the inland country, for reasons that will be discussed in Chapter 18, traders and governors went into the business of fraud. They mixed so much copper with the gold they sent overseas that this metal was described, in an official document of 1652, as being less gold than copper. Roguery and corruption now undercut the whole Portuguese effort in these lands.

Mombasa: The revolt of Yusuf bin Hasan

The Africans watched all this with growing hope of being able to free themselves from Portuguese controls and taxes. But they were badly placed to help themselves. Even along the northern coast, where the Portuguese were weaker than in the south, the city-states were seldom prepared to work together. They were divided, it is true, by miles of land or sea: more serious still, they were also divided by rivalries for trade and power. Whenever one rebelled against the Portuguese, the others usually left it to its fate; weak though they were, the Portuguese could concentrate against a single rebel city without running much risk of revolts elsewhere. This is what happened when Mombasa rebelled again in 1631.

For years the Portuguese had ruled Mombasa, from their great castle of Fort Jesus, in the manner of men who squeeze lemons for their juice. A Portuguese priest who visited Mombasa in 1606 described how local merchants who had once been wealthy were living "in utter poverty," while Portuguese merchants had as many as seventy comfortable houses. At the same time the Portuguese continued to pay the king of Malindi, their puppet in Mombasa, a part of the money they got from taxes, hoping in this way to keep him on their side. But this sharing of taxes led to disputes which were further envenomed by intrigues within the king's own family.

In 1614 these troubles led to the killing of King Hasan bin Ahmad at local Portuguese instigation. A rival was then put in his place. Finding this still unsatisfactory for their purposes, the Portuguese switched ground five years later, and offered reparation for Hasan's murder by enthroning his son, Yusuf, then twenty years old.

Yusuf bin Hasan had been educated as a Christian in Goa,[2] at that time still the Portuguese headquarters for all their positions around the Indian Ocean. Made king at Mombasa, he decided to return to the Muslim faith and avenge his murdered father. But Yusuf proceeded cautiously, concealing his intentions from the Portuguese who garrisoned Mombasa. When he was ready he gathered some three hundred followers in Mombasa town, entered Fort Jesus with a handful of these in holiday clothes, and then, having got within the gates, called in his warriors. Overrun, the garrison could show no fight. Except for the captain himself all the Portuguese and their African Christian followers were given the choice of embracing Islam and continuing to enjoy life and freedom, or accepting death. Many refused to give up their Christian faith, and the number killed in one way or another is said to have been about 250, of whom seventy were Africans and some others were mulattoes.

The Portuguese were not slow in reacting against Yusuf. Early in 1632 they arrived with a fleet to retake Mombasa. In this they failed. Yet the city remained alone in its revolt, and Yusuf now lost his nerve. Believing that the Portuguese would return in greater force, he abandoned Mom-

[2] And so is usually known by his baptismal name in the Portuguese records: Dom Jeronimo Chingulia.

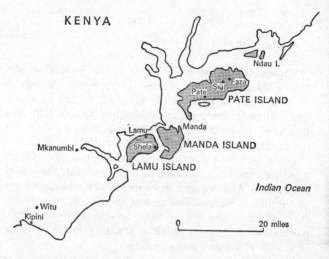

18. The Lamu archipelago

basa in May 1632, and the Portuguese were able to regain control there a few weeks later.

Only the people of Pate, always eager to resist the Portuguese if they could, gave Yusuf aid. But they were made to pay for their defiance. In 1636 the Portuguese set out from Mombasa to punish Pate. They landed, cut down some ten thousand coconut trees, killed many people in the fighting, and beheaded two hundred local men of importance. They also attacked the towns of Siu and Manda,[3] and exacted a heavy tribute. But the people of Pate did not lose heart. Not long afterwards, when the Omani appeared as allies, they again opposed the Portuguese, and for this, too, they were to pay a bitter price.

[3] Siu on Pate Island, Manda on Manda Island.

Rise of Oman

Encouraged by the enfeeblement of the Portuguese, the Omani Arabs took the offensive in their own homeland in 1643. Their leader Nasir ibn Murshid, the first of a new line of imams, captured the Portuguese fort of Sohar in that year. In 1650 they capped this success by throwing the Portuguese out of the trading port of Muscat.

Learning from European tactics, the new state of Oman rapidly turned itself into a sea power. Once more the sailors of southern Arabia began to command the western waters of the Indian Ocean. Testing their new military strength, they sailed to the aid of their Swahili fellow-Muslims, partly from a sense of religious solidarity but even more in search of commercial advantage.

In 1652, only two years after making themselves masters of Muscat and setting up their capital there, the Omani were invited by the citizens of Mombasa to bring help against the Portuguese. They accordingly raised a fleet and despatched it southward from Muscat. Landing on Zanzibar, they sacked the Portuguese town. They were welcomed by the queen who then ruled Zanzibar; and she, together with the ruler of Pemba and the chief of Otondo, on the mainland near Bagamoyo, accepted the overlordship and protection of the imam of Oman and agreed to pay him tribute.

Other city-states made ready to do the same. But this time the Portuguese were too quick for them. Mounting an expedition from Mombasa, they landed three hundred men on Zanzibar, fired the queen's town, and attacked a fleet from Pemba. Yet the Swahili-Oman alliance was by no means at an end.

Its next action came in 1661 when an Omani fleet raided the Portuguese base at Mombasa, drove the Portuguese out of the town into the shelter of Fort Jesus, and departed with a promise that they would soon come back and finish the job by taking the castle as well. In 1670 another Omani fleet, this time of eighteen ships, went as far south as Mozambique Island. There they landed and sacked the Portuguese town, but, like the Dutch before them, found the fort too strongly placed for capture.

Weak though they now were, the Portuguese could still retaliate. Gathering what little strength in ships and soldiers they could, they replied in 1678 with an expedition against the city-state of Pate which they regarded, with some reason, as the ringleader of the Swahili alliance with Oman. With help from the ruler of nearby Faza, now on Portugal's side because he had quarrelled with the ruler of Pate, the Portuguese captain Almeida took Pate city by storm, adding insult to injury by setting up his headquarters on the sacred ground of a mosque. Other units raided the neighboring island-city of Siu, as well as Manda and Lamu cities, all of which opposed the Portuguese, and seized their rulers.

All these four cities, Pate and Siu, Lamu and Manda, were looted for their wealth in gold and silver, ivory and tortoise shell, and their four kings were beheaded on Almeida's orders. But, as so often in the record of these wars, the Portuguese triumph was a brief one. While the Portuguese soldiers were still going from house to house, robbing and wrecking, four Omani ships hove in sight. The next day these ships landed Omani soldiers who went into action against Almeida's men, and three days later the Portuguese were put to flight. They retired to their ships and sailed back the way they had come, leaving most of their loot behind them. It was to be the last of their big piratical actions along the Coast.

Eviction of the Portuguese

The ravages of the Portuguese were not quite over. Pate city once again fell to their attack in 1687. But the Swahili-Omani alliance now moved swiftly against them.

The allies gained ground. In 1694 the island of Pemba rebelled successfully against Portuguese overlordship. In 1696 an Omani fleet laid siege to Mombasa, the last Portuguese stronghold on the northern coast. Its garrison managed to send a small boat southward with eight seamen to raise the alarm and ask for help.

This time it was the queen of Zanzibar, no doubt fearing that the Portuguese would otherwise again send an expedition against her town, who came to their aid. She despatched three ships with supplies for the Portuguese in Mombasa, illustrating once again the fatal disunity of these city-states. There followed a long siege which lasted from March 1696 until December 1698 and ended in Arab victory. So reduced were the defenders of Fort Jesus that at the end of the siege they are said to have numbered only eight Portuguese soldiers, three Indians, and two African women.

At last the Swahili were in sight of freedom from the Portuguese. The final actions took place in 1728, when the Portuguese reoccupied Mombasa, and in 1729, when they were once more thrown out, this time never to return. Along the entire Coast there now remained to them only their base on Mozambique Island, and a few lesser stations near the mouths of the Zambezi river.

10. THE COAST AND ISLANDS
1700–1800: YEARS OF REVIVAL

This chapter is concerned mainly with events and developments between 1729, when the Portuguese were at last evicted from Mombasa, and 1806, when Sayyid Said came to power in Oman and embarked on the chief phase of Omani expansion. During this period there was a considerable recovery among many city-states. But these now found themselves faced with fresh demands for overlordship over them, this time from the Omani Arabs: immediately after their capture of Fort Jesus in 1698, the Omani appointed governors at several important cities along the coast, and soon afterwards built at Zanzibar the fort which may still be seen there. Before following this new phase of conflict, it will be useful to review some of the achievements of Swahili civilisation during this period.

The civilisation of the Swahili

Detailed research over the past twenty years has much increased the respect of historians for this civilisation of the Swahili-speaking people of the East African Coast and Islands. Though always a variant of the Muslim civilisation of Arabia, it was one with a clear distinction of its own that was expressed in its own specific forms of language, literature, architecture in coral stone, and other ways. Here as in West Africa, Islam brought new trading opportunities, new concepts and methods of government, new systems of thought. Africans took all these and worked them into patterns of their own. And although much troubled by outside interference after the coming of the Portuguese, this civilisation regained some of its old strength and distinction after 1700, when it flowered in fresh ways.[1]

Though undoubtedly African, Swahili civilisation was limited to the city-states, towns, and villages of the Coast and Islands. Swahili traders journeyed inland every year on business, and some of them settled for long periods in the Interior. But the peoples of the Interior continued to develop in their own separate ways. When they built large trading systems, as for example the Shona and Malawi did, these owed little or nothing to the Swahili except the opportunity for engaging in long-distance trade.

From first to last, over more than a thousand years of thriving enterprise before the colonial period began, the Swahili remained a string of trading communities. Their power did not depend on conquest of territory but on their ability to act as middlemen between the sea merchants of the Indian Ocean and the gold or ivory producers of the Interior.

They usually failed to unite against their enemies, as has been noted. Their coastline, after all, was nearly three thousand miles in length. Yet at the same time the troubles of the sixteenth and seventeenth centuries gave many of these communities, faced as they were with an outside enemy far stronger than any one of them, a deeper sense of

[1] The essentially African nature of Swahili civilisation has been gracefully expressed by the modern Swahili poet, Shaaban Robert, when speaking of himself:

Mwafrika madhubuti	I am an honest African
vingine nisidhaniwe	do not think of me otherwise
Sikuchanganya nasaba	I am not of mixed lineage
kwa mama wala kwa baba	neither on my mother's nor my father's side
ingawaje ni haiba	however fine other lineage may be
mimi sina asiliye	I am not sprung from it
Si Mwarabu si Mzungu	I am no Arab nor a European
Hindi si jadi yangu	I am not of Indian lineage
naarifu walimwengu	I tell this to the world
wadadisio wajue	so that the curious may know.

participating in the same civilisation. Even those few states which befriended the Portuguese, notably Malindi, lived to regret it. Malindi was spared the sufferings of Mombasa, but it fell into ruin all the same.

This revival of Swahili civilisation after 1700 occurred, predictably, along those parts of the coast where resistance to the Portuguese was more successful, and where the Portuguese remained weaker than in the far south. It was here —chiefly at Pate, Lamu, Mombasa, and a few other places —that the language of the Swahili now underwent a new expansion. Even to this day it is generally the kiSwahili spoken along the northern and central coast that has led the way in development of the language: in enriching it with new words, and in writing it. It is thus no accident that the earliest piece of writing known in kiSwahili, an heroic poem called the Utendi wa Tambuka, was composed and written in Pate. It was done for the king of Pate city-state in 1728, the very year when the Portuguese made their final but unsuccessful effort to regain control of the northern coast, and when the people of Pate knew at last that their many battles had not been in vain.

How early the Swahili adopted the use of Arabic script for their language is not yet known. As the Utendi wa Tambuka shows, verse was certainly being written at the beginning of the eighteenth century, while the earliest known prose work is a letter dated 1771 which has lately been found[2] in the French archives in Paris. Yet it may be reasonably assumed that the writing of Swahili began before the coming of the Portuguese, even though no writings of that period have survived or, at any rate, have as yet been identified in private libraries along the Coast.

In this connection it should be remembered that Arabic, throughout the Great Age of Islam and even in later centuries, had high prestige among Muslims as the language of the Faith. Among the Swahili, as among the scholars of such cities as Timbuktu in the Western Sudan, Arabic

[2] By Dr. G. S. P. Freeman-Grenville.

enjoyed much the same position as Latin in medieval Europe. When they began to write in their individual languages, Europeans continued to use Latin script. This is evidently what happened to the Swahili-speaking peoples during the revival of their culture after 1700. They seem at no time to have thought of themselves as a separate and single nation; but they undoubtedly became more aware of the value of the civilisation they had built and fought to defend, and, reflecting this pride, they produced in kiSwahili a written literature of an often remarkable distinction.

Their poets and singers had composed verses and traditional stories, long before they wrote them down, for the delight and instruction of kings and courtiers, traders, farmers and fishermen. By 1700 this language had acquired much power and beauty. Though early forms of poetry were modelled on the verse styles of the Arabs, Swahili writers soon broke away into styles of their own. These were and are of different kinds for various purposes. All poems composed for public performance are called *mashairi,* but there are several kinds of these: *nyimbo,* which are songs of one sort or another, *hadithi,* which are tales, and best known, perhaps, *utendi,* the heroic poems about the deeds and lives of famous men and great events. All these styles are very old, but they were much developed in the revival of Swahili culture.

Since the Swahili language belongs to the heritage of the whole of Africa, and is now in daily use by more than 30 million Africans, it may be well to give at least one small example of its achievements in the field of epic verse. An *utendi* which has won renown, even outside East Africa, was written in Pate by a poet called Sayid Abdallah, a member of an honored family of poets, between 1810 and 1820, and is called the Utendi wa Inkishafi, sometimes translated as "The Soul's Awakening."

Writing when the old glories of Pate had vanished from the scene, but were still alive in the memories of men, Abdallah describes the brilliance of Pate city-state at the

height of its wealth and comfort, and speaks his sorrow
for the splendour that is gone:

Uwene wangapi watu wakwasi	How many rich men have you seen
walo wakiwaa kama shamasi	Who shone like the sun
wa muluku zana za adharusi	Who had control of the weapons of war
dhahabu na fedha wakhiziniye	And stored up silver and gold?
Malimwengu yote yatwatiile	All the world paid them homage
na dunia yao iwaokele	And their world was straight ahead of them
wachenda zitwa zai zilele	They walked with heads held disdainfully
mato mafumbuzi wayafumbiye	And eyes closed in scorn
Wakimia mbuni na zao shingo	Swinging their arms and arching their necks
na nyuma na mbele ili miyongo	While behind and in front crowds accompanied them
wakaapo pote ili zitengo	And everywhere they had seats of honor
asikari jamu wawatandiye	And troops of soldiers to attend them
Nyumba zao mbake zikinawiri	Their lighted houses were aglow
kwa taa za kowa na za sufuri	With lamps of crystal and brass
makiku yakele kama nahari	The nights were as the day
haiba na jaha iwazingiye	Beauty and honor surrounded them
Wapa, biye sini ya kuteuwa	They decorated their houses with choice porcelain
na kula kikombe kinakishiwa	And every goblet was engraved
kati watiziye kuzi na kowa	And in the midst they put crystal pitchers
katika mapambo yanawiriye . . .	Amongst the decorations that glittered . . .

Yet pride, Abdallah reminds us, comes before a fall, and those who grow powerful and wealthy at the cost of their fellow-men must expect the same end:

Ukwasi ungapo na tafakhuri	For even though wealth has its boasting
wakanakiliwa ili safari	They were taken on the great journey
washukiye nyumba za maka-buri	And went down into the mansions of the grave
fusi na fusize liwafusiye	Where the crumbling earth demolished them

And what now remains behind is only the shell of former luxury and power, just as ruins stood in Pate city during Abdallah's time, sadly displaying the vanished glory of the past:

Nyumba zao mbaka ziwele tame	Their lighted mansions are without people
makinda ya popo iyu wengeme	The young of bats cling up above
husikii hisi wala ukeme	You hear no whispering nor shouting
zitanda matandu walitandiye	Spiders crawl over the beds
Madaka ya nyumba ya zisahani	Where once the porcelain stood in the wall niches
sasa walaliye wana wa nyuni	Wild birds make nests for their young
bumu hukoromoa kati numbani	Owls hoot within these chambers
zisije na kotwe waikaliye	Birds and ducklings are their guests

Only the memory of the bold rulers and flourishing merchants of old Pate is left to tell the story of what is gone:

Wa wapi ziuli wa Pate Yunga	Where are the brave men of strong Pate

wenye nyuso ali zenya mi- anga	Men of noble and of brilliant life?
wangiziye nyumba za tan- gatanga	They lie in the mansions of the sands
daula na ezi iwaushiye . . .	Power and strength are taken from them.[3]

Lyrical Swahili verse such as this forms a vivid part in the general heritage of African civilisation.

Fine buildings were another Swahili achievement. The stone they used is the grey coral rag, or coral stone, of the coastland, which their masons were highly skilled in carving. Excellent mosques and palaces were raised to the honour and comfort of kings and merchants in Kilwa, Mafia, Zanzibar, Pemba, Gedi, Malindi, Mombasa, Pate, Mogadishu and other cities. Nearly all are ruined today, but even their ruins are worth visiting.[4]

With the ravages of the sixteenth and seventeenth centuries, wrecking the trade on which the cities had depended, building in stone declined and gave way to wood and clay and thatch, which were cheap to use. Yet a few good stone buildings were erected after 1700, and some others, such as the Kizimkazi mosque on Zanzibar, were restored. But the towns in this later period generally lacked the comfort and sophistication of taste which had existed in earlier times. Continually harried by raiders from the sea, robbed of their share in the Indian Ocean trade, threatened by many dangers, the Swahili seldom now had the wealth to carry on with their fine architecture. But while the material signs of their civilisation fell slowly into ruin, verse and prose seem to have reached new heights of literary skill.[5] They suggest that this civilisation possessed

[3] This translation is by Lyndon Harries, *Swahili Poetry,* Oxford, 1962.

[4] No good library of African culture should be without Peter Garlake's finely illustrated monograph: *Early Islamic Architecture of the East African Coast,* Nairobi, 1966.

[5] Whether the new Swahili literature was really better than the old we cannot now be sure, however, because the old is nearly all lost, or yet to be recovered from private libraries.

an inner strength which was greater than its material decay, and that this was the strength which enabled these coastal peoples to survive and contribute to the civilisation of Africa as a whole.

Conflicts with the Omani

After evicting the Portuguese, with the help of the Omani Arabs, from the northern coast in 1729, the leaders of the Swahili city-states found themselves in a new position. The Omani Arabs now revealed that they wished to be more than allies. Like the Portuguese, they also wanted to be overlords. The cities began to see that they had exchanged one master for another. This newcomer might be more acceptable than the Portuguese, since the Omani were Muslims as the Swahili were, and their overlordship promised to be less burdensome. But still the cities preferred their own freedom, and they tried to secure it.

They returned to their old policy of playing off one foreign power against another. They had called in the Omani against the Portuguese. Now some of them began to think of calling back the Portuguese against the Omani, or, if the Portuguese should fail, any other European power with warships in the Indian Ocean. For a long time this had little or no effect. The Portuguese would have liked to return to the Coast, but lacked the necessary ships and men. The English and French had a few warships in the Indian Ocean, but were at this time far too interested in India and the Far East to bother much about Africa. Swahili resistance to Omani overlordship continued through the eighteenth century, but with little success.

Omani garrisons were sent to Pemba, Kilwa, and several other cities after the freeing of Mombasa from the Portuguese in 1698. These were commanded by Omani governors, called *walis*, who were sent to rule these places. They were not popular. The king of Kilwa was especially active in trying to get rid of his Omani wali and garrison of about fifty soldiers who occupied the old Portuguese city, and in 1724 sent messengers to Mozambique Island with a request for aid, which proved vain. In 1765 he sent another such request. But in 1771, during a moment of Omani weakness, their governor was forced to leave by popular pressure in Kilwa. For several years after this Kilwa was left alone. At this point a new partner appeared.

By now the French had established themselves on Mauritius and nearby islands in the Indian Ocean. In 1776 the French captain Morice arrived at Kilwa. He wanted to buy slaves for the French plantations in the islands. King Hasan of Kilwa signed a treaty with Morice, agreeing to sell slaves captured from the mainland in exchange for French protection against the Omani, and even offering to allow the French to build a fort on his island. This French fort was never built; but the king of Kilwa now went into the slave trade on a much greater scale than before, supplying captives to the French plantation islands, especially Mauritius, and the European colonies in North America. Later, when the Omani returned, Kilwa became part of the dominions of Sayyid Said of Zanzibar.

Along the northern coast the Swahili were in a somewhat better posture. They knew more about the Omani, and, as time went by, they were able to take some advantage of conflicts between different Omani rulers. These conflicts came to a head in 1741, the year in which the governor of Sohar, Ahmad bin Said al-Bu-Saidi, managed to get himself chosen as ruler of Oman, and, soon afterwards, took the throne as the first of a new line of imams, known as the Busaidi.[6]

The Omani who ruled Mombasa, members of the Mazrui lineage, at once refused to recognize the new line of rulers, for they had ambitions of their own. The first of the Mazrui in East Africa had been Nasir ibn Abdallah, who had taken part in the Omani siege of Fort Jesus in 1698. Another Mazrui became deputy governor in 1727,

[6] *Bu-* is a shortened way of saying *banu,* Arabic for tribe. The correct name of all this family was Aulad al-Imam.

ruling with such a heavy hand that the people of Mombasa
revolted against him. But the Mazrui remained in power.
When Ahmad al-Bu-Said became imam, their ruling member, Muhammad bin Uthman at once proclaimed himself
independent, saying that his family were as important as
the Busaidi. "The new Imam is an ordinary citizen like
myself," he declared. "He has taken the power in Oman.
I have taken it in Mombasa." In 1745 the Portuguese on
Mozambique Island heard news that Pate, Malindi, Pemba,
Zanzibar and Mafia had all thrown off their allegiance.

The new imam set out to recover these break-away fragments of the Omani empire, moving first against Mombasa.
In 1746 he sent agents there to murder the ruling Mazrui,
Muhammad bin Uthman, and imprison his brother, Ali
Mazrui. This they did. But Ali made a daring escape down
a leather rope from the high walls of Fort Jesus, called
successfully on the people of Mombasa for support, and
attacked the new governor, Saif bin Khalfan. The latter
held out for three days, but was defeated. Ali Mazrui became independent ruler of Mombasa.

Pate followed much the same policy, and with much
the same success, under their long-established rulers the
Nabahani, and especially under Bwana Mkuu, who came
to power in 1745. (The first of the Nabahani lineage appear
to have arrived at Pate in 1482, when a leading family
of that name was expelled from Oman.)

Once again the cities proved unable to unite their forces.
Pate and Mombasa went on quarrelling as they had often
done before. Zanzibar contested Pate's claim to rule
Pemba. Kilwa plotted against Mafia and Zanzibar. Yet each
on their own were strong enough to reduce or contain
local Omani power, and not until 1784 did events begin to
take a new turn.

In that year the Imam Ahmad al-Bu-Said died in his
capital of Muscat, and the succession was disputed among
Omani lineage leaders.[7] Dissensions spread to the Swahili

---

[7] The next imam was Said bin Ahmad, who ruled until 1791. Sultan bin Ahmad (the word Sultan being a personal name, not a title)

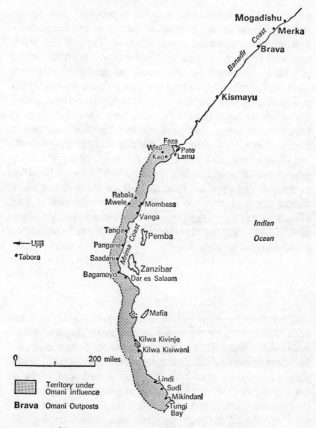

19. Omani overlordship in East Africa

coast, and an unsuccessful rival for the throne of Oman
sailed southward to carve out a new kingdom for himself
among the Swahili. Kilwa accepted this ambitious man, no
doubt hoping to use him against Oman; but Zanzibar re-

then deposed him and ruled until 1804, when he was killed. He was
followed by a regent, Badr, who was assassinated in 1806, when
the renowned Sayyid Said became ruler of Oman.

fused. In 1785 there came another expedition from Oman, with orders to regain control. It partly succeeded, but the new control proved no more effective than the old. It became clear to the rulers in Muscat that they must either pay closer attention to the Coast, or gradually lose their positions there. This opened a new phase. Basing themselves mainly on Zanzibar, the Omani strengthened their garrisons. From 1822 onwards, a new Omani system of commercial power and military overlordship emerged at certain points along the East African seaboard. The building of this "empire" was mainly the work of Sayyid Said,[8] who came to power in Muscat in 1806 when only fifteen years old. The most intelligent of all the Arab rulers of the nineteenth century, Said was to dominate the life of Zanzibar and parts of the Coast for many years and especially after 1840, when he transferred his political headquarters from Muscat to Zanzibar.

A new slave trade

Sayyid Said's achievement is important for several reasons which will be discussed in the next chapter. Meanwhile there was one notable development, when Said and his Zanzibar merchants rose to power and wealth, which calls for special attention. This was a vast and rapid increase in the capture and selling of people into slavery.

Between about 1750 and 1880 a large number of young men of several African peoples, and a smaller but still considerable number of young women, were wrenched from their village homes and marched to the Coast, where they were sold as slaves. The numbers greatly expanded after about 1800. Nobody knows how many were taken away: the total was certainly many hundreds of thousands of people, not counting all those who died in raids and battles caused by this ruthless trade. Wide regions of East

---

[8] *Sayyid* meant lord or prince. Sayyid Said did not himself use the Omani title of imam.

and Central Africa were plagued with its cruelty and violence. Because of its far-ranging effects, the new slave trade needs to be looked at in a framework.

The reasons why some Africans engaged in the business of capturing and selling other Africans belong to economic rather than political history, and are discussed in Chapter 21. Here it will be useful to consider several other questions. Why is this development in Sayyid Said's time called a *new* slave trade? How did it come about? Where were the captives taken, what did they work at, and for whom?

East Africa had a small part in the worldwide slave trade of ancient times. As early as about AD 120 the Greek merchant who wrote the *Periplus of the Erythraean Sea* said that it was possible to buy slaves along the Coast. This continued to be true in later centuries. Every year a few Africans were sold to the sea merchants, and were taken across the Indian Ocean to Arabia and India and even as far as China, where they were used as house servants, field-workers, doorkeepers and soldiers. Gradually, here and there, groups of African slaves and their descendants became quite numerous. There were enough of them in Iraq, by about 800, to launch an important revolt. But this eastern slave trade was still a very small one.[9]

Much the same thing, one may add, occurred in West Africa. Every year a number of West Africans were taken as slaves across the Sahara, where they were sold to North Africans and Europeans. This western trade was larger than the East African slave trade, but it was small when compared with the ocean trade of later times. Similar trading, of course, went on in Europe and Asia. All through the European Middle Ages, from the ninth century until the fourteenth, European kings and merchants were in the business of selling European slaves to the kings and merchants of North Africa and Western Asia.

[9] It was small because slaves were a luxury commodity in the Arab and Indian worlds, and because, with the exception of southern Iraq in the 8th–9th centuries, slaves were not used as plantation labor.

When the Portuguese sailed to the coasts of Western Africa in 1440 and after, they soon began capturing a few Africans and taking them back to Portugal for sale as slaves. After a while they found they could also buy captives from willing African kings. But the total numbers were very small. Then, with the discovery of the New World, there came a tremendous change.

The Spanish and Portuguese soldiers and settlers in the Americas began by enslaving the native Indians, many of whom they worked to death in mines and on plantations. Later, they asked their own home governments for slaves, but although some were sent there were never enough of them available, while the enslaving of Christians was condemned by the Christian Church.[10] Then, with the idea of importing slaves from non-Christian lands, they turned to Africa. To begin with they got their African slaves from among those who had already been taken to Spain and Portugal. But of these, too, there were not enough, so they began to take them directly from Africa. Soon after 1500 the first cargo of African captives was taken directly from West Africa to the Spanish-ruled island of Hispaniola, and put on sale in the Spanish slave-markets there.

Where the Spanish and Portuguese had led, other European seagoing nations soon followed. Between 1609 and 1630 the English, French, and Dutch got hold of several islands in the Caribbean Sea and started growing sugar there. Not long afterwards they settled in the eastern part of North America and began to grow tobacco and other crops. Their products were eagerly bought in Europe, and the trade became immensely valuable, especially the trade in sugar. But it depended on slave labor. Every year after about 1650, tens of thousands of Africans were taken in chains across the Atlantic and forced into plantation work in the Americas under inhuman conditions.

[10] The Muslims also thought it wrong to enslave other Muslims. But like most Christians of those days, they also thought it quite all right to enslave people who were not of their own religion, and they did so without scruple.

These Africans laid the foundations of modern American civilisation just as other slaves, long before them, had enabled the building of ancient civilisations in Europe and Asia. As many as a million Africans labored in the sugar plantations of Brazil at the end of the eighteenth century. Another six hundred thousand toiled in the Brazilian mining industry. Other millions gave their work, and their lives, in North and Central America and in all the countries of South America. Nobody can say how many Africans were enslaved before about 1880, when this infamous trade at last came to an end, but the total was certainly many millions.

They came from many parts of Africa, but mostly from western African lands near the sea. Thus the East African peoples did not suffer much, and the Central African peoples scarcely at all, until after 1800. A few East Africans had, however, been taken to the New World in earlier times, as baptismal records show. In Mexico, for example, such records mention two East African places as providing a few slaves before 1600: these were the city-state of Malindi and the Portuguese base of Mozambique Island.

Yet the East African part in this traffic remained very small, even insignificant, until about 1750. Then new developments began to encourage its growth, one of these being the activity of the French on Mauritius and neighboring islands. They opened plantations and went to the Coast—to Kilwa and elsewhere—for slaves to work them. Next, the Portuguese began to acquire slaves in Mozambique in large numbers. Between 1800 and 1850 they were exporting people from Mozambique to Brazil at the rate of about 25,000 captives a year.[11]

[11] The main reason for this increase was that the Portuguese found it difficult, after 1807, to export slaves from western Africa, because in that year the British, until then the biggest of the European slaving powers, abolished the slave trade in their own ships. When other slaving nations, notably the Portuguese, did not follow suit, the British tried to force them to do so. British warships patrolled the Atlantic and captured every slave ship they could find. They took the slaves to Sierra Leone or other points in Africa, and

Another powerful spur to the growth of the new slave trade along the Coast was the building of the Omani empire. The Omani opened clove plantations on Zanzibar and elsewhere, and worked them with slaves who were captured in the Interior. They also sold large numbers of captives for slave-labor in Arabia and Iraq. In 1811 a British captain named Smee reported, after visiting Zanzibar, that the Omani governor, Yakut, was supplying the French on Mauritius, and the Arabs in Oman, with from six to ten thousand slaves a year.

This new slave trade, whether in Mozambique through the Portuguese, or in Tanzania and other parts of East and Central Africa through the Omani and their Swahili fellow merchants, grew by leaps and bounds. North of Mozambique it became very large after about 1830. Its consequences, as we shall see, were often appalling. At the hub and center of the trade was Sayyid Said of Zanzibar, and Sultan Majid after him. By 1840, when Said transferred his government from the scorching city of Muscat to the pleasant island of Zanzibar, the Omani and their fellow merchants were selling several tens of thousands of Africans every year, as well as buying other thousands for their own use. Rich men in Zanzibar flourished, but poor men paid a bitter price.

---

released them. So the Portuguese turned to Mozambique, because the British had as yet few or no warships along the East Coast. Later this changed, and the Portuguese towards 1880 were finally forced to end the oversea slave trade from East Africa as well.

11. THE COAST AND ISLANDS AFTER 1800: NEW INVADERS

After 1800 there came years of deepening trouble for the Coast and Islands. Said's empire was not built easily, or without violence. Rulers and merchants did well under it, but ordinary people suffered. Gradually, too, there came new pressures from the Indian Ocean as European powers moved towards colonial invasion. The eighteenth century had been a time of revival and comparative peace. Now the nineteenth brought a period of upheaval.

The Omani-British alliance

Sayyid Said was a boy of thirteen when his father, Sultan bin Ahmad, died in 1804, and his cousin Badr seized the throne. But Badr was assassinated in 1806, and Said became ruler. Though still only fifteen, he at once showed skill in government. He ruled for fifty years, dying only in 1856.

At first he was neither able nor eager to strengthen Omani control over the northern Coast and Islands. He had plenty of work at home, building up his own position in Muscat, supervising the despatch of Arab trading ships to every part of the Indian Ocean, and dealing with other powers.

Throughout the Indian Ocean Said faced a delicate diplomatic problem. The British and French were fighting for supremacy in these waters. He understandably wished to be on good terms with the victor, but was just as understandably doubtful who this would be. In 1738 the British East India Company, then ruling most of India, had persuaded Sultan bin Ahmad to sign with them a treaty of trade and friendship. Coming to power in 1806, Said ac-

cepted this treaty. But he took care to remain on good
terms with the French. By this time, true enough, the
British had already won their naval victory at Trafalgar
in 1805, and were far stronger than the French at sea.
But the battles on land continued, and if the French could
emerge supreme there, they might yet take control of the
ocean.

Said went on balancing between the two until 1815,
when the last army of Napoleon was shattered by the British and their allies on the bloodstained field of Waterloo,
and the wars ended in French defeat. Thenceforth Said
became Britain's firm ally. The alliance was to have important consequences for the Swahili rulers of the Coast
and Islands, and especially for the Mazrui.

Not content with their independence at Mombasa and
their overlordship of Pemba where they kept a governor,
the Mazrui aspired at a little empire of their own. In 1807
they ousted the Omani candidate for the throne of Pate
and installed their own candidate. In 1813 they attacked
Lamu, though this time they were smartly defeated. In
1819 they again intervened in Pate for their own advantage. They now ruled over a strip of the northern coast
about one hundred and fifty miles long.

It began to look as though they might be able to seize
control of the whole northern Coast from Said. Taking the
position that the Mazrui were in fact disloyal subjects of
Oman, Said began to prepare for action.

The Mazrui fight back

The Mazrui had long expected a clash with Said, and
had sought allies against him. As early as 1807 they decided to try calling in the British, and sent an embassy to
Bombay, then the capital of the British empire in India,
with an offer to the British of the overlordship of Mombasa. In 1809 they offered Pemba as well.

In so doing the Mazrui were following in the footsteps

of earlier Swahili rulers who had called in first the Turks, and then the Omani, against the Portuguese. By this time, in fact, the Mazrui were much more Swahili than Arab. The first of them, after all, had come to Mombasa a hundred years earlier. Many sons of the Mazrui had Swahili mothers, and many of their customs were Swahili, as was their language. When a British officer visited Mombasa in 1824, he found that they customarily spoke Swahili, and that a local history of Mombasa, written not many years before, was in Swahili and not in Arabic. Though proud of their Arab ancestry, being in this respect like other descendants of Arab settlers along the Coast, the culture of the Mazrui had become Swahili.

The British refused the overlordship that was offered to them. They were not yet interested in Africa. Besides, they had a treaty with Oman. Were they now to break the spirit of that treaty by acting against Omani interests on the Coast? They thought not, and politely said so. The Mazrui were left to save themselves if they could.

Their clash with Said began in earnest in 1817, when he ordered an attack on the Mazrui-held city of Pate. It succeeded after bitter fighting; five years later, in 1822, Said followed this with another on Pemba, whose Mazrui governor, Rizike, was driven out with the help of the local population. At the same time another Omani fleet sailed down the Somali and northern Kenya coast. Brava and Lamu at once accepted Said's overlordship. Omani control of Pate was confirmed. But there still remained Mombasa, the Mazrui stronghold. Said quietly got ready to attack Fort Jesus.

Again the Mazrui appealed to Britain. Sheikh Abdullah Mazrui offered his whole kingdom to the British Crown. What the ruler of Oman wanted, he wrote in 1823 to the British at Bombay, "is to get possession of my country. To him I will not give it, but to the King of England . . . Send me a flag that the nations may know that my kingdom is subject to you, and write to the Imam (Sayyid Said) to tell him not to attack us . . ."

But again the offer was declined. Only six months earlier the British had made another treaty with Oman. This time their aim was to persuade Said to abolish the oversea slave trade from the ports of Oman, and from those ports of East Africa, notably Zanzibar, where Said was in control. "It is contrary to our policy," the British at Bombay therefore replied to the Mazrui, "to enter on such intimate connections in Africa as those proposed by you. Besides, faithfulness to our engagements with His Highness the Imam (Sayyid Said) would prevent our agreeing to your proposal." Sixty-seven years later, such are the strange ways of history, the British were to declare themselves the "protectors" not only of Mombasa, but of all the Omani positions along the Coast. But that came far too late to save the Mazrui.

Events moved slowly. In December 1823 a British naval ship put into Mombasa harbor, and the Mazrui asked its captain for permission to fly the British flag. This was refused. Two months later the long-feared Omani fleet at last came over the horizon, entered the harbor, and began bombarding the castle. It seemed that the Mazrui must be defeated. Yet help arrived in the nick of time, and from an unexpected quarter. As Sheikh Suliman Mazrui ordered the guns of Fort Jesus to shoot back at the Omani fleet, a British warship sailed in. Both sides stopped firing, and waited to see what the British would do.

Now it happened that the commander of this warship, Captain Owen, was no ordinary kind of man. His main task was to make naval surveys of the Coast, and in doing so he had seen much of the slave trade and had come to hate its horrors. He shared the ardent wish of many of his countrymen that the trade should be stopped. Sailing into Mombasa harbor he saw that Fort Jesus, under fire from the Omani, was flying a British flag, one in fact that the Mazrui had made for themselves. Believing the Omani to be the worst of slavers, Owen stormed ashore to see if he could save Mombasa from them.

Inside Fort Jesus he found Sheikh Suliman and his council of Mazrui chiefs. They renewed their request for British protection against Oman. Acting on his own responsibility —"taking my own line," as he afterwards told the British Admiralty—Owen thrust aside the earlier British rejections of this request and agreed to the immediate setting up of a British protectorate over Mombasa. For the moment, the Mazrui were saved. Not caring to attack a British warship, the Omani fleet sailed away.

But Owen insisted on one important condition: that the Mazrui should abolish their own slave trade at Mombasa. They agreed, though without really meaning it, and Owen departed. Behind him, as British representative and governor, he left a young naval officer, Lieutenant John Reitz; when Reitz died of fever, another young officer, Acting-Lieutenant James Emery, took over from him. These two men governed Mombasa, at least in theory, for nearly three years. They had no easy time of it, for the Mazrui had no real intention of ending the slave trade. All they wanted was British protection against Oman.

Unhappily for them, Owen had possessed no authority to make Mombasa a British protectorate. The colonial period was still far ahead, and at this time the British government was opposed to the idea of forming new colonies or protectorates in Africa. But in those days news could take weeks to reach Bombay, the British capital in India, and months to reach London; and when at last the distant British authorities learned what had happened, they were unsure what to do. It seemed too late to undo the situation, so they let matters slide.

But only for three years: in 1826 they ordered the evacuation of Mombasa. Now the fate of the Mazrui was sealed. They capitulated to Said in 1827, only to rebel against him in 1828. Said himself came to Mombasa with another force from Muscat, and made a treaty with them. Then he bided his time, waiting for the Mazrui to quarrel among themselves. This they obligingly did in 1835, and two years later Said obtained full possession of Mombasa. The last act of violence was unfolded within those grey old walls of Fort Jesus where, for more than two hundred years, bold or desperate men had lived and governed, laid their plots or fought their bitter battles. Every leading member of the Mazrui family was arrested and deported. Every one of them died in prison.

Said was now free to build up his commercial power along the northern and central Coast. Soon he had established his authority from Cape Delgado in the south to Pate and Lamu in the north. His successes were recognised by the outside world. In 1837, three years before Said moved his headquarters from Muscat to Zanzibar, an American consul took up residence in Zanzibar. In 1841 he was joined by a British consul, and in 1844 by a French one. Four German trading firms set up offices there.

A trading empire

"I am nothing but a trader," Said once told a European visitor. Trade was certainly the main work of his empire. Having established his governors and tax collectors in the principal Swahili cities, Said had no interest in further conquest, and used his small army only as garrisons for his various forts and city-states along the seaboard. Outside the neighborhood of Zanzibar town, his military and political power was nowhere sure or strong.

Trade ranged far and wide under Said's political system. Agents were sent to eastern countries beyond the Indian Ocean to restore the old traditional markets for East African produce. Several European countries joined in. Goods from Asia and Europe began to flow into Zanzibar, with European guns high on the list.

These goods were bought with ivory and slaves. Several peoples of the inland country were now in the lead in the long-distance caravan trade to the Coast: the Yao to Kilwa, the Nyamwezi to the ports opposite Zanzibar Island, the Kamba to Mombasa. For a long time Kilwa remained the most important center for slaves; these were brought as captives from the Interior and sent on to Zanzibar for sale abroad, or for use in Zanzibar itself.

Said met the expenses of his government, his ships and soldiers, officials and personal needs, by means of a tax on the import of goods from abroad. Here he showed himself a skillful man of business. He swept away all the complicated export-and-import taxes of the Swahili cities, abolished export taxes except on slaves, and imposed a single import tax of five per cent on the value of every cargo of incoming goods.

Exactly how much he derived from this tax is unknown. It was reckoned in a coin called the Maria Theresa dollar, then worth a little more than a fifth of one English golden sovereign. In 1828 it was said that the Zanzibar Coast was yielding Said, every year, a total tax revenue of about 35,000 of these dollars. This rapidly expanded. By 1833 it had risen to more than double that amount.

Said ruled as simply and cheaply as possible. On most days of the week he met his leading men at a conference and discussed matters with them, giving personal decisions on questions of importance. There were no social services, and education was available only in Muslim schools, which taught religion and a little arithmetic. There was no highly organised system of ministers and officials. Finding it difficult to collect taxes through his own men, Said employed Indians instead.

He encouraged Indian traders to come and settle, so that trade with the East should flourish, and farmed out the business of collecting taxes to an Indian firm which received a small percentage of the amount it gathered. The first Indian firm to take on this job was the Wat Bania, which agreed to hand Said 70,000 dollars every year from the import taxes it had the right to collect. By this time many Indians were trading on the Coast. They acted as bankers for Arab and Swahili caravan traders, advancing them money so that they could take goods into the Interior and buy African goods, mainly ivory and captives, in ex-

change. These activities were centered in Zanzibar, but
went on in all the cities of Said's empire.

Said left the coastal rulers to themselves as long as they
accepted his overlordship. He simply appointed a governor
in each place, added a few officials, and sent a small garrison of soldiers to protect them. The soldiers were usually
from Baluchistan, a Muslim territory lying between the
Persian Gulf and India.

In these ways, Zanzibar became a capital for wealthy
merchants from many lands. After about 1830, their influence began to penetrate far into East Africa. "When
you pipe at Zanzibar," men used to say in those days
about Zanzibar's commercial influence, "they dance at the
Lakes": the great lakes of Tanganyika, Nyanza, and
Malawi. As will be seen, there was a good deal of truth
in this.

Zanzibar and Pemba under Sayyid Said

In the early 1830s, when Said had begun thinking that
he might make his capital at Zanzibar instead of Muscat,
the island had two local rulers. Northern Zanzibar and the
small island of Tumbatu were governed by a chief called
the *Sheha,* usually a man but occasionally a woman. He
lived on Tumbatu, and his people bore the same name. The
rest of Zanzibar was ruled by another chief, called the
Jumbe or the *Mwenyi Mkuu,* whose people were the
Hadimu. These were and are a mixture of local inhabitants
and of mainland folk who have migrated into Zanzibar at
various times.

They spoke (and speak) various dialects of Swahili.
Thus kiUnguja became the dialect of the town of Zanzibar
and the central part of the island, kiHadimu the dialect of
the southern part of the island, while kiTumbatu became
that of Tumbatu island. All these dialects of Swahili were
affected by other nearby African languages.

Said chose the Shangani peninsula, where the modern

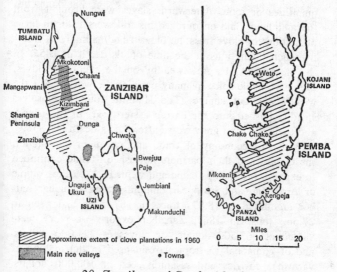

20. Zanzibar and Pemba islands

city of Zanzibar now stands, for his place of government; and so it was the Hadimu, or Shirazi as some of them afterwards called themselves, who felt the full weight of Omani presence. Like the Sheha of the Tumbatu, the Mwenyi Makuu of the Hadimu thought it best to accept Said's overlordship. He had long received a salary from the rulers of Oman as the price of his friendship, and Said promised to continue paying it. In return Said asked him to provide gangs of workers to cut down forest land and help in building houses for the Omani.

The Hadimu lived badly under the Omani. Things became hard for them after Said introduced the cultivation of the clove tree in 1818. Most of Zanzibar has little soil to cover its foundation of coral rag. The best soil is on the western part of the islands, where in those days there were thick woods. When clove plantations were opened, these forests had to be cut down, and it was the Hadimu who were at first forced to do the work in return for meagre quantities of food. Afterwards slaves were brought from the mainland. Said encouraged his followers to open large plantations of clove trees; he himself had as many as forty-five such plantations at the time of his death in 1856. In this way the Arabs grew wealthy on the export of cloves, then a valuable spice in many parts of the world.[1] But the wealth was not shared. The Hadimu found themselves steadily pushed into the barren eastern part of the island, and their situation grew worse after Said's death in 1856.[2]

With this economy of trade and cheap or slave-labor, the Omani and their partners flourished. Trade continued to expand. More ships came and went. In 1859 the volume of American and European shipping using Zanzibar harbor amounted to 18,877 tons. In 1871 this had risen to 27,662 tons. In 1867, Zanzibar exports of ivory were valued at 663,500 dollars, of cloves at 321,000 dollars, and of gumcopal (a tropical resin used in the making of varnish), cowries and sesamun seed at 100,000 dollars. Large profits continued to be made from the slave trade, and taxes on it brought useful sums into the Sultan's treasury: an amount equal to about 25,000 dollars in 1845 and 50,000 dollars in 1871.

Much the same train of events took place in Pemba, which was ruled from Zanzibar under a local governor. Pemba had two important traditional rulers in Said's time, the Diwani Ngwacheni and Diwani Athmani. Their power was not great. Under them, but often acting independently, were lesser chiefs, called shehas, each of whom ruled a village, assisted by a council of elders called Watu Wazima.

These chiefs accepted Said's overlordship as the price of getting rid of government by the Mazrui, and agreed to

[1] Zanzibar today has about 4,000,000 clove trees, and supplies about 80 per cent of the world's consumption of cloves.

[2] After Said, the rulers were: 1856–70 Majid; 1870–88 Barghash; 1888–90 Khalifa; 1890–93 Ali; and then five more sultans down to Jamshid, who came to the throne in 1963 and was deposed in 1964 when Zanzibar had become independent and shortly before it joined with Tanganyika to form Tanzania.

Others went still further, and some of them, by now, had reached Buganda: after 1851, as will be seen, the trading flag of Oman was already far west of the Great Lakes. Other end stations of the Mrima coast were Vanga, Saadani, Pangani, and Bagamoyo. Pangani, as big as Tanga, was exporting as much as 35,000 lbs. of ivory every year. Bagamoyo specialised in caravans going to the land of the Nyamwezi, in western Tanzania, and onward to Ujiji on Lake Tanganyika.

Kilwa regained some of its old importance towards 1750, when its king built himself a new palace,[3] and began to look for allies, including the French, against the Omani. This recovery was based on the slave trade. By 1800 Kilwa had become the biggest slaving port between Zanzibar and Mozambique, dealing mainly in captives from the Makua, Yao, Nyanja and other neighboring peoples. This continued to be true for many years.

Once the "queen of the south," rich and comfortable on the trade in ivory and gold, Kilwa had sadly seen its ancient brilliance fade. Now it had become little more than a squalid market for the sale of human beings, who were packed into coastal sailing ships, sometimes on rows of shelves with room only to lie in, and taken up the coast to Zanzibar. After the slave trade ended, Kilwa had nothing to replace it with, and when the city was struck by an epidemic of cholera in 1857, and again in 1870, its fall was complete. Little more than its ruins are left today.

South of Cape Delgado the Portuguese had clung to their dusty little trading stations. They were few and miserable. Landing on Mozambique Island in 1812, a British officer found the Portuguese governor's residence "more like an old warehouse; and we were first led to it by the clashing of billiard balls, and the confused noise of quarrelling voices, so that we thought it must be a drink shop or gambling house." Yet the governor, who rejoiced in

[3] At Makutani, on the south-western side of the old town on Kilwa island.

the high-sounding name of Dom Antonio Manuel de Mello Castro e Mendoza, was said to have made a personal fortune of $200,000, an immense sum of money in the values of that time. He had made it mostly out of the slave trade, now the only important interest left to the Portuguese. Every great claim about "bringing civilisation to Africa" had been reduced to a traffic in human suffering. Portuguese expeditions scoured the inland country for captives whom they took by violence, destroying families, burning villages, caring nothing for the ruin in their wake. These captives were brought to Inhambane, Sofala, Angoche, Mozambique Island, and, most important of all, Quilimane.

In 1822 the same Captain Owen who went afterwards to the aid of the Mazrui at Mombasa inspected Quilimane on behalf of the British Admiralty. He reported that "from eleven to fourteen slave ships come every year from Rio de Janeiro to this place, and go back again with, on the average, four to five hundred slaves each . . . They buy these slaves for blue dungaree, colored cloths, arms, gunpowder, brass and pewter, red colored beads in imitation of coral, cutlery, and various other things . . . To contain the slaves they have collected for sale, every Portuguese house has a big yard or enclosure, called a barracoon, usually surrounded by a high brick wall . . ."

All this brought ruin to wide areas. Not only were the people taken away; the land also suffered. The country round Quilimane had once grown grain for export to other parts of the Coast, but because of the slave trade, Owen noted, the area no longer had enough even for its own needs. Much of northern Mozambique was reduced to poverty even before the colonial period began.

Madagascar and Mauritius

The Hova people, remote descendants of Indonesian settlers, now ruled over a distinctive Malagasy civilisation in much of Madagascar. A smaller and less powerful Malagasy people, the Sakalava, appeared briefly on the scene. Under their queen, Tsihometa, they were centered on the little island of Nossi Bé near the north-western coast of Madagascar. A trading and raiding people, they were regarded by the Swahili as dangerous enemies. In 1822, living up to their reputation, the Sakalava raided Juani island in the Mafia group, and sacked the Swahili town of Kua, which never recovered. Only its ruins in thick bush are left to show that a town once existed there.

Fearing conquest by the Hova, the Sakalava needed allies to help them. In the 1830s, Queen Tsihometa offered to accept the overlordship of Sayyid Said if he would protect her. Said actually signed a treaty with her, under which she surrendered "all her dominions in the island of Nossi Bé," and agreed to pay Said 30,000 Maria Theresa dollars. In return Said sent her a red flag of Oman. But he sent nothing else, and when he asked her for soldiers to help him against the Mazrui, the bargain fell apart. Queen Tshihometa complained that a red flag was no use to her without soldiers to fight for it, and of these Said sent none: on the contrary, he asked her for fighting men. In 1841 the queen found a new protector. She surrendered her little island to the French in exchange for protection against the Hova and a yearly salary of 1200 francs. Said asked the British to prevent this deal, but the British declined, for their quarrels with the French were over.

More than the other Indian Ocean islands that are distant from the Coast, Mauritius entered African history at this stage because of its demand for slave labor. When the French first seized the island as part of their dominions in 1714, they found only a few hundred Africans, together with a small population of people who were the descendants of Indians and Africans. French settlers began to open sugar plantations, and soon they were seeking slaves. By 1767 there were as many as 15,000 African slaves there; 37,000 in 1789; and 49,000 in 1807. Much the same occurred on a smaller scale upon the nearby island of Bourbon, afterwards renamed Réunion. This too was settled by the French who imported slaves, some from East Africa, some from Madagascar, and some even from West Africa. After Britain had defeated France in 1815, the British took Mauritius for themselves, while Bourbon (Réunion) remained to the French.

Missionaries and explorers

For many years before the colonial period began, the British and some other European peoples were interested in spreading the Gospel in Africa. The Portuguese had indeed brought missionaries as early as the sixteenth century, but these had achieved no wide influence. A new Christian effort began in the nineteenth century. The first missionaries to travel into East Africa were two German pastors in the service of the British Church Missionary Society, Johann Krapf and Johann Rebmann. Krapf came to Zanzibar in 1844, and was joined by Rebmann two years later.

Apart from their missionary work, they did much exploring. Krapf was the first European to visit Shambalai and its neighborhood, while Rebmann was the first to visit the Chaga. They wrote interesting reports about these and other peoples. Later on, other missionaries took up the work of Christian conversion and education. Particularly successful among them were Scottish missionaries who began their work in Malawi with the founding of a settlement by the Established Church of Scotland in 1875.

The best known of all the missionary-explorers was David Livingstone. His first long journey took him right across Africa from west to east, ending at Quilimane in 1856. Later he returned and began his last major journey in 1866 at Mikindani on the southern coast of Tanzania.

The missionaries were followed by other explorers, who came for the sake of adventure, and because European powers were now becoming interested in the Interior. They followed the caravan trails of the Swahili, Nyamwezi and other trading peoples. In this way Richard Burton walked from Bagamoyo to Lake Tanganyika in 1857. John Hanning Speke, who accompanied Burton, went on northward and reached the southern shore of the lake which was renamed Victoria. James Grant followed him to the upper waters of the White Nile. Soon the geography of the Interior began to be known. When colonial expeditions pushed inland from the Coast towards the end of the century, they already knew a great deal about where they were going.

Britain takes over

The Omani political system based at Zanzibar never grew into a full-scale empire such as the European Powers were later to impose on Africa. Its military and police control existed only in a few towns and ports, and Sayyid Said and his successors had no interest in extending it. They were content with a business empire of the kind that the kings of Kilwa had exercised along the southern seaboard in earlier times.

Occupied with his African ventures, Said had little time for far-away Oman, but troubles there caused him to visit Muscat in April 1854. Before setting sail, he went with his son Khalid to see the British consul, Hamerton, and reaffirmed his reliance on British friendship. By that time, the British Navy was the most powerful force in the Indian Ocean, and Zanzibar had fallen gradually into the status of a British protectorate. Said died at sea during his return voyage from Muscat in 1856. Khalid having also died, Said's fourth son Majid was appointed ruler with strong British support.

Not long before his death Said had declared that his two "empires"—of Oman and of Zanzibar—were to be ruled separately after he died. In 1856 Majid took over in Zanzibar, but the son who took over in Muscat, Thuwain, was far from satisfied, because, as he rightly thought, the Zanzibar part of Said's domains was far more valuable than the Oman part. Thuwain therefore attempted to gain control of Zanzibar as well, sending an expedition in 1859 that was intercepted by a British warship and turned back. Later the same year the British Navy again intervened, on Majid's behalf, bombarding the Zanzibar shore where some anti-Majid rebels were gathered, and helping to scatter them. In 1861 the two rulers, Thuwain and Majid, agreed to ask Britain to settle their dispute. By an award of April 1861 the British decided that the two political systems, Oman and Zanzibar, were to remain separate. Majid was to go on ruling Zanzibar and its dependencies, but would compensate Thuwain by paying him 40,000 crowns a year. Both rulers accepted this award, and it was followed in 1862 by a British-French agreement by which these two imperialist Powers agreed to recognise and respect the independence of the two rulers.

All this was part of the prelude to European partition of East Africa. As things turned out, however, the Zanzibar "empire" was divided not between Britain and France, but between Britain and Germany. This reflected the "share out" which the big imperialist Powers arranged between themselves at a conference of 1884–85 in Berlin. The arrangement was made, of course, without consulting any Africans. Sultan Barghash (1870–88) even offered Britain the whole mainland area under Zanzibar control or influence as a protectorate, but the British, for reasons of European politics, preferred to divide the spoils of imperialist expansion with the Germans. By the time that Zanzibar Island was declared a British Protectorate, in 1890, the mainland of East Africa had been divided into two main spheres of interest, British and German, and the building of colonial empires had begun.

12. EAST AFRICA: THE INTERIOR AFTER 1500–1: KENYA

This chapter and the two that follow describe the background, after 1500, of the inland peoples of Kenya, Tanzania and Uganda. In reading them, two important points should be kept in mind.

The first is that all these peoples, like their neighbors to north and west and south, belong to a single large process of historical development. The second is that frontiers, as they exist today, had no meaning for them. Quite different frontiers then divided their communities and states.

These communities and states, which were very numerous, had come into existence as farming and cattle-raising populations grew in size, occupied more land, and built up separate homelands. They were varied in their ways of life. Growth of populations led to movement, and movement to change. Small groups broke away from their parent peoples, in migrations such as described in Chapter 3, and went away in search of new fields or pastures.

As these breakaway groups settled in their new homelands, they faced new problems: how to farm in the uplands round Mount Kenya, how to grow bananas in the valleys of Uganda, how to breed and keep cattle in the dry plains of Tanzania, how to improve fishing methods in lakes or rivers. Other problems were in social life: how to organise a new community in a new homeland, how to choose leading men, how to fix rules for keeping law and order, how to live at peace with the other peoples who might be already living in the area. In solving these and other problems, breakaway groups grew into new peoples, who often mingled with the populations whom they had found. They became different from their parent peoples in many ways: in beliefs, customs, laws, and sometimes in language.

By 1500 the peoples of East Africa and their neighbors already varied greatly in their social and political systems. Chapter 3 discussed how some of the more important of these variations came about: for example, the shaping of such peoples as the Kikuyu and Kamba in central Kenya, the adoption of *ntemi* chiefs in Tanzania, the growth of early kingdoms in Uganda. It was noted at the same time that all these differences in ways of life arose on foundations which had been laid down before AD 1000 by farmers, metal-workers and cattle-breeders of the Early Iron Age. All these peoples, however differently they lived in the details of everyday life, may be said to have shared a civilisation that was common to them all. After 1500 they developed it much further, and although their civilisation remained simple in most of its material things, in tools and weapons, in means of transport, in housing, in lack of reading and writing, in methods of producing goods, its everyday life became rich and complex in certain other ways. It became a civilisation of dignity and value in its spiritual beliefs, in methods of self-rule, in arts such as dancing and singing, in skills that were needed for the solving of the problems of everyday life.

It was also, for the most part, a peaceful civilisation, generally far more so than that of Europe. Battles with immigrant peoples such as the Masai certainly bulk large in the political record, but it should again be remembered that the political record can be misleading in this respect. Most of the ancestors of Kenya's peoples were troubled only occasionally by wars and raids. They lived at peace among themselves, thanks to methods of self-rule that were often powerfully democratic; and they lived at peace with their neighbors because there was usually enough land for all, at least until the eighteenth century. Most African peoples, especially those without kings and large powerful states, had no reason to be aggressive.

But all this went hand-in-hand with continued population growth until in some areas, there began to be a short-age of land, especially for cattle-raising peoples who needed more pastures. This shortage, together with other factors such as the pressure of stronger peoples, caused new and important migrations, some of which, especially after 1600, had profound effect on certain areas of East Africa, notably in Kenya and northern Tanzania. After 1800, other intruders came from Arabia and Europe, and were to have an even greater effect.

Another general point may be kept in mind about most of these migrations. Like the somewhat earlier movement of the Luo into southern Uganda, they chiefly involved cattle-breeding nomads who moved into lands occupied by soil-working farmers; they brought clashes, that is, be-tween nomads and sedentaries. Generally the nomads proved stronger, because their fighting bands were bigger, better trained, and more used to raiding warfare than those of any village or group of villages they attacked. Sometimes they settled down and mingled with the original population, as in southern Uganda. Elsewhere, as with the Masai, they continued to live separate lives.

The Masai, Turkana, and others

Among the important movements after 1500 were those of the Masai. Pushing gradually southward from their homeland in northern Kenya, groups of Masai reached the highlands of central Kenya and the neighborhood of modern Nairobi. Some of them went on pushing to the south in later years, raiding for cattle and grazing new pasturelands. The exact reasons which first set the Masai in motion are not yet clear: broadly, however, these lay in the need to find larger grazing grounds for a steadily if slowly expanding population, and in the fact that the best pastures lay to the southward of the original Masai homeland.

Like other nomads, the Masai used methods of warfare

which farmers who lived in little isolated villages, or even
in groups of villages, found hard to resist. Armed with
long spears and clubs made of hard wood, protected by
broad shields of buffalo hide, the ostrich-plumed warriors
of the Masai rushed without warning on defenceless villages, often putting the farmers and their families to death,
or driving them away and seizing their cattle.

These warriors were young men trained from boyhood.
Cattle-breeding and cattle-raiding were at the heart of
Masai life. Many farming peoples living east of Lake
Nyanza, and as far away as the Tana river, suffered losses
from their raids. But while these were painful and destructive, it is also true that they were soon over. They were
not conquests, for the Masai had little or no interest in
ruling other peoples. What they wanted was cattle and
pastureland, and the damage they did was of a limited kind.

It was further limited by geography. Being cattle folk,
the Masai stayed mostly in the broadening valleys and
plains. As their groups came steadily southward, they
passed down the Rift Valley to the west of the main areas
of the Kikuyu, Kamba, Taita and Chaga of the wooded
highlands, and east of the hills where lived the Nandi and
other Kalenjin peoples, and the Tatoga, Goroa and Iraqw.

But the peoples whom they met in their path they
crushed or thrust aside. Not until they were well into the
plains of northern Tanzania, during the 1830s, were they
halted by the Gogo, a farming but warlike people who
had come, in earlier years, from Unyamwezi and Uhehe.[1]
Their fluctuating northern frontier became the southern
limit of the Masai.

By the time that the ivory trade with the Coast became
important, after 1750 and even more after 1800, the
Masai were in occupation of a broad wedge of pastureland
in southern Kenya and northern Tanzania. They were so

[1] Unyamwezi and Uhehe mean "lands of the Nyamwezi and Hehe
peoples." *U-* is a Bantu prefix meaning "land of." Some Bantu languages have other such prefixes. Thus, Buganda for the land of the
Ganda people, Lubemba for the land of the Bemba people.

placed that they could control some of the main caravan
trails eastward to Mombasa, and even south-eastward to
the Mrima coast, and they used this control to their own
advantage. They did not go into the caravan trade themselves in any important way, but allowed other traders to
use the trails on payment of a tax. In this way they could
buy much cloth, tobacco, beads, and the brass wire which
they greatly prized as personal ornaments, especially for
their wives. The wife of a leading Masai man would often
wear a great quantity of brass-wire necklaces and bangles.
The Masai also sold large quantities of ivory. Usually they
did not hunt the elephants themselves, but obtained their
ivory from another people living in their neighborhood,
the Dorobo, famed for their hunting skills.

The Masai ceased expanding after the middle of the
nineteenth century. Southward they were stopped by the
tough resistance of the Gogo, while to west and east there
were upland farming peoples who could also defend themselves. When it became more difficult to raid other people
for cattle, the Masai began to raid each other. They suffered much in doing so. Later again they were badly hit
by cholera in 1869 and by smallpox in 1883, at the same
time losing many cattle from pleuro-pneumonia. They
were still making raids on their neighbors, as well as on
one another, when the British and Germans came on the
scene, but no longer with the strength of earlier years.

The Masai were not the only wanderers to enter Kenya
after 1500. There also came groups of Luo from north-
west of Lake Nyanza, some of whom continued to move
around for many years, eventually forming the Kenya Luo
and Padhola peoples. Later again, towards 1850, a branch
of the Karimojong, the Turkana, began shifting southward as far as Lake Baringo. As the Masai had done, they
set other peoples in violent motion; among these were the
Suk and the Samburu.

Other migrations occurred in Somalia and north-eastern
Kenya. Various groups of the Somali, belonging to the
Darod branch of that people, moved southward to the

Tana river in search of pastureland. Here they collided with the southern Galla in the plains to north and south of the Tana, and by 1850 there was much scattered fighting between them. Attacked also by the Masai and the Kamba from the south-west, the Galla had the worst of it. They lost heavily in cattle and pastureland, and many were forced to work for Somali overlords.

Different forms of leadership: The Nandi and others

These peoples had a rich variety of forms of self-rule. Different from the *ntemi* chieftainships of Tanzania, or from the kingships of Uganda, those of Kenya are often of great interest. They were developed from earlier customs of headmanship or rule by the senior men of families in the same group, and were influenced by the movements and new settlements that occurred after 1500. These methods of self-rule varied according to the problems of each people and went on changing and developing as time brought fresh problems. Often they were successful in meeting the needs of both settled peoples and nomad peoples.

Though the Masai certainly grew in numbers, they never adopted a system of rule by chiefs, probably because of the wandering life they lived. Enlarging, their groups simply split up and moved to new pastures, so the problems that come with growth never seriously arose. Besides, each group had rules for behavior developed in the past, based on guarding their own cattle and raiding for the cattle of other people, which could strongly unite the members of a group.

Yet even the Masai found it necessary to develop a degree of over-all unity. This they did through the appointment of priests, known as *laibons*, who were given the authority to take important decisions for a number of groups. After the wars among the Masai of the mid-nineteenth century, mentioned above, the power of the *laibons* grew, partly as a means of making peace between different groups, and partly as a way of uniting all the Masai against the invading British and Germans.

The Nandi group of Kalenjin were another people who became strong in or near their present homeland in about 1600, and stronger still after 1700. They ruled themselves by much the same method as the Masai, from whom, perhaps, they borrowed it. They were divided into many different groups, but achieved a certain degree of unity through the recognition of religious leaders, called *orkoiik*. The power of the *orkoiik* tended to grow, like that of the Masai *laibons,* during the nineteenth century, and for the same reasons. By the 1880s, the Nandi had become one of the strongest peoples in the country east of Lake Nyanza.

As elsewhere in eastern Africa (see Chapters 14 and 15), the nineteenth century brought new pressures on many of the smaller groups in Kenya. A British traveller in the land of the Baluyia during 1883 found at least one people of that group, the Tiriki, living in villages surrounded by stone walls and ditches of water because, they told him, they needed protection against Masai raiders.[2]

The Kikuyu, Luo, and others

The Kikuyu and Kamba of central Kenya were among the peoples who had no chiefs or kings, but who none the less worked out successful ways of running their affairs, keeping law and order, defending their villages, and expanding their prosperity. Their system was one of village councils; the task of their counsellors was to uphold standards of public behaviour, to act as judges in courts of law, and to advise on matters of general interest in the separate villages where they lived. These peoples felt no need to bring all their villages under one rule, and, not

[2] Joseph Thomson, *Through Masai Land,* p. 278.

being interested in conquest, they had no armies. But they gradually occupied more land as their numbers grew. After 1800, for example, Kikuyu farmers occupied southern Kiambu.

They, too, were affected by what was going on around them, and, especially after 1800, by the spread of warfare and upheaval. They began to appoint leaders who, in case of need, could command the men of fighting age of a number of villages. These leaders were not priests or prophets, as were the *orkoiik* of the Nandi and the *laibons* of the Masai, nor were they chiefs like the *ruoths* of the Luo, but fighting men who had proved their courage and fitness to command in time of danger. Among the Kikuyu, they were called *athimaki*. These never became chiefs or kings, but were able to unite different villages in self-defence. The Kamba also developed a kind of *athimaki*, in their case not only for self-defence but also for the better running of the caravan trade to Mombasa. Machakos and Kitui, two districts of modern Ukamba, were named after leaders of this type.

Because of the increasing dangers to everyday life in the nineteenth century, caused by the spread of warfare, people were beginning to want more unity among themselves. The *athimaki* of the Kikuyu and Kamba might even have become regular chiefs in the course of time, if the colonialist invaders had not come at the end of the century and taken all the power themselves. This general increase in the power of chiefs, or of men who could command other men, is well shown in the case of the Kenya Luo.

These descendants of wanderers from the north are said to have arrived in the Nyanza district of western Kenya shortly before AD 1500. Here they settled without much trouble in a country already inhabited by a few Stone Age hunters, Sudanic cattle folk, and Bantu farmers. Kenya Luo traditions say that their founding ancestors in this land were Ramogi and Jok, and that later, about 1600, these and their followers were joined by other Luo-speaking groups under Owiny and Omolo. Towards 1750, growing more numerous, and needing more pastures for their herds, they pushed down into south Nyanza. For a long time they were content to live in small independent groups. Only in comparatively modern times did these Luo begin to think of themselves as a single people.

It was much the same with their neighbors the Baluyia, another people of western Kenya, though belonging to the Bantu language-group. Their early ancestors were probably settled in this land to the east of the Lake long before the coming of the Luo, but they too were afterwards joined by other groups who spoke the same language; and all these, gradually, also began to think of themselves as a single people and to accept, for better self-defence and other reasons, the rule of strong local chiefs. During most of the colonial period they were known as the "Bantu Kavirondo" after the place where they lived, but in 1935 they began to call themselves Baluyia, a name that was generally accepted after 1945.

By 1800 the Kenya Luo had for a long time ruled themselves with local chiefs called *ruoths*.[3] Each *ruoth,* who had religious as well as political powers, ruled over an *oganda*. There were about a dozen of these sections, which had come into existence during the wanderings of the ancestors of the Kenya Luo. Each *ruoth* governed his *oganda* with the help of a council of elders which included various officials such as the military leader.

During the nineteenth century these Luo *ruoths* were growing stronger among their people. At the same time that they were acquiring more political power, some of their counsellors became important religious leaders or prophets. Between the dozen main sections of the Kenya Luo, Professor Ogot tells us, "no political superstructure, such as a federation or a confederation, existed. But many of the famous prophets, who acted as counsellors

[3] All the branches of Luo-speaking people use the word *ruoth,* which means chief or king, but its spelling and pronunciation differ in different Luo-speaking branches. Among the Shilluk of the southern Sudan, for example, it is *reth.*

to the chiefs, and whose main function was to look after
the spiritual well-being of the tribe . . . were known and
consulted all over Luoland. This tended to emphasise the
unity of the Luo . . ."[4] So religious leaders among the
Luo began to play the same part as the *laibons* of the
Masai, or the *orkoiik* of the Nandi, speaking in the name
of a whole people.

It is easy to see why. By this time the crisis of the nineteenth century, the reasons for which are discussed at
greater length in later chapters, had caused insecurity and
danger to the welfare and independence of the Luo and
their neighbors. As the needs of self-defence increased,
with trouble and warfare spreading across the Interior, a
few of the *ruoths* began claiming the command over
weaker ones among them. The Luo were now moving towards the appointment of strong chiefs who could unite
several of their sections. Here, as elsewhere, the imposition
of colonial rule put an end to new political forms and
larger reorganisations of power among African peoples.

Foundations of nationhood

Generally, the principal change to be noted during the
nineteenth century was the trend towards a greater concentration of power in the hands of chiefs or kings. Though
not everywhere present, this trend made itself felt among
many peoples. It is not difficult to trace the reasons.

Formerly there had been few chiefs, or only weak ones,
because there had been peace in the land, or the wars had
been no more than raiding conflicts. Now the dangers
vastly grew, and, as strong leaders became necessary, so
also did the power of chiefs. The same kind of change
occurred, much later, among the Kikuyu and other fighters in the forests during the great anti-colonial uprising
of the 1950s, the so-called "Mau Mau." There then arose

[4] B. A. Ogot: "British Administration in the Central Nyanza District," *Journal of African History*, 2 of 1963, p. 252.

athimaki, famous war leaders such as Dedan Kimathi, who were able to command large numbers of guerilla fighters in powerful resistance to continued colonial rule.

It was this kind of unification that foreshadowed the foundation of modern nations. In the nineteenth century each people tended to come together under its own separate leadership. Yet none proved strong enough to win the twentieth-century struggle for independence from colonialism. Out of this arose nationalist movements which sought and eventually succeeded in unifying many previously divided peoples under the leadership of national spokesmen. As the colonial period wore on, and new national entities took shape within frontiers which the Europeans had drawn, people began thinking of themselves in radically new ways: not only as Kikuyu or Luo or Masai, but also as Kenyans; not only as Hehe or Nyamwezi or Chaga, but also as Tanzanians; not only as Banyoro or Baganda or Lango, but also as Ugandans. It was to prove a long and difficult process of unification, leading on as it did to a still greater unity of identification as people began thinking of themselves not only as Kenyans, Tanzanians or Ugandans, but also as Africans. This was the process, one of the greatest political developments of the twentieth century, that marked the birth of modern Africa.

13. EAST AFRICA: THE INTERIOR AFTER 1500—2: TANZANIA 1500–1800

This chapter continues the history of the peoples of Tanzania, and is devoted to those who lived in the inland country. They had links, through trade, with the Swahili of the Tanzanian Coast and Islands, just as the inland peoples of Kenya had links with the Swahili of their seaboard; but, again like the people of Kenya, they developed separately from the Swahili.

Further spread of ntemi

More peoples appointed chiefs or kings after about 1500, partly for reasons discussed in Chapter 4, but also because here, too, there was growing need for self-defence, especially against raiders such as the Masai.

The Gogo were the people who brought to an end the southward spread of the Masai. Even before that time they had adopted chiefs, a development they seem to have borrowed from the Hehe. When the Masai attacked them on the southern plains, they were able to offer a successful resistance.

Further north, as will be seen, the Chaga also adopted *ntemi* chiefs, who gradually grew stronger. It would be wrong, however, to think that political development always passed from one people to the next. There was local invention and initiative as well. This may be seen in the case of Ugweno, a solid little state with political methods of its own that was formed in the Pare Mountains, after AD 1500 by Bantu people who had come from a "dispersal area" in the Taïta region during earlier times. Ugweno is believed to have developed under metalsmith-chiefs for two main reasons: the growth of local population as more people moved in from the north, and the need for better self-defence against hostile neighbors. But often, in this period after 1500, the spread of *ntemi* chiefs does seem to have moved from central Tanzania into the north-eastern parts of the country. One answer to the interesting problem of how the idea of appointing *ntemi* chiefs passed from one people to another is well shown in the case of Shambalai (Ushambara), described with vivid detail in a Swahili book called the *Habari za Wakilindi*.[1] It tells how the people of Shambalai, towards 1700, accepted from the Kilindi people a new ruler whose name was Mbega.

The example of Shambalai

Before the coming of Mbega to Shambalai, the people of this land of rolling hills and pastures say that they lived in many villages, each of which ruled itself through its own headman. Their largest settlement was at Vuga, and, at the time when these events took place, around 1700, the headman of Vuga was a man called Turi. The *Habari za Wakilindi* says that Turi was a skilful metalsmith of good repute.

At about this time the people of Vuga and neighboring villages began to feel they would be safer, and better off, if they had a strong chief to unite them. So they looked around for someone from another people who could help them, and heard about a wise man of the Kilindi whose name was Mbega. This is how the *Habari za Wakilindi* tells the story:

"Tidings reached Vuga, and Turi its headman, that there was in Bumburi a great magician, who knew charms for success in war, who could bring clouds of rain over the land, and who could heal any man who was ill. So Turi

---

[1] The *Habari za Wakilindi* was first written down, so far as is known, in 1900; as oral history, however, it undoubtedly dates from earlier times. Its title means "News of the Kilindi People."

gathered all his people together, young as well as old, and
said to them: 'I have called you all, men of Vuga, because
I have heard that a man has come to Bumburi from Kilindi
. . . who is a great hunter and master of charms. In war
he can throw a spell upon his enemies so that they see
neither towns nor people. And we hear that he is a fine
and friendly person . . . And now he has freed all the
people of Bumburi. There is no doubt of that, for they
have given him a wife, and he has married her. Now, my
friends, what shall we do? What is your judgment?' The
peoples answered, 'Turi, it is for you to choose. If you
wish to bring this man here, then send men to spy out the
truth about him . . .' "

After making careful inquiries, the people of Vuga decided that it would be good to ask Mbega to come and
rule over them. So they instructed Turi to go to Bumburi
with a following of Vuga people, and persuade Mbega to

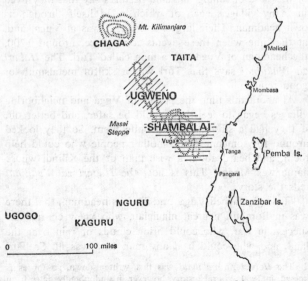

21. Shambalai and some of its neighbors

do so. Then Turi "set out with the men of Vuga, a very great army, young men and elders, with two war-horns and his flute and his signal-horn . . . And they came to that place (where Mbega was) with singing and dancing, and every man spoke of his own bravery and praised his country, and boasted of his own importance. Turi, their headman, was received with loud shouts of applause."

Then Turi spoke to Mbega and the men of Bumburi. "He proclaimed his skill in his craft, and glorified the fire of his forge, and boasted how he slew the men of Pare with his spear, and how he beat out arrows and axes and hammers and knives . . . And he boasted that he was rich in oxen and goats and sheep, and he claimed that it was he who protected all his people and cared for them with gentle kindness. And at every word he asked his people, 'Is this that I say true or false?' And his people answered as with one voice, 'It is true.'" No doubt Turi was doing his best to show that the people of Vuga were good and valiant, well worth ruling over, and that they possessed fine skills in crafts such as metal-working, and enough wealth in cattle to support a chief such as Mbega would be.

Mbega was impressed by what Turi and the elders of Vuga had to say about their country. He received them well. "They went in and they saluted Mbega and saw him: they saw his handsome appearance and the beauty of his face and smile and tall stature. Of all the men of Shambalai there was not one who was up to him by half a head in height. He overtopped them all . . . The men of Vuga said, 'He is our king without a doubt.' . . . and others said, 'We cannot help wanting him to be our king because of his skill and beauty and eloquence . . . The matter is ended: he is our king. Let us bring him out and take his hand and let all the people see him.'

"So they brought him out into the courtyard where all the people who had come from Vuga with Turi and the elders were waiting. And they took his hand to show that he was indeed their king . . ."

Mbega went back to Vuga with them. "And the men of

Vuga dwelt with their king, and he governed them and
enforced the laws, and the people (of Shambalai) brought
their problems to Mbega, and he settled these problems.
No one could dispute his laws but all approved of them."
This, of course, is the story from Mbega's point of view;
no doubt there were people in Shambalai who did dispute
his laws and disagree with his judgments. But Mbega's
rule was undoubtedly successful, and he gradually spread
his command over the whole of Shambalai and its neighborhood, and built up a new state. "Their control," says
the *Habari za Wakilindi,* "ran as far as the coast at Tanga
and Pangani and Marangu; and as far as Vanga they were
the masters. In those days there was no higher authority.
Every judgment (in important matters) came from Vuga,
the capital, and everyone paid tribute (to the king at
Vuga), even freemen and Arabs paid tribute . . ."

In this way one may see how the people of Shambalai
borrowed the idea of kingship from their neighbors, and
used it to their own advantage. Others did the same. In
changing times they sought means of reducing the dis-
persion of political and military power, and, through
kingship, found the way to greater unity, better self-
defence, and more trade.

The southern Interior before 1800

Most of the peoples of the southern interior of Tanzania
were left in peace until the nineteenth century. Their many
small struggles were evidently settled without much blood-
shed; even the slave trade from Kilwa had small effect on
most of them until after 1800.

The old traditions still speak about those peaceful times.
"In the old days," claim the traditions of the Yao, "the
Yao were in accord with each other . . . If a quarrel
arose, they used to fight without bitterness, avoiding blood-
shed . . . If strangers came to a village, would they have
to pay for their food? No, it was given to them free. Di-

rectly a man heard that a stranger was at his door, he would rejoice and say, 'Truly, I have the plant of hospitality at my door, bringing guests.' "[2]

What was true of the Yao was also true of their neighbors. Even as late as 1880, when much of eastern and central Africa was plunged in violent tumult, the British traveller Joseph Thomson could still see what life in the old days had been like. One of the southern peoples among whom he travelled were the Nyakyusa. They live near the northern end of Lake Malawi, in an isolated area where they were able to avoid the raids and killings of the slave trade of the nineteenth century. Thomson was impressed by the smiling peacefulness of the peoples whom he found, and compared their country to Arcadia.

In truth the Nyakyusa had their troubles. Yet these were small; and it was not difficult for Thomson to think of them as living in a kind of Arcadia. "Imagine," he wrote, "a magnificent grove of bananas, laden with bunches of fruit, each of which would form a man's load, growing on a perfectly level plain from which all weeds, garbage, and ugly things are carefully cleared away. Dotted here and there are a number of immense shady sycamore trees, with branches each almost as large as a separate tree. At every few paces are charmingly neat circular huts, with conical roofs, and walls . . . with the clay worked prettily into rounded bricks, and daubed symmetrically with spots . . ." Living there he found a peaceful and hospitable people.

In these lands, still beyond reach of outside invasion or disturbance, the quiet years went by with little change or need for change. Peoples untroubled by their neighbors, and content with the lands and lives they had, cultivated their gardens and banana groves, fattened their herds of cattle, worked at their village crafts in the ways of their ancestors, and were generally at peace. Though their technical knowledge was of a simple kind, it was

<hr>

[2] Quoted from Y. B. Abdallah, *The Yaos*, 1919, p. 11, by Alison Smith in *History of East Africa,* edited by R. Oliver and G. Mathew, 1963, vol. 1, p. 256.

enough to ensure a living. These peoples knew how to
terrace their hillsides so as to keep the soil from being
washed away, how to make the best use of the rains by
digging water channels in their gardens, and enough about
metal-working to supply themselves with the tools and
weapons they needed. Among the Fipa, for example, a
people noted for their metal-working knowledge, a group
of men and women could produce from a single furnace
two hoes a day and a few smaller tools.

This was clearly far from being a modern civilisation,
especially in its technologically simple methods of production. Yet it was a civilisation in which small communities
had been able to solve all the problems of everyday life,
and to allow for the amenities of social intercourse. Among
the Nyakyusa, we are told, nothing was more valued than
ukwangela, which means the enjoyment of good company:
not only good manners and friendliness, as Monica Wilson
writes about the Nyakyusa, "but also discussion between
equals, which the Nyakyusa regard as the principal form
of education . . ."[3] A good man should practise *ukwangela,* but he should also have *ubusisya,* dignity. It was
only such a man who deserved the respect of others. And
in thinking this the Nyakyusa were far from being alone.

[3] M. Wilson, *Good Company,* 1951, p. 66.

14. EAST AFRICA: THE INTERIOR AFTER 1500—3: TANZANIA AND NEIGHBORING COUNTRIES AFTER 1800

The nineteenth century brought a time of general crisis and suffering to many groups in East and Central Africa. Soon after 1800 they faced events of new and often terrible meaning. This chapter looks at these events and their causes, part of the essential background to the history of the nineteenth century not only in East Africa, but also in Central Africa.

The crisis of the nineteenth century

Much of traditional civilisation, whether in East or in Central Africa, was seriously damaged or submerged by a rising tide of violence. Many old states or communities were ruined, long-established customs and beliefs were undermined, ancient systems of law and order were set aside.

Determined peoples did their utmost to keep out this flood, fighting hard against it. But the tide was too strong for them. By 1900 even the strongest and most intelligent resistance had proved in vain. By then the old independence of inland Africa was lost, and would remain so for difficult and costly years.

There were several reasons for this upheaval, some local and others with Arab or European sources. These will be discussed in their proper order; but one general point of background explanation, to which we shall return in Chapters 21 and 22, needs mention here.

The end of the eighteenth century was also the end, as it happened, of the centuries of Iron Age growth during

which most inland peoples of Africa were little touched
by the doings of the rest of mankind, and, seldom disturbed by outside interference, followed their own paths
into the future. But developments of revolutionary importance evolved soon after 1800, and then, for one reason
or another, the whole of inland Africa was drawn step
by step into the affairs of a wider world. Yet these peoples
were badly placed to meet this harsh and sudden challenge
from outside. They had fallen far behind the strong nations of other continents in the technology of production,
whether for peace or war.

Europe after 1500 had entered a time of far-reaching
mechanical and scientific discovery and development. Inland Africa, in growing contrast, had not. Inland peoples
continued with the steady but slow development of their
own cultures; and they could, as these pages have shown,
point to many achievements. There was much advance
and invention in the arts of community life, in the adopting
of new crops, in the spread of metal-working skills, in the
growth of trade, and, still more important, in methods of
self-rule and ways of keeping the peace. These were important gains, but they could not match the growing power
of the industrialised peoples of the outside world. Between
these and the inland peoples of Africa, the power gap
ceaselessly widened.

By 1800 the technological power of the Europeans was
far greater than that of the Africans. By 1900 this gap
had become enormous. This deepening contrast in systems
of production underlay much of the history of the nineteenth century, and goes far to explain the crisis which
opened after 1800. Though it made itself directly felt only
after 1850, it had an indirect effect on the inland country
long before that date.

Direct pressures of change and upheaval came at first
from inside Africa. Among them was the arrival of the
Ngoni. These bands of wanderers from south-eastern Africa, seeking new homelands in the north, caused many
troubles before they settled down again. They disturbed

the peace of southern Mozambique, overthrew the ancient
kingdom of Urozwi, crashed into the lands of the Malawi,
and finally arrived in southern Tanzania.[1]

Zwangendaba and the Northern Ngoni

In 1818, two thousand miles away from Tanzania in
south-eastern Africa, two groups of the Ngoni people, the
Mtetwa and Ndwandwe, fought each other in one of the
decisive battles of southern African history. There on the
banks of the Mhlatuze river the tireless warriors of Shaka
closed in hand-to-hand combat with their battered rivals,
and broke the last great resistance to Shaka's overlordship.
Swept from the field by the stabbing spears of Shaka's regiments, the Ndwandwe fled. Knowing they could no longer
survive in their own country, their defeated leaders took
many warriors with them on the search for new homelands in the north.

In different groups under Soshengane and Zwangendaba, they pushed around the lands of the Swazi and entered southern Mozambique. There Soshengane took the
lead and built the Ngoni empire of Gaza. Others continued
on their way, some westward into Urozwi, others northward into Malawi. Those under Zwangendaba, after many
wanderings, finally crossed the Zambezi in 1835, seven-
teen years after their defeat at Shaka's hands. They were
by now, of course, a group which had absorbed warriors
and wives from other peoples among whom they had
fought or settled for a while. But they remained under
strong Ngoni leadership. Their chiefs or war leaders continued to be drawn from the foremost Ngoni lineages
among them.

Early in the 1840s the Ngoni under Zwangendaba's
leadership reached the lands of the Fipa and their neigh-

[1] The background to their movements is described in Chapter 20,
and their consequences for Central Africa in Chapters 16, 17, and
18.

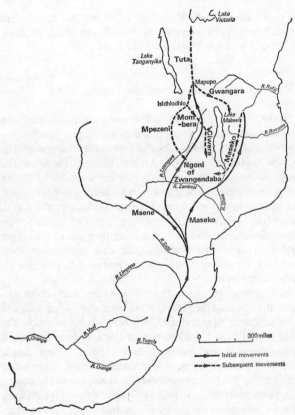

22. *Northward movements of Ngoni under Zwangendaba and others*

bors in southern Tanzania. There, in 1845, Zwangendaba died. Deprived of his command, these Ngoni split up into several groups. Some of them, under Mombera and Mpezeni, went southward from Ufipa into what is now north-eastern Zambia, divided there once more, and pushed south again in two groups across the Luangwa river, where they settled. Others went northward or east-

ward. Those who went northward, under Tuta, raided as
far as Unyamwezi and the trading settlement of Ujiji on
Lake Tanganyika. Two other indunas, or military commanders, Zuru and Mbonani, thrust boldly eastward
through the lands of the Safwa, Kinga, and Pangwa. They
and their warriors clashed with the Gwangara, another
Ngoni group under Mputa, who was killed in the fighting.
They then set up two new Ngoni states, of Songea and
Njombe, in the hill country of what is now southern Tanzania. Mputa's son Chikase retreated south across the
Ruvuma river and established yet another little Ngoni state,
along the modern frontier of Malawi and Mozambique,
which became known by the name of his son, Gomani.

For much of southern Tanzania and parts of Malawi
these invasions had two consequences of historical importance. One was that they disturbed the peace of many peoples, shattered villages and homesteads, brought into existence a large number of men who had lost homes and
families, and so paved the way for the rise of the *ruga ruga*
mercenaries who lived by war and plunder. Secondly, and
constructively, they influenced a change in methods of self-
rule among a number of peoples who felt the shock of
Ngoni raiding and warfare.

Until that time the usual method of self-rule in these
countries was by *ntemi,* with each *ntemi* ruling over a
group of villages. This method had been good enough for
the peaceful days of the past, but it proved weak in face
of Ngoni onslaught. Something stronger was needed. Unless these small *ntemi* states could somehow unite, they
were bound to fall, one by one, to Ngoni conquest. Some
of them were overrun in this way, and their lands laid
waste. But others made shift to help themselves.

Early in the 1840s, driven out of Ufipa, groups of Sangu
began to unite their strength. They had retreated into
Uhehe, but now they came together under Mwahawangu,
mtwa or chief of Mapunga, and returned to Ufipa when
they heard news of the Ngoni break-up after Zwangendaba's death in 1845. There they founded a new state com-

posed of small units which had previously ruled themselves separately. King Mwahawangu was followed in power by his grandson Merere, and Merere built himself a strong fortified settlement at Utengule, which became the center of this people's power.

Where some led, others followed. Eastward of Ufipa, a group of Bena chieftainships now came together under a single government of their own, so as better to defend themselves. This effort at unity was soon surpassed by a greater one, when about thirty chiefs of the Hehe united under Muyugumbwa. Uhehe became a strong state. King Muyugumbwa took over the military methods of the Ngoni: he trained regiments, as they did, in the tough discipline of assault tactics, and armed them with the Ngoni stabbing-spear, for hand-to-hand combat, in place of the long-range throwing-spear they had formerly used.

Using these new types of self-rule and warfare, the Hehe next united some of their neighbors with themselves, absorbing most of Ubena and its chiefdoms. They were then strong enough to throw back an invasion of Ngoni from Chipeta's new state of Songea, and later on, under their heroic King Mkwawa, they held firm against German invasion. Only after Mkwawa's death, in 1898, were the Germans able to gain the upper hand in Uhehe.

East and north-east of Lake Malawi the Yao were less affected by the Ngoni, but they too felt the same influence. Like other peoples, they bought firearms from the Coast, learned to use them, and put them to effect both in self-defence and in the slave trade. After 1850 the Yao were able to control most of the trading trails between the southern interior and Kilwa.

Arriving in a time of growing crisis caused by the spread of the slave trade and of firearms from the Coast, the Ngoni destroyed much, but they also gave a lead in the forming of stronger states, a valuable step for those who took it. The peoples who suffered most during the upheavals of the nineteenth century were those who stayed in small groups. They could not always protect themselves, nor keep out the slave raiders. But peoples such as the Hehe, who had strengthened their systems, were able for a long time to defend themselves and conserve their independence.

Rise of the inland trade

Before 1500 the Swahili cities of the Coast had traded with some of the peoples of the Interior for ivory, gold and other products, selling them cotton cloth and other imports in exchange. Most of the gold and ivory came from Central Africa and Mozambique. Few of the peoples of northern Tanzania or Kenya, and none of those of Uganda, were involved in this commerce.

After 1700, with the decline of Portuguese interference along the central and northern Coast, trade with the Interior picked up again and began to expand. A much greater expansion followed in the nineteenth century. The Omani Arabs along the Coast, under Sayyid Said's energetic leadership, reopened the old channels of trade between many countries of the Indian Ocean seaboard, notably Arabia, India, South-east Asia, and East Africa. Demand for African products, and ivory above all, rapidly grew. At first it was met by Arab and Swahili merchants who travelled into the Interior on trading missions, but soon these were joined by several inland peoples who also became active in the caravan trade, notably the Kamba and Chaga in the north, and the Nyamwezi in central Tanzania.

These trade-links quickly extended farther inland. The Nyamwezi, for example, had their trading agents as far away as the land of Kazembe, in Katanga and northern Zambia, soon after 1800. They bought ivory which was carried along the trails to Ujiji or to Unyamwezi, and there sold to Arab or Swahili merchants, or else was taken by other Nyamwezi dealers to the ports of the Mrima coast, such as Pangani and Tanga opposite Zanzibar. Other traders, as will be seen, were active in linking the kingdoms of Uganda with the Coast after about 1860.

By about 1830 the network of inland trade had become far more developed than at any previous time. Arab or Swahili merchants had set up permanent trading stations as far to the west as Ujiji, on Lake Tanganyika, and in Unyamwezi and Unyanyembe near modern Tabora. They lived on good terms with the Nyamwezi, who were also to some extent their competitors. Among the earliest of these important inland merchants in Unyamwezi was a certain Juma bin Rajab, whose grandson was the famous Tippu Tip, a warrior-trader who ranged far westward into the Congo. Most of the merchants were Swahili, like Tippu Tip, though they were often called Arabs because of their Muslim religion, and also because many of them liked to think of themselves as being part of Arab civilisation. Later on they were joined by a number of Indian traders, who built up an important business, as they had already done along the Coast, by giving credit to lesser traders as well as by direct trading on their own account. Of these Indian merchants the best known was Musa Mzuri, "Musa the Handsome," who first moved inland from Zanzibar in 1823, and who lived in Unyamwezi until his death in 1861.

But whether they were Swahili or Arab or Indian, these coastal dealers greatly helped to open the trade of all the inland country of Tanzania and its neighboring lands to the west and south-west. A glimpse of how they lived is offered in the writings of the British traveller, Richard Burton, who passed through the inland country in the late 1850s. In Unyanyembe, he reported, the coastal merchants "live comfortably, and even splendidly . . . (Their) houses, though single-storied, are large, substantial, and capable of defence. Their gardens are extensive and well planted. They receive . . . regular supplies from the Coast. They are surrounded by troops of concubines and slaves, whom they train to various crafts and callings. Rich men have riding asses from Zanzibar. Even the poorest keep flocks and herds."

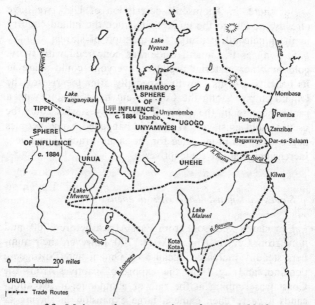

23. Main trade routes after about AD *1840*

Such men as these travelled widely. In 1844 they
reached the court of Buganda, following in the footsteps
of earlier traders, where they were welcomed by King
Suna. But their main inland bases were always at Unyanyembe and Ujiji on Lake Tanganyika. The traveller Joseph Thomson described the scene at Ujiji in 1880, though
it must have been much the same in earlier years as well.
He spoke of "the frequent appearance of Arabs in their
flowing garments . . . bands of Swahili, strings of slaves
laden with grain or ivory, flocks of sheep and goats, and
small herds of cattle, together with canoes on the waters
of the Lake. All this gave the place an appearance not
unlike a village of the Mrima Coast."[2]

---

[2] The Mrima Coast, one may recall, enclosed the Swahili trading
towns and ports of most of the modern Tanzanian seaboard.

But there, in Thomson's description of Ujiji, we have already the key to the curse that struck the inland country in the nineteenth century: the mention of slaves.

So long as the inland trade was concerned with ivory, gold or other material products, everyone could share in its benefits. But its growth, especially after the rise of the Omani empire along the Coast, went hand-in-hand with a rapid increase in the demand for captives who could be used or sold as slaves. When this happened, some peoples began to pay a bitter price for the inland trade. They were increasingly raided for captives.

Slaves and guns: The crisis deepens

Few slaves were sold from East Africa before 1700, and none from Central Africa. After 1700, however, their numbers steadily increased because of Omani and Portuguese demand, and by 1750 the export of captives from the Coast was running at the rate of about one or two thousands a year. Then came a large expansion in slaving as the French opened plantations on Mauritius and Bourbon, North American ships began sailing to East Africa in quest of slave-labor, and the Portuguese turned to Mozambique for the captives they could no longer take in sufficient numbers from Angola. By 1800 the Coast was exporting far more than ever before. By about 1830 the total had swollen to several tens of thousands every year. It had become an enormous business.

Gradually, and especially after 1830, large regions of East and Central Africa as far as the forests of the Congo were ravaged by the slave raiders. Many of the smaller or more weakly organised peoples suffered terribly. Slave-raiding became one of the principal causes of this deepening crisis of the nineteenth century. It was destructive not only to the captives who were taken away and sold, but also to the peace and welfare of countless villages. Because there had been no slaves in the Interior before the coming of the inland merchants, the merchants had to take captives by force, and savage attacks and minor wars burst in fury across these inland countries. This is why the nineteenth century, for many inland peoples, often became a time of misery and suffering.

Guns began to be used in large numbers for the first time, bought by the coastal merchants in exchange for captives whom they sold to Europeans and Arabs. By the middle of the century, comparatively huge quantities of guns were entering the Interior in the hands of soldiers employed by caravan merchants. In 1847 the missionary Johann Krapf saw coastal caravans going up into Masailand that had as many as one thousand guns among the soldiers who escorted them. A few years later, it is known, one European firm in Zanzibar was selling as many as 13,000 guns a year for use in the Interior. In 1883 it was estimated that the Nyamwezi ruler of Unyanyembe, near modern Tabora, possessed as many as 20,000 guns.

At first these guns were far from effective. Until the 1880s they were nearly all loaded at the muzzle. The bullets they fired could not seriously hurt anything at more than a hundred yards or so; even within that range, their aim was far from reliable. They were often called "gas pipes"; and war-experienced peoples such as the Kamba scornfully preferred to fight with spears. Even so, these guns were widely used, and they helped to spread fear and warfare across the inland country.

In 1866, however, breech-loading guns came into use in Europe, and the European powers' haste to supply them to their forces meant that there were a lot of the older models available for sale. Tens of thousands of these were annually sold to Africa; perhaps as many as 100,000 a year were going inland from Zanzibar in the 1880s. Then some of the new breech-loading guns also began to find their way into the area, although the Europeans, aiming now at conquest in Africa, made repeated and sometimes concerted efforts to stop this improved weapon from getting into African hands.

By this time guns were being used not only in slave raids, but also by one inland state or kingdom against another. Thus the insecurity of many peoples deepened.

Other pressures were also at work. Some of these, as the next chapter will show, were the result of Egyptian invasion of the Sudan and its consequences for Uganda. Others arose from the growing power of Ethiopia, now enlarging its southern boundaries and pressing on the peoples of that region. Ethiopian pressure, for example, helped to set the Turkana on their southward move in Kenya. Yet another set of pressures were a bitter fruit of the Ngoni invasions and the rise of the *ruga ruga* companies, tough military units put together from men who had lost homes and families, from runaway captives, and from all manner of adventurers. These operated in southern Tanzania and northern Malawi. Backed by *ruga ruga* fighters, who served for pay or for plunder, inland merchants or other ambitious men went into the slave trade without mercy for anyone whom they found in their path.

And then, in the final and most fateful stage of the nineteenth century crisis, there came the Europeans, at first as travellers or missionaries but soon as soldiers and invaders. They marched into lands already shattered by years of raiding and fighting. There they gradually imposed a new peace, speaking in the words of God but thinking, all too often, in a different language: in the language of conquest and domination.

New Chaga leaders: Horombo and Rindi

Various peoples of the inland country sought better ways to defend themselves. Some, as we have seen, adopted Ngoni methods; others found other new patterns of leadership. Another constructive example of these changes in methods of self-rule was the case of the Chaga who lived then, as they do today, in the neighborhood of Mount Kilimanjaro.

For a long time they had governed themselves under a number of chiefs of the *ntemi* sort. But now, like other peoples after 1800, groups of Chaga began to unite under a single leader so as to combine their strength. The first of these leaders to become powerful was Horombo. During the late 1830s or early 1840s, in the course of many tough little wars against the Masai and other neighbors, Horombo gradually extended his authority from his base at Chimbii, his own chiefdom, and soon had overlordship in some two-thirds of Chaga country.

To improve their means of defence, the Chaga under Horombo's rule built stone forts that were commanded by Horombo and his brother. The walls of some of these forts were as much as six feet thick, and several hundred yards long, another proof of the growing perils of warfare.

When Horombo was killed in battle with the Masai, other chiefs tried to unite the Chaga as he had done. Of these the most important were Rengwa and Masaki. But they seem not to have possessed Horombo's political skill, and largely they failed. Another strong leader appeared in the 1860s. This was a local chief of the Moshi Chaga, Rindi, who eventually managed to unite many of the Chaga groups. He might perhaps have become the first of a line of kings to rule over them all. But the Europeans arrived instead.

The Nyamwezi: Fundakira, Mirambo

The Swahili of the Coast were not the only people to grasp the new trading opportunities of the nineteenth century. Long before the coming of the coastal merchants there were others, as we have noted, who used the long trails across East and Central Africa. Among these were the Kamba in the north, the Nyamwezi in the central and western country of Tanzania, and the Malawi and the Shona in the south.

During the nineteenth century the most important of

these trading trails were those controlled by the Nyamwezi. There were several reasons for this, the most important being that the Nyamwezi were geographically well placed to send their trading companies into distant parts of Central Africa. They proved able to reach more peoples of the inland country than anyone else, and their bold caravans ranged far and wide, eastward to the Mrima Coast and westward to the Katanga and north-eastern Zambia.

The Nyamwezi had not formed an empire in the past. They had not needed to. Their different sections were each ruled by an *ntemi* chief, usually chosen because he had shown skill and courage in the caravan business; and all these trader-chiefs kept on good terms with one another. They welcomed the Arab and Swahili merchants from the Mrima Coast and Zanzibar, and allowed them to settle down in Unyamwezi and its chiefdoms such as Unyanyembe. But soon they found themselves in growing competition; and competition led to rivalry, and rivalry to disputes. Some of their *ntemis* of the middle part of the nineteenth century began to find it necessary to strengthen their little states, and there emerged more powerful kings, prominent among them King Fundakira of Unyanyembe. Another important Nyamwezi chief of this period was Kalasa, who was also the father of Msiri, who later carved out a kingdom for himself in Katanga.[3]

The work of unifying the Nyamwezi was carried much further by Mirambo, who had spent his youth in learning the caravan trade and became the ruler of most of Unyamwezi. Far-seeing and determined, Mirambo believed that the Nyamwezi could make the best of the caravan trade only if they united against their Arab and Swahili competitors, and came together under a single ruler, who was to be himself. He began his career as political leader by combining his father's small chiefdom, Ugowe, with another chiefdom ruled by a member of his mother's family, Uliankuru. Little by little, he brought more territory under

[3] See Chapter 16, at the end of *The Kingdom of Kazembe*.

his control. This hurt the coastal merchants who tried to hit back by placing a boycott on trade with Mirambo. Not in vain: as a result, Mirambo and his followers lived through hungry years, but gradually he got the upper hand. There followed a time of irregular fighting between the two sides until an agreement was reached in 1876.

By this time Mirambo's capital, Urambo, was as strong a trading center as that of the coastal merchants at Unyanyembe, and here Mirambo continued to rule and extend his power until the 1880s. To enlarge his army, he began to employ companies of *ruga ruga* fighters. Dressed in their uniforms of red cloaks and feathered headdresses, these tough mercenaries were soon able to give him the military strength he needed, a power which he shrewdly reinforced by alliance with the formidable Tippu Tip.[4]

Other trader-chiefs of the inland country, less powerful than Mirambo or Tippu Tip, followed the same path of commercial expansion by force of arms. As their warfare spread, and free-booting companies of *ruga ruga* grew in number, the weaker peoples of the Interior went in peril of their lives and liberty. In the later years of the nineteenth century, it became the custom for chiefs to build strongholds or big *bomas* not only for themselves, but also for the safety of their people and cattle. Mirambo's own capital was described in the 1880s as being a walled enclosure big enough for the huts of ten thousand people. Other capitals were not so large, but each was surrounded by strong defensive hedges of thorn and *miyombo* (euphorbia), pierced with loopholes so that the defenders could aim at their attackers through them. Sometimes, to frighten attackers, chiefs would put human skulls on poles above their defensive walls. Inside their strongholds they

[4] The remarkable story of Tippu Tip, a man of outstanding political and military gifts for whom the slave trade was always secondary to the ivory trade, has been vividly told by himself in his Swahili autobiography, *Maisha ya Hamed bin Muhammed etc,* republished and translated by W. H. Whiteley, East African Literature Bureau, Nairobi (repr.) 1966. This should be read by all who want to taste the firsthand flavor of those tumultuous years.

also built little forts in which they could continue to resist
if an enemy got through the outer walls.

Resistance to invasion

These states of inland Tanzania, like the trading system
of Mirambo, became victims of the German invasion of the
end of the nineteenth century, and their later history lies
within the colonial period. But we may note that the Germans, like other colonialist invaders in East and Central
Africa, did not find it easy to beat down the resistance of
African peoples. Pushing inland from their coastal bases
in southern Tanzania, German troops were met with stub-
born and combined resistance by peoples along the coastland as well as in parts of the Interior.

Many peoples resisted, and sometimes for long and bitter years. This happened in Kenya and Uganda as well as
in Tanzania, in Zambia and Malawi as well as in the lands
to the south of the Limpopo that were afterwards to become Rhodesia. It happened in Mozambique, Congo, Angola; indeed in every part of Africa.

This resistance was powered by many drives—by proud
traditions of independence, by skill and courage, but also
by political and military strength. In Tanzania, for example, the toughest resistance came from those peoples who
had succeeded in uniting themselves during previous years,
especially during the early and middle years of the nineteenth century. So it was that the Germans found the Hehe,
who had united after the Ngoni invasions of the 1840s, a
very hard nut to crack. Only in 1894, after three years of
fighting, did the main fort of the Hehe at Kalenga fall to
German onslaught.

It would be easy to multiply examples. One of the most
notable, for Tanzania, was a Swahili resistance movement
along the Mrima Coast that was led by Abushiri bin Salim
of Pangani. For a whole year Abushiri and his followers
had the better of the Germans along the coast and as far

south as Lindi, even though other colonialist powers refused to supply them with arms and ammunition. But perhaps the last word in the story of Tanzanian resistance may be left with a chief of the Yao, named Masemba, who spoke not only for himself but for many others as well.

Though Masemba was a notorious slave-trader and raider, he was nonetheless able to win much African support. In 1890 the German military commander, Hermann von Wissmann, demanded his submission to German rule. Masemba's reply, in kiSwahili, was afterwards filed in the German colonial records, and is still there. It reads in part:

"I have listened to your words, but I can find no reason why I should obey you. I would rather die . . . I look for some reason why I should obey you and I find not the smallest.

"If it should be friendship that you want, then I am ready for it, today and always. But I will not be your subject . . . If it should be war that you desire, then I am also ready . . . I do not fall at your feet, for you are God's creature just as I am . . .

"I am sultan in my land. You are sultan there in yours. But listen to me: I do not say that you should obey me, for I know that you are a free man . . . As for me, I will not come to you, and if you are strong enough for it, then come and fetch me . . ."

The Germans did prove strong enough for it in Tanzania, like the British in Kenya and others elsewhere. They had more and better guns and stronger military organisation. Yet their success was also, in some degree, the result of the troubled condition of the inland country, ravaged as it was by years of slaving warfare.

All in all, the crisis of the nineteenth century had done much to undermine the old order and stability of Iron Age civilisation. A new start was clearly needed, but it was to be long delayed. Only in the 1960s, after more than half a century of obstructive colonial rule, were East and Central Africans, like other Africans, at last able to make this new start. Then they took over the wide frontiers established by the colonial Powers and began, within these frontiers, to build new nations of a strength and size that might at last be able to confront the problems of transition to the modern world.

15. EAST AFRICA: THE INTERIOR AFTER 1500—4: UGANDA

After 1500 the peoples to the west of Lake Victoria, and southward along the hills and pastures as far as Lake Kivu, continued to develop their own forms of self-rule and everyday life. Except in northern Uganda, these were especially the work of ruling groups such as the Hima and Tutsi. After 1600 new kingdoms grew in strength, and Buganda became the largest of these.

Bunyoro-Kitara

At some time between 1450 and 1500 a number of groups of Luo arrived from the north, as described in Chapter 3. They settled in the fertile country of central Uganda, merged with local Iru farmers and others, and made war on the Hima rulers. By 1500 the strongest of these rulers, the Chwezi, were displaced by a new line of kings, partly of Luo origin, called the Bito. These formed a new empire with its center in Bunyoro.

From Bunyoro the Bito kings, beginning soon after 1500, sent out raiding parties and placed their chiefs over neighboring peoples—the Haya of Kiziba, for example, and the small kingdoms of Koki and Toro. Other Bito princes ruled Busoga and Buganda. Yet it was not long before the descendants of these outlying chiefs of Bunyoro-Kitara broke their links with their homeland, and set up independent kingdoms.

In the south the Bito were resisted by the Hima rulers of Ankole. Here another kingdom came into existence under one such ruler, Ruhinda, who founded a line of Hima kings, known as the Hinda, which continued to reign there until recent times. Eighteen rulers after Ruhinda are remembered in local traditions, down to King Gasynonga II who came to the throne in 1957. Each of these rulers, according to their ancient custom, settled in a new location where he built a palace of thatched reeds and established the grazing grounds where he kept his royal cattle. The sites of these old palaces are well remembered today, although the buildings have long since disappeared. Ankole then was a country of considerable wealth in cattle, but a new spread of tsetse fly since the end of the nineteenth century has obliged its people to rely mainly on cultivation.

At the time of the rise of the Bito empire of Bunyoro, the Ganda were centered in a small part of the country to the north-west of Lake Victoria. There they were fortunate in having good soil for growing bananas, a fruit that can be harvested the year round, and it is clear that they used this advantage with skill and energy. Around 1600 they were attacked by a Bito army that was stronger than their own, and, although they were still a small state, they proved strong enough to beat it off.

Rise of Buganda

By 1650 the fortunes of Bunyoro had reached their greatest point under the Bito kings, and were beginning to decline. They no longer had enough strength for the wide-spread power they tried to exercise. Their armies were defeated by other kingdoms, notably Ankole. At about this time the Ganda embarked on their own history of conquest.

Around 1650 the Ganda were ruled by King Katerega. He proved to be a determined leader in war; under his rule the Ganda more than doubled the size of their territory, expanding westward into Mawokota and Gomba, Butambala and Singo. By 1750 the king of Buganda, whose title was *kabaka,* was supreme in all the Lakeside country between the mouth of the Kagera river and the exit of the Nile. The map shows the stages of this and of later ex-

pansion of Ganda power. The reasons for this expansion
are important.

There was first of all the fact that the Ganda were extensive banana-growers, counting on bananas as the staple
of their diet. This meant that the task of supplying food
could be left largely to women, so that the kabakas were
able to call on many warriors who were always more or

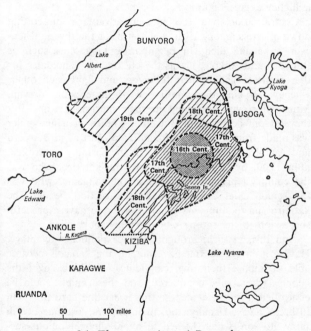

24. *The expansion of Buganda*

less available for service. They thus enjoyed a military advantage over most of their neighbors. Among the Bunyoro, for example, men were engaged in caring for their
cattle and, at certain seasons of the year, in tilling the soil,
for they regarded it as wrong for women to do such work.

Next among reasons for Ganda success was their politi-

cal system. In early times their kabakas had been little
more than senior religious chiefs among the batokas, the
leading lineage heads. But the wars of the seventeenth century taught the Ganda that they could do better if political
power was concentrated in the hands of their king. Such
concentration seems to have developed more effectively in
Buganda than elsewhere. This gave the Ganda a political
advantage over their neighbors: generally, they possessed
a higher degree of unity.

Centralisation had the further advantage of cutting
down quarrels among rival candidates for the throne whenever a kabaka died. In neighboring kingdoms, such as
Bunyoro and Ankole, it was the custom for candidates for
the throne to gather their followers and fight each other,
whenever a king died, until one of these could prevail.
Much effort was expended in such succession wars. But
they seldom occurred in Buganda. Choice of a new ruler
was made from a number of candidates, just as in Bunyoro
and Ankole, but the selection was increasingly controlled,
after 1700, by two senior officials, the katikiro, who was
the country's prime minister, and the mugema, who was
the senior chief among the batoka section heads. The
katikiro and the mugema generally tried to have a peaceful
succession to the throne whenever a kabaka died.

And this, in turn, brought another political advantage.
Having a strong central government, the kabakas became
able to impose their own candidates, as chiefs, over the
peoples whom they conquered, and these chiefs could be
controlled from the center, so that it became hard for them
to break away. Usually, too, their powers descended from
father to son, which helped to avoid quarrels about succession, and to conserve Ganda energies for warfare on
their neighbors.

Control over trade was another reason for Ganda royal
strength. In the eighteenth century their kings began to
open a trade route with the Coast for the first time. Ganda
traditions say that Kabaka Kyabuga, who reigned from
about 1763 until 1780, imported tableware such as cups

and plates, while his son Semakokiro, who reigned from about 1797 until 1814, sold ivory to Swahili traders in exchange for Indian cottons, cowrie shells to be used as money, and copper bracelets. The route these traders used is believed to have come south of Lake Nyanza by way of Unyamwezi and Karagwe into southern Buganda.

Inside Buganda the long-distance trade was controlled by the king, who was thus able to increase his power by rewarding his soldiers and officials with goods from abroad, as well as with gifts of land. This is another example of the way in which kings could use the long-distance trade for their own advantage.

By the beginning of the nineteenth century the Ganda kingdom lived increasingly by war on its neighbors. Its political system lost the equality and democracy of earlier times, and the kings became increasingly despotic. "It was in war," M. S. Kiwanuka tells us, "that lay the sources of (Buganda's) wealth such as livestock, slaves, ivory: in sum, the very things of which there was a shortage in Buganda." Up to that time, moreover, Buganda had been short of iron. It had had to buy its hoes from neighboring Bunyoro, which had large supplies of iron in its territory and good metalsmiths. But during the nineteenth century "the conquest of Eastern Kyaggwe by King Mawanda, the annexation of Buddu by King Junja, and the friendship of Koki, had all increased Buganda's sources of iron, and had also obtained a new large number of smiths."[1]

All this helped to develop Buganda into a rich and powerful kingdom. A description of everyday Ganda life in those days would speak of many prosperous and peaceful villages where there was seldom any lack of food; where disputes and legal cases were quickly settled in long-established courts and by customs known to all; where the passing of the seasons was marked by festivals and dancing, and the rivalries and violence of kings or great officials made only a distant and occasional echo.

[1] *Basekabaka be Buganda*, by Apolo Kaggwa, translated and edited by M. S. Kiwanuka, 1965, p. 332.

But the political record tells a different story. The royal
traditions show that life was often far from peaceful or
pleasant for the men of leading families. These lived dangerous and often very short lives, for in spite of the care
they took to prevent quarrels about who should rule, the
kings were always worried about plots against them. King
Semakokiro's greatest worry, according to the royal traditions of Buganda, was to stop anyone else from pushing
him off the throne. "He himself had obtained it through
violence by killing his brother Junja. So he made certain
that such a catastrophe did not befall him. Because he had
fully grown sons, he executed all of them except three, and
when he learned that his in-laws . . . were plotting to overthrow him . . . he executed about seventy of them."[2]
Other kabakas of the nineteenth century did the same.

Other types of kingdom: Okutoizha, *a two-way loyalty*

Buganda's smaller neighbors had less interest in conquest and warfare; when they went to war, it was mainly
for wider pastures and more cattle. These wars are often
mentioned in the political record, but they were small and
cost little in lives or property. Writing at the beginning of
the colonial period, when conditions were much the same
as in somewhat earlier times, a European observer noted
that "only on rare occasions are there wars . . . (Then)
the combatants shoot arrows and sling stones, they seek
cover and strive to get within shooting-range unobserved,
and again at times one or two men from either side will
rush out and engage in a hand-to-hand fight while the armies look on, till possibly one man is seriously wounded
or perhaps killed. Such a combat of champions will end
the battle, and the winning side will dictate the terms of
peace." Among the Basoga, this observer continued,

---

[2] *Loc. cit.* p. 442: from *Ebifa* of 1910–11 by Apolo Kaggwa.

"there have never been any prolonged wars of a serious nature . . ."[3]

But states which had strong kings, in Africa as elsewhere, tended to have more wars and sharper ones. This was partly because the kings strove for more power over their own subjects or over neighboring populations; and the Ganda, in this respect, were not the only people to become aggressive. What happened in the Haya kingdom of Karagwe during the nineteenth century also sketches the picture for other peoples who had strong central governments. King Ndagara of Karagwe fought several successful wars during his reign, which lasted from about 1832 to 1855, and so did his son Rumanika. Unlike the Ganda rulers, however, the Haya were usually content to leave the peoples they conquered under their own rulers. These rulers had to pay tribute to their conquerors, but they were not, as in Buganda, made into part of the Karagwe ruling system.

In their social structure these kingdoms also differed from the *ntemi* kingships of Tanzania. Unlike most of the latter, each of these kingdoms had several clearly separated social strata. The uppermost stratum consisted of the rulers: the king and his chiefs; the second of the mass of Hima and Tutsi cattle-owners. Only these two classes enjoyed political rights. Each cattle-owner had to swear loyalty to the king, to promise to fight for him, and, from time to time, to pay him tribute in cattle. In return, the king undertook to govern the country, lead the army in warfare, and decide important legal cases. This tie between the king and the cattle-owners was called *okutoizha* among the Hima, and *ubuhake* in Ruanda. These words have reference to systems of dependence; but, as noted, this was a two-way dependence.

Under the Hima, in Ankole, there were a far greater number of Iru farmers, potters, and blacksmiths. They had no political rights, however, and they were not generally

[3] J. Roscoe, *The Northern Bantu*, 1915 (repr. 1966), in various chapters.

regarded as being citizens. Yet there was a similar two-way tie of dependence, a form of *okutoizha,* between the Hima cattle-owners and the Iru soil-cultivators. The Iru had to work for the Hima and also pay them taxes, but the Hima were under an obligation to fight in defence of the Iru in times of danger.

In Ankole and some other kingdoms there was still another class beneath the Iru. These were called *abahuku,* a word which means something like "slave." Most of the *abahuku,* of whom there were few, consisted of Iru who had been captured in raids on neighboring kingdoms. These unfortunate people sometimes had their ears cut off, so that they could be recognised if they should run away.

To the south of Ankole the large kingdom of Ruanda was ruled in much the same way, as was Burundi to the

25. (*a*) *Uganda Kingdoms around* AD *1700*

south of Ruanda. There the two upper strata were the
Tutsi king and cattle-owners, while the farmers and field-
workers were the much more numerous Hutu. Beneath
them were the Twa, wandering Pygmy hunters who pre-
served a life of their own, and who often used the Tutsi
and the Hutu for their own benefit just as they in turn were
used.

It would be a mistake to think of any of these societies
as being rigidly frozen into these classes. As time went by,
and especially in the nineteenth century, there was a steady
lessening in the social gap between the Hima and the Iru
in Ankole, as between the Tutsi and the Hutu in Ruanda.

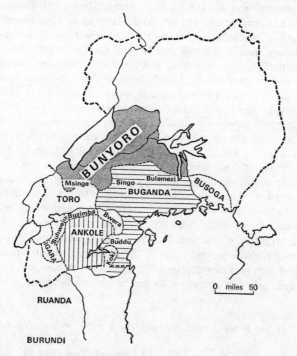

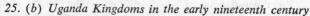

25. (b) Uganda Kingdoms in the early nineteenth century

During the colonial period, unhappily for the consequences, the German and then the Belgian colonialists relied heavily on the Tutsi at the expense of the Hutu. When the colonial period came to an end in the 1960s the Hutu felt great bitterness against the Tutsi, and warred on them with tragic results.

Northern Uganda

The peoples of northern Uganda—Madi, Lugbara, Acholi, Lango, Alur and others—differ in certain ways from those of the rest of the country. They speak Central or Eastern Sudanic and not Bantu languages. They depend largely on cattle but, unlike the southern Ugandans, they do not have much soil that is good for cultivation. Their methods of self-rule have not been kingdoms, but looser forms of government, largely because these northern peoples have always been forced to move around a great deal, seeking fresh pastures in their rainless land. They have therefore developed structures of dispersed authority that are somewhat similar to those of their neighbors in Kenya, the Kenya Luo, the Kalenjin, and Baluyia.

Most of these northern peoples, as noted in Chapter 3 (*Coming of the Luo*), were formed by the migrations and minglings during the fifteenth century. Not until the nineteenth century was there any major interruption in their political and social life. When it did come, however, the interruption was severe. It formed, for Uganda, one of the causes of the general crisis of the nineteenth century mentioned in previous chapters. To understand it, however, one must turn for a moment to the history of Egypt.

Egypt in the Sudan: Consequences for Northern Uganda

Egypt was conquered by the Ottoman Turks in 1517 and ruled after that by viceroys in Cairo who were appointed by the imperial sultan in Istanbul. Cairo remained an important center of trade for North Africa, buying gold from the western Sudan as in earlier times, but taking small notice of the eastern Sudan. The new rulers of Egypt had little interest in tropical Africa.

This changed early in the nineteenth century. In 1820 an unusually ambitious viceroy, Muhammad Ali, undertook the building of new imperial provinces in the distant south, despatching there an army commanded by his third son, Ismail, with some 4000 soldiers drawn from many parts of the Turkish Empire as far as Albania. It even included an American converted to Islam, who was in charge of the artillery.

These various but efficient units pushed southward up the Nile, and defeated the Sudanese whom they found in their path. They had brought all the central Nile valley under their control, by 1821, as far as the country of the Funj whose capital was at Sennar on the Blue Nile. These annexed territories were held for many years, and ruled by Egyptian governors appointed by the viceroy in Cairo. The governors were not popular, and there were many revolts.

One of Muhammad Ali's interests in promoting the conquest of the Sudan was to milk the wealth of the Sudanese by obliging them to pay taxes. Even more, he wanted a supply of Sudanese and other captives who could be turned into slaves, and used in the Turkish Empire as domestic servants, laborers or soldiers. Every general sent to the south was told to concentrate on sending back captives. "You are aware," Muhammad Ali wrote to one of them in 1825, "that the reason for all these efforts and expense is to get blacks. Please show zeal in carrying out our wishes in this most important matter."

The Egyptian commanders and governors did show zeal. They showed appalling zeal. Soon the whole middle part of the Sudan as far west as Darfur was being searched by raiding forces. Very large numbers of captives were taken, and sent north for sale as slaves. From this time the settlement of Khartum, now the capital of the modern Republic of the Sudan, became a center for government and trade.

But it was not only the middle part of the Sudan that was ransacked for captives. Soon the commanders began pushing down into the southern Sudan, where they raided the Nuer, Dinka, and neighboring folk for captives and ivory. Eventually, their operations approached the country of the northern peoples of Uganda. In 1841 a Turkish captain named Selim went as far up the Nile as Gondokoro, only thirty miles north of the modern frontier of Uganda and the Sudan.

Gondokoro became an Egyptian base for new raiding operations in the far south, enabling the "Khartumers," as they were afterwards called, to strike at the peace and security of a wide region. Many of these peoples, of northernmost Uganda and the southernmost area of the Sudan, were poorly organised to defend themselves. They were cattle-raising nomads who lived in scattered villages and hamlets which could be attacked one after the other. Here was another case, in those painful years of the nineteenth century, when weak peoples had to pay a bitter price to those who had guns and stronger organisation. And here, too, religious pride and prejudice played a sorry part. The raiders from the north were Muslims whose maltreatment of the peoples of the south was "justified" by one or another form of racial or religious prejudice such as, for example, the belief that people must wear clothes.[4]

[4] Myths about a natural inferiority of black Africans were as old and as prevalent among Muslim Arabs as among Christian Europeans, and led to opinions no less absurd. Even the great Hejazi geographer of the tenth century AD, al-Mas'udi—we are told by the still greater Berber historian of the fourteenth century, Ibn Khaldun —"undertook to investigate the reason for the levity, excitability and emotionalism in Negroes, and attempted to explain it. However, he did no better than to report [on the evidence of previous writers], that the reason is a weakness of their brains which results in a weakness of their intellect." Himself an African, though of Muslim Spain, Ibn Khaldun adds brusquely: "This is an inconclusive and unproven statement." (*The Muqaddimah*, trans. F. Rosenthal, New York, 1967,

The plague of violence spread further. In the late 1850s a trader from the Mediterranean island of Malta, an adventurer called Debono, led an expedition into Acholi country north of Bunyoro. Some fifteen years later another "Khartumer," Ali Husain, did the same in Lango country. Both expeditions plundered and killed, destroying villages, driving off cattle, enslaving men, women and children. The northern Ugandans tried to defend themselves. When the next raiding expedition came south, the Lango fought them and drove them out. But destructive raids continued for many years.

Late in the 1860s the Turkish-Egyptian viceroy in Cairo, the Khedive Ismail, decided to bring the "Khartumers" under government control, and, at the same time, to push the colonial frontier still further south. In 1869 he appointed a British explorer, Sir Samuel Baker, as leader of an official expedition to the lakeland country of western Uganda. In this way there came into being the most southerly of the Turkish-Egyptian provinces. This was governed for a time by another Englishman, General Gordon, who was afterwards killed by the northern Sudanese in their great resistance movement under their Mahdi, Muhammad Ahmad ibn Abdullah; and then by a German who took the name of Emin Pasha. Emin was still in the country, though with little control over any of it, when the British arrived from Kenya in the 1890s.

Southern Uganda after 1850

The pressures of warfare continued to strengthen the power of the southern kings, especially those of Buganda. That kingdom now reached the height of its power under two outstanding kabakas, Suna II, who reigned until 1856, and Mutesa I, who reigned until 1884.

---

vol. 1, pp. 175–76.) Which has not, alas, prevented many others, whether Muslim or Christian, from repeating it.

King Suna took the bloodthirsty but familiar royal pre-
caution of killing all his brothers, about fifty-eight of them,
in case they should plot against him. He further reduced
the power of leading Ganda priests and officials, tightened
his direct control of the country by appointing more chiefs
under his direct command, and reorganised the Ganda
army by beginning the use of long-service soldiers. He
kept the commander of the army, the mujasi, under strict
watch; and all its officers, in turn, were closely controlled
by the mujasi.

Suna was the first king in Uganda to import guns in
any quantity. He bought them from Zanzibar traders and
kept them normally in his own armoury, handing them
out to his troops only under strict supervision. They were
old-fashioned muzzle-loaders, and far from reliable, but
they made a great deal of noise; and they easily frightened
people who knew, as yet, far less about firearms than they
were to learn in the future.

Mutesa I used the same methods of rule as Suna II, and
further exploited the Ganda political system in the interests
of royal authority and of royal despotism, previously a
rare and even impossible phenomenon. He likewise made
military changes. In 1872 he had more guns at his dis-
posal, perhaps as many as a thousand in all, than any of
his neighbors. These were used by a special regiment
composed of young men who had served at the king's
court. They fought as part of a much larger army
equipped with spears. These mixed regiments raided in
many directions, attacking Busoga, Bunyoro, Ankole, Toro
and other kingdoms.

At the same time Mutesa improved Ganda control on
Lake Victoria by organising a canoe navy under an official
called the gabunga. Armed canoes raided the islands of
the Lake, as well as lakeside villages, for cattle, ivory and
captives. No fewer than sixty such raids for loot, whether
by land or water, are recorded for the twenty-seven years
of Mutesa's reign. Even as late as 1884, a land-and-water
operation against Buzinza is said to have returned to the

kabaka's capital with five thousand cattle and several hundred prisoners.

Few were able to withstand such raids. Among those who resisted with success was Bunyoro. This old kingdom had steadily declined in power since its great days in the sixteenth and seventeenth centuries, but towards 1850 it began to be ruled with a new energy by a mukama, or king, called Kamurasi. Helped to his throne by the Lango, who had joined the Bunyoro in fighting against attacks from Buganda, Mukama Kamurasi defeated a Ganda invasion and established firm control over the trade routes which ran northward to the "Khartumers," or eastwards to the Coast and Zanzibar, from the neighborhood of Lake Kyogo. He died in 1869 and was followed by another energetic mukama, Kabarega.

Kabarega knew that he was in for trouble from Buganda, and looked around for outside help, concluding that if the king of Buganda could buy guns from the Zanzibaris, then so could he. He proceeded to do so; and at the same time he began buying them from the "Khartumers" as well. He went further, enlisting a number of "Khartumers" in his military service; and he, too, like his rival Mutesa of Buganda, reorganised his army and formed new regiments.

By the 1870s Buganda and Bunyoro faced each other in more or less equal strength. But the balance between the two was soon overturned, once again by foreign intervention. Kabarega came into conflict with the official agents of the Turkish-Egyptian viceroy in Cairo, the first of whom was the Englishman Baker. This man, with the high contempt for Africans characteristic of his origins and period, thought that the Bunyoro were far too independent in their attitude towards him; while Kabarega, rightly in this case, feared that Baker and his followers might easily turn hostile. Carefully watching all this, Mutesa of Buganda tried to win Turkish-Egyptian support for himself. In this he failed. But in the moment of his failure there arrived from the Mrima Coast another Englishman, the

traveller Henry Stanley; and Stanley, much impressed by
Ganda political and military strength, at once suggested an
alliance to Mutesa. This made little immediate difference
to the balance of power between Mutesa and Kabarega,
but it was afterwards to have a profound effect. Admiring
Mutesa and the Ganda kingdom, Stanley was listened to by
the British government, then embarking on colonial conquest; so that when the British arrived in force, during the
1890s, they were prepared to regard Buganda as their
friend and Bunyoro as their enemy. They made an alliance
with Buganda, and Kabarega and the Bunyoro were left
to resist the British as they could. By this time Kabarega
had an army well-equipped with guns, including some of
the new breech-loading type. He was able to hold out until
1899, when he was captured and imprisoned in the
Seychelle Islands of the Indian Ocean, a place of distant
exile often chosen by the British for African kings who
resisted them and whom they captured.

Another kingdom to adopt new methods of warfare in
these troubled years was Ruanda. There, too, the widening
crisis of the nineteenth century reached westward from
the Mrima Coast with advantage for the strong, but disaster
for the weak, beginning under Mutara II in the 1840s and
continuing under his successor Kigeri IV. To keep a bal-
anced view, one should remember once again that most
people were affected by these troubles only occasionally,
and that wars and raids were seldom more than brief interruptions in otherwise peaceful lives. Like its neighbors,
Ruanda had developed a strong local civilisation reinforced
by well-accepted laws and customs.

Yet the nineteenth century undoubtedly brought a rapid
increase in the amount of warfare, as well as making war
more destructive. Rivalries sharpened. Royal ambitions
grew stronger. Dangers increased. Having attacked Burundi in the south without success, King Kigeri turned
his armies northward and raided far into Ankole. Buying
guns from the Zanzibaris, he made every able-bodied man
in Ruanda do military service in regiments that were used

by turns, one after another, so that Kigeri always had a force mobilised for action. Continued import of guns added to the spread of insecurity and violence, helped to transform peaceful states into warring states, and spread destruction from one country to another.[5]

No one can tell what solutions might have been found to this general crisis of the nineteenth century if the colonial invaders had not appeared on the scene. New forms of unity among peoples were clearly needed, new ways of avoiding warfare, new methods of keeping the peace over wide areas. No doubt all these would have been found in the course of time: here and there, indeed, they were already on the scene. As it was, the colonial invaders came instead, the British to Kenya and Uganda, the Germans and then the British to Tanzania, the Germans and then the Belgians to Ruanda and Burundi. And they dictated their own colonialist solutions, breaking into African development for more than half a century.

[5] The quantity of guns sold every year to East Africa became larger than ever in the 1880s. Dr. R. W. Beachey has estimated that about one million guns, more than four million lbs. of gunpowder, and many million rounds of ammunition were imported, between 1885 and 1902, by the peoples living in what had now become the British and German spheres of interest; that is, the later territories of Kenya and Tanzania ("The Arms Trade in East Africa," *Journal of African History,* 3 of 1962).

IV

Central Africa after 1500

Chapters 16 and 17 are concerned with the development, after 1500, of the peoples whose descendants live in Zambia and Malawi, while Chapter 18 describes the rise and fall of the ancient kingdoms of Mwanamutapa and Urozwi in the countries which became, in 1923, the British Crown Colony of Southern Rhodesia.

Although these peoples had built up their own separate cultures in the past, they were not isolated. Many of their neighbors were useful to them, and the same was true in reverse. At certain times and places they had valuable connexions with East Africa, chiefly by means of long-distance trade with peoples such as the Swahili, Nyamwezi and Yao, another factor which explains why their history needs to be considered together with East Africa.

Other neighboring countries similarly proved important for Central Africans and call for some mention here: notably the Congo grasslands, central Mozambique, and the southerly lands beyond the Limpopo (modern South Africa). Chapter 19 accordingly gives a brief sketch of the political history of the Western Congo and Angola after 1500. Chapter 20 does the same for South Africa with special reference to the settlement of Europeans, the penetration of the Boers (Afrikaners), and the background to the Ngoni migrations.

16. BETWEEN THE CONGO AND THE ZAMBEZI AFTER 1500— 1: ZAMBIA

It was described in Chapter 4 how thinly scattered groups of Bantu farmers and metalworkers in the territory of modern Zambia became more numerous during the Early Iron Age, developed new social and political systems such as the Kalomo Culture, embarked on some long-distance trade, and laid foundations for their future expansion.

The Tonga, Ila, and others

These peoples were distant ancestors of the Tonga, Ila, Nsenga and others. In scattered communities they continued with their village economy after 1500, ruling themselves by headmen or local chiefs in settlements which seldom numbered more than a few hundred people each. They grew millet and a few other crops, raised cattle, hunted for many kinds of game, and generally had plenty of land to move around in despite a lot of trouble from tsetse fly. They had little trade, whether local or long-distance, so there was no particular reason why they should form themselves into larger units of self-rule. Then came two developments of great importance.

At first mainly in western and northern Zambia, farmers after about 1600 began growing some of the American food-crops which the Portuguese had initially carried to West Africa. Of these new crops the most valuable were maize and cassava, which made useful additions to existing food supply, helped the growth of population, and increased the demand for farming land.

Around 1650, pushed perhaps by this growing demand

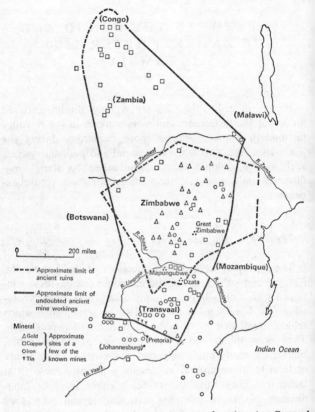

26. *Main areas of ancient mines and ruins in Central Africa*

for farming land as well as by lineage disputes or other political motives, groups of people began moving south from the Congo grasslands, and made their homes in the territories which were to become the Republic of Zambia in 1964. These newcomers, notably the Lozi and the Bemba, brought new ideas about government. Under powerful leaders they settled in western and north-eastern

Zambia, and in some eastern Zambian lands then occupied by the Malawi. In so doing, they greatly changed the history of the area, and it is worth looking at the background to these movements and changes.

The Luba-Lunda states of the Congo grasslands

A wide country of grass and trees, watered by many rivers, spreads to the south of the dense tropical forests of the Congo. The eastern part of this grassland belt, as explained in Chapter 2, may have been an early homeland and dispersal area of the Bantu peoples. Flourishing Bantu populations have in any case inhabited these grasslands for at least two thousand years. Chapter 4 described their early history.

They too received new crops from the Americas. Brought by Portuguese ships to the western kingdoms near the mouth of the Congo river, maize began reaching them around 1550. Cassava (manioc) came in a little later. The size of populations grew, here as elsewhere, and so did their need for farming land. With this growth, there came political changes.

Even before the introduction of new crops, the Congo grasslands were the scene of interesting developments of a new type. Local chiefs in Katanga had ruled small states here in the Early Iron Age. Now others began to combine groups of villages into new states. After about 1450 adventurous leaders set out with warrior bands in conquest of their neighbors. They led them further afield as time went by. More states were founded, several of which were to be important in later history.

The people who chiefly set this process going were the Luba of Katanga. After about 1500 they built a fairly large state, ruled by a Luba king, where before there had only been several small states, such as those of the Kaniok and the Kalundwe. Not much is known about all this; but the process began, according to Luba traditions, when a people called *balopwe* arrived from the north, perhaps from the area where the town of Kongolo now stands. The *balopwe* are said to have been led by a chief called Kongolo, whom the Luba remember today as one of the founders of their people.

Kongolo made his headquarters at Mwibele near Lake Boya, brought nearby villages under his control, and sent out warrior bands who conquered some of the country south of Mwibele. These conquests were continued by one of Kongolo's sisters' sons, another Luba hero called Kalala Ilunga. By about 1550, the Luba *balopwe* had won control over many lesser chiefs and a broad stretch of territory west of Lake Kisale, and had founded a new system of self-rule which gave more power to the Luba king than any chiefs of this grassland country had previously possessed. The king now had a strong central government, especially for matters concerning warfare, tribute to be paid by other peoples, and trade. At his court there were chiefs who acted as ministers for different departments. One was the *twite,* in charge of military affairs and commander of a special force assigned to police duties throughout the kingdom; another was the *inabanza,* who kept the sacred spears and other regalia pertaining to the kingship, and who also ruled an important province; while a third was the *sungu,* who gave the king's orders to other chiefs, and was therefore a kind of prime minister. Another leading official, the *nsikala,* had the task of acting as temporary ruler in the interregnum between the death of one king and the enthronement of another.

What happened here after 1500, we may note, was much the same kind of political change as was taking place at about the same time in southern Uganda, Ruanda and Burundi, and also, to a lesser extent, in western Tanzania and Malawi: the steady growth in the power of chiefs, together with the development of loosely governed states into kingdoms with stronger central governments. It may be that all these Bantu-language peoples drew their new ideas about self-rule from the same source, and that this

source was the first homeland of the Luba in the eastern
Congo. We should observe, in any case, that the beliefs
and customs underpinning all these kingships had much
in common. All these kings were important sacral figures,
and were believed to have decisive spiritual powers. Each
possessed a sacred regalia in the form of special spears or
drums, presided over special ceremonies of interest to everyone in each community over whom they ruled, and was
buried with special ceremonies of mourning. Like some
of the kings of southern Uganda, each Luba king built
himself a new capital, or *kitenta;* and, again as in Uganda,
each old *kitenta* was left in charge of a woman-priest who
presided over a shrine there. In all this we see the essential
unity of ideas which underlay so much of Africa's traditional civilisation.

As in other kingdoms, too, power was kept in the hands
of a few ruling families or lineages. This was achieved by
insisting that all chiefs must be *balopwe*: descendants, that
is, of the lineages of Kongolo and Kalala Ilunga. Their
chain of command, moreover, resembled that of Bunyoro
and other northern kingdoms: the kings ruled through
chiefs who commanded lesser chiefs, right down to headmen of villages, in a system that was in some respects comparable with the feudal hierarchies of medieval Europe.
Later on, again as in Europe, some of these kings began
to rule directly through appointed officials instead of
through vassals, and to gather quasi-despotic powers.

Most Luba chiefs were lineage-heads appointed for life,
but they had to resign whenever a king died, and the new
king might then replace them by other chiefs: in contrast
with Europe, that is, the right of succession by primogeni-
ture was never accepted as automatic.[1] While the strength
of these kingdoms lay in their clear chain of command,

---

[1] See, on this point, an interesting discussion by Ronald Cohen,
"The Dynamics of Feudalism in Bornu," Boston University Papers
on Africa, vol. 2, 1966, p. 85; and, for succession problems over a
wider African field, J. Goody (ed.), *Succession to High Office,* Cam-
bridge 1966.

their weakness resided in the difficulty of settling which men should hold the various positions of power. Disputes between leading families were not uncommon. Dethroned chiefs became dissatisfied, as did other ambitious men who had failed to win power. These disappointed or unsuccessful chiefs then gathered their warriors together and led them forth to the conquest of a new kingdom of their own.

This sort of thing occurred frequently. Around 1600, for example, a chief called Kibinda Ilunga, who was the disappointed brother of the reigning Luba king, Ilunga Walefu, left Lubaland and went away to the westward, where he laid the foundations of what was to become a much larger kingdom, the empire of the Lunda. In later years, as will be seen, other chiefs went southward with their followers into the lands of modern Zambia.

Besides the Luba kingdom formed by Kongolo and enlarged by Kalala and his successors, there were three smaller kingdoms in Katanga which all adopted Luba methods of self-rule—Kikonja, Kalundwe and Kaniok. All were ruled by the same system of village headmen, junior chiefs and senior chiefs, each rank taking its orders from the one above, with the king at the top of the pyramid of power. As elsewhere, the sacral qualities of the kingship were the buttress of its political authority.

But Luba methods were not limited to Katanga. They proved useful to neighboring peoples as well. In particular, they spread westward to the Lunda peoples of the Kasai river and its neighboring tributaries of the Congo. When Kibinda Ilunga led his followers into Lundaland around 1600, they settled in a country ruled by a queen called Rweej, whom Kibinda married. Possibly the Luba *balopwe* conquered this area, or perhaps they were welcomed for their skills in government and warfare. In any case their methods were adopted by the Lunda, and gradually a new center of power took shape along the banks of the Kasai river.

This was the work of Luseeng, Kibinda's son, and of Luseeng's son Naweej. Lunda traditions say that it was

Luseeng who laid the foundations of Lunda power, adopting Luba ways of rule through a strong king and lesser chiefs, and who gave these chiefs the titles which have survived into modern times. After Luseeng, *Yaav* or king Naweej carried on this work, strengthening the new system and extending its power over neighboring lands. Yaav Naweej is remembered as the first Mwata Yamvo, or emperor of the Lunda.[2] By 1700 the Mwata Yamvo ruled many Lunda and subject peoples who paid him tribute, and to whom he gave military protection.

But the rulers of the Lunda did not simply copy Luba ideas; they also developed them, and did so in a way which made it easy for subject peoples to become part of the Lunda empire. In this, the Lunda rulers were more ambitious than the Luba. When the Luba conquered other peoples living around them, they were content to have the chiefs pay tribute to the Luba king. They did not try to enclose the lands of these chiefs within the Luba kingdom, or to build a Luba empire.

When Lunda kings, on the other hand, conquered other kings or chiefs living near them they brought the conquered lands within their own system. Conquered chiefs could become Lunda chiefs simply by changing their titles. Once defeated, chiefs had to pay tribute every year and were controlled through special representatives or commissioners whom the Mwata Yamvo kept permanently at their local capitals. But these conquered chiefs were not deprived of their own local importance. On the contrary, they were restored to their dignity, given new titles, and asked to carry on as members of a larger and more impressive system of government. Central to this Lunda system were the ideas of enduring kinship among chiefs, and of "positional succession." All appointed chiefs were thought of as being closely related to others in the chain of command, and titles such as Mwata Yamvo (the king), Nswaan Mulopwe (the heir to the king, or crown prince),

[2] The words come from *Mwaant Yaav*, Lord of the Viper.

as well as those of lesser chiefs, were passed down from one generation to the next. This unusually stable system helps to explain why the Lunda kings were successful in extending and maintaining their power for many years.

After 1600 these Luba-Lunda methods of rule spread a long way to west and east. Bold leaders at the head of warrior bands trekked far afield, and formed new kingdoms by force and by persuasion. Famous among these leaders was Kinguri, a brother of the Queen Rweej who had married the Luba *mulopwe*, Kibinda Ilunga, the founder of the first Luba-Lunda kingship.

Kinguri led his people westward into what is now Angola, where they took the name of Imbangala, and played a part in the history of the Angolan wars between Ndongo and the Portuguese.[3] Another brother of Rweej, Chinyama, is said to have gone southward with his followers, and founded a kingdom near the headwaters of the Zambezi river. The Luvale state of north-western Zambia took shape in this way, and so did several others.[4]

Another parallel with East African history may be observed here: the westward expansion of the long-distance trade. Just as the Nyamwezi forged trade links between East-Central Africa and the East Coast and the Indian Ocean, so also did the Lunda connect West-Central Africa with the West Coast and the Atlantic. In this way new opportunities for trade and development were opened up. But at the same time, as in inland East Africa, there were also opened up new opportunities for disturbance or destruction when guns became more numerous after 1800, and when dealing in ivory was joined by raiding and trading for slaves.

Among leading pioneers of the trade route to the At-

[3] See Chapter 19.
[4] As late as the 1950s, even after long years of colonial rule, Luvale chiefs were still getting their ritual crowns from hat-makers in the service of the Mwata Yamvo, whom their ancestors of long ago had recognised as their distant overlord.

lantic were the followers of Kinguri, the Imbangala who
settled in eastern Angola. The name Imbangala was already in use by another people who had already come
from Lundaland, some thirty years earlier, the Yaka or
Yaga. In course of time, the Yaka and the followers of
Kinguri became the same people.

These western pioneers were not the only groups who
marched out of Lundaland to make their fortunes elsewhere. Others went eastward and southward.

The Kingdom of Kazembe

By 1700 the grassland country to the south and east of
the old Luba kingdoms was controlled by several strong
chiefs of Lunda origin. Their grandfathers or fathers had
come from Lundaland in the early years of the seventeenth century with small warrior bands and had imposed
their Luba-Lunda rule on village peoples already living in
the region. So the whole great area of Katanga and northern Zambia was now ruled by a number of independent
kingships, each of which had a capital of its own, and a
court from which the king ruled through appointed chiefs
or ministers. Most of these rulers exercised little control in
the outlying areas of their kingdoms; their powers dimin-
ished as the distance from their capitals increased. But
occasionally these kingdoms clashed with each other.

In the eighteenth and nineteenth centuries the most important of these states was that of the Kazembe. This word
was the inherited title of the king, like Chitimukulu among
the Bemba of Zambia and Undi among the Chewa of
Malawi: or, in a constitutional parallel that is remote but
not unfounded, the President of the United States. The
first Kazembe is said to have been a Lunda chief of that
name who founded the kingdom soon after 1700. There
were in fact two other states ruled by kings whose title
was Kazembe, but the greatest by far was the Mwata

Kazembe[5] who ruled on either side of the Luapula river south of Lake Mweru. By 1800 his chiefs controlled all the country southward into Zambia as far as the headwaters of the Kafue river, and eastward beyond Lake Bangweolu to the country of the Bisa.

By 1800 this large kingdom of Kazembe was beginning to be interested in trade with East Africa. Here the Nyamwezi provided the eastern link just as the Imbangala and other Lunda were providing the western: traders could now exchange goods all the way across Central Africa between the Atlantic and Indian oceans. Two African traders in Portuguese service actually made the whole journey from Angola to Mozambique, and back again, in 1805–11; and one of them wrote an account of what he and his companion had seen. He reported that the kingdom of Kazembe was rich in food and strongly governed.[6]

How strongly it was governed was again revealed by the first Europeans to reach its capital, a Portuguese expedition under Major Monteiro and Captain Gamitto who visited the court of Kazembe in 1831. Gamitto wrote a good description of what he saw. The Portuguese were greeted ceremonially by a military display of five or six thousand warriors. They found the Mwata Kazembe enthroned in dignity upon a royal stool placed on "many leopard skins, which served him as a carpet." On his head he wore a tall hat with scarlet feathers. His other garments were decorated with brilliant beads, jewels of glass, ornaments of ivory, and a necklace of mirrors. "This necklace fell around his shoulders and over his chest, and when it was struck by the rays of the sun, it was too bright to look at."

"The Mwata Kazembe," Gamitto remembered, "looks fifty years old, but we were told he is much older. He has

---

[5] *Mwata* meaning lord or king, and *Kazembe* being the royal title inherited by succession to the throne.

[6] Cf. Journey of the *Pombeiros,* trans. B. A. Beadle, in R. F. Burton, *Lacerda's Journey to Kazembe,* London, 1873, p. 167. Their baptismal names were Pedro João Baptista and Amaro José.

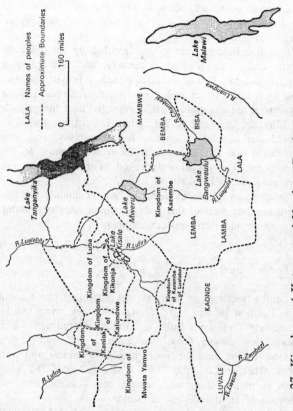

27. *Kingdoms of Katanga and Northern Zambia in about* AD *1800*

a long beard, already turning grey. He is well built and tall, and has a strength and energy which promise a long life. He looks agreeable and majestic. His style is splendid in its fashion. Certainly we never expected to find so much ceremonial, pomp and show in the ruler of a country so far from the coast, and over a nation which appears so barbarous and savage."

This flourishing country was invaded by the Belgians at the end of the nineteenth century, and reduced to a Belgian colony. Before that happened, however, another link with East Africa had been forged. Towards 1870 a Nyamwezi merchant-king, Msiri, repeated here the exploits of Mirambo in western Tanzania. He and his followers carved out a solid little state for themselves, and won control of the long-distance trade from Katanga to the East Coast. The Belgians destroyed Msiri's kingdom and severed Katanga's links with East Africa.

Other Luba-Lunda movements had meanwhile been at work in other parts of this wide grassland country, notably in western and north-eastern Zambia.

Bemba power

Bemba traditions of today do not altogether agree about who the first Bemba were. Some hold they were Lunda, others say they were Luba—a conflict of tradition which shows how closely those two cultures had become entwined. In any case they were breakaway chiefs and warriors, whether Lunda or Luba, who followed the same path as many others who sought new homelands where they could build independent states.

Embarking on their adventures soon after 1650, they marched eastward over the Luapula river and settled in the high plains of what is north-eastern Zambia today. On their way, it is said, they gave chiefs to the Lala and Lamba, though these peoples disagree on this. In their new homeland of Lubemba they had certain disadvan-

tages; the soil was poor, and tsetse fly prevented the breed-
ing of cattle. But they had advantages as well. There was
plenty of room, especially as the Bemba were militarily
stronger than the scattered peoples already living there,
some of whom were obliged to take refuge in the swamps
of Lake Bangweolu or the hills to the north. Lubemba
also had a good central position for trade with neighbors
who were in some ways better off. In the north-west the
Tabwa had salt deposits and good stocks of elephant which
they hunted for ivory. The Bisa to the south and south-
west were able to provide fish as well as salt. Several of
these neighbors lived in country with less tsetse, and
better pastures, and so were able to breed cattle. These
the Bemba obtained by trade or warfare.

In the course of time the Bemba became numerous, expanding their own population by marrying and mingling
with neighboring peoples. Their methods of government
were generally derived from the Luba-Lunda pattern, although, for a long time after 1700, they did not form a
single kingdom. Power in Lubemba was shared among
chiefs who were all descended from a single royal clan,
very much like the *balopwe* who had founded the Luba
kingdom more than a hundred years earlier. Over all these
chiefs there was a paramount chief or king. His royal
title was Chitimukulu, so named after the founding hero
of the Bemba people, Chief Chiti Maluba, who is remembered as having led the ancestors of the Bemba out of
Lundaland across the Luapula to found Lubemba, and
who was given the praise-title of Makulu, "the Great."
The Chitimukulus who followed the first of their name
had for a long time only an important religious position
in Lubemba: as representing, that is, the living link between the Bemba and the spirits of their founding ancestors. But soon after 1800 this began to change. As they
strengthened their hold over Lubemba, and enlarged it
by conquest, the Bemba began to need more power at
the center. One of the sections of the royal lineage now
gained control over the appointment of the Chitimukulu,

and kept it; this enabled them to influence the appointment of other senior chiefs as well. Gradually, the ruling Chitimukulu acquired more political power, and the Bemba came to have a kingdom with a central government such as that of Kazembe.

Thanks to this stronger organisation of their power, they were able to continue to expand. They already had several reasons for wishing to do so, but a new one was now added. After 1850 Lubemba became increasingly linked to the East African trade by Nyamwezi and Swahili travelling merchants. But this trade, by now, was increasingly for slaves, and raiding warfare grew more frequent, threatening the weak with destruction or captivity but provoking the strong into an effort to become stronger still.

Pushed by the pressures of trade and warfare, the Bemba again reinforced their system of government. Their main period of expansion began soon after 1850 when a chief called Chileshe, who had become wealthy in trade and who was invited by other chiefs to revolt against the ruling Chitimukulu, whose name was Chimbola or Chitenta. Chileshe assumed power at the center, and strengthened it by bringing all senior chiefs under closer control. New provinces were added. Chileshe also took charge of Lubemba's valuable ivory trade with the Nyamwezi and Swahili: characteristically, he became a merchant-king; and now, in exchange for ivory, he began importing guns. These enabled him to expand his power still further and, in 1856, to beat off attacks by the incoming Ngoni.

Chileshe was followed by Bwembia. Remembered as a weak ruler, Bwembia was ousted by a warrior called Chitapankwa, who ruled Lubemba from 1866 to 1887. Lubemba was now a powerful structure. But the agents of another, still more powerful, were already on the scene: the explorer-businessmen sent in by the British South Africa Company and the harbingers of the British Empire.

In 1893, while the Bemba were still an independent people, the distant British declared a protectorate over their whole country and that of their neighbors to the south. Partly because of the persuasions of a missionary, Bishop Dupont of the White Fathers, the Bemba rulers accepted this without resistance. Lubemba became part of the new Protectorate of North-eastern Rhodesia, and the colonial period began.

Foundation of Bulozi

Zambia knew one other large result of Luba-Lunda development: the foundation of the kingdom of the Lozi. As with the Bemba, traditions of the Lozi do not agree about who their first ancestors were. But nearly all these traditions assert that their ancestors came from somewhere else, and most of them say that the Lozi came from the northern grasslands, and were chiefs and warriors in search of a new home, just like other groups from the savannah country of the southern Congo. This happened soon after 1650, at about the same time as Kinguri was founding a new kingdom in eastern Angola and Chiti Maluba was leading his Bemba followers across the Luapula.

Their first leader is remembered as Queen Mwambwa.[7] She was succeeded by Mbuyu, who in turn was succeeded by Mboo; and Mboo is reckoned by the Lozi as their first *litunga* or king. At this time they did not call themselves Lozi. They had become known as the Aluyi, a name which is sometimes said to have been given them by local peoples, and meant simply "the foreigners." Only much later, after the Kololo conquest of their country, did they become known as the Lozi. One explanation for this change of name is that the Kololo pronounced Aluyi as Aluwize, out of which the word Lozi came into general use.[8] After the Kololo conquest, moreover, the Lozi began

---

[7] Also known as Mwambonjema Kati.

[8] I am following here the opinion of a modern Lozi historian, Mr. Ndembu of Itufa near Senanga.

to use the language of the Kololo, which they still mainly speak today.

These newcomers settled in the flood plain of the Zambezi river in the far western part of modern Zambia. They found the area thinly populated by hunting peoples such as the Manantwa, Manyengo, Muenyi and other groups. These knew their country by the name of Ngulu; this name it retained until the Kololo conquest, after which it was called Bulozi. When the Europeans arrived at the end of the nineteenth century, they called it Barotseland.[9]

Ngulu, afterwards Bulozi or Barotseland, was in some ways a strange and difficult homeland because it was centered on a plain which is flooded every year, to a depth of several feet, by the Zambezi river flowing through it. The Lozi adapted their way of life to this annual inundation. They built villages on low mounds in the plain, but transferred themselves during the flood season to other villages along the ridge of hills which dominates the eastern border of their plain.

On one such mound the litunga's capital, Lealui, was established; but the litunga also had another capital, Mongu, on the eastern hills. Once a year he was taken in a great ceremonial canoe, the *nalikwanda,* from Lealui to Mongu, and then back again when the floods went down. This ceremony is still observed, although nowadays, of course, the journey during the dry season can be made in a few minutes by car.

While the litunga was formally in charge of all Bulozi, there was a political difference between the southern and northern halves of the country. The southern half was mainly under the control of a queen who belonged to the royal family, and was sometimes independent. This internal division derived partly from the pattern of Lozi political institutions, which gave great influence to queen-

---

[9] Either because they confused "Lozi" with "Rozwi," the leading lineage of the Shona south of the Zambezi, or "l" with "r" in the word Lozi—a familiar source of different pronunciations of Bantu words.

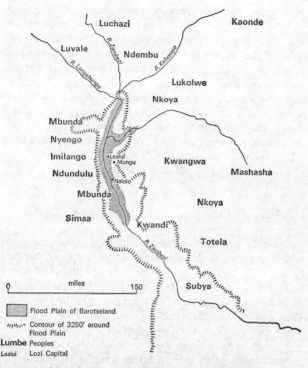

28. The Lozi kingdom around AD *1830*

mothers, and partly from rivalries between north and
south Bulozi that derived from the earliest times of Lozi
settlement here.[10]

Like other kingdoms ruled by Luba-Lunda methods,
Bulozi was governed by chiefs of leading families who
all owed a close and ritual loyalty to the litunga. Under
these families was the mass of the Lozi people, and, under

[10] For detailed accounts of the complex story of Lozi settlement
in Ngulu, see M. Mainga, "The Origin of the Lozi: Some Oral Traditions," and L. S. Mkuu, "The Colonization of Barotseland in the
17th century," in *The Zambesian Past*, Manchester, 1966.

them again, the local peoples whom they had conquered. As time went by the Lozi grew in numbers, intermarried with local peoples, and increased their strength. All sections of the population, whether Lozi or non-Lozi, paid tribute to the litunga and his senior chiefs, who became wealthy and lived comfortable lives. Here again it may be seen how a small group of newcomers[11] could impose their power over a new land, multiply in numbers, and build a strong kingdom where none had existed before. Unlike the Lunda, however, the Aluyi or Lozi did not admit their subject peoples as equals with themselves, and this was to prove a source of political weakness.

Sebituane of the Kololo, and the Ngoni in Zambia

Dramatic events shook Bulozi in 1833. Once more the widening crisis of the nineteenth century spread outward to engulf a peaceful land. This time the upheaval came neither from the slave trade nor from the spreading use of guns, but from other distant happenings: the rise of the Zulu empire and the continued northward movement of white farmers from the Cape districts of South Africa.[12]

Though remote from the center of this storm, Bulozi became involved in it only fifteen years after Shaka had vanquished the Ndwandwe more than a thousand miles away. Among the wanderers who moved away to the north were various sections of the Ngoni, but also a Tswana people under Chief Sebituane who became known as the Kololo. The Kololo were several thousand strong by the time they settled on the south bank of the Zambezi, opposite Bulozi. But they were repeatedly attacked by the Ngoni Ndebele (Matabele) under Chief Mzilikazi, and the Ndebele proved the stronger. Beating off Ndebele raids, the Kololo broke away northward again, and crossed the Zam-

---

[11] The early ancestors of the Lozi, like those of the Bemba and other migrating groups, were certainly few in number.

[12] See Chapter 20.

bezi, moving up through the wooded plains around Mulo-
bezi to the west of the Kafue river. Yet there was little
food in that area, and the Ndebele were already on their
heels.

The Kololo were fortunate, however, in having an outstanding leader in Sebituane. He decided to seek refuge
for his people in the country of the Lozi. Marching westward into Bulozi through a gap in the hills, they came
down to the edge of the plain at a time when the floods
were high. The Lozi army arrived in canoes to repulse
this invasion. But the Lozi were weaker than they might
have been because their new litunga, Mubukwanu, had
failed to settle a quarrel with a rival to the throne, Silume-
lume. The Lozi commanders were also less experienced in
warfare than Sebituane and the Kololo chiefs; they made
the mistake of leaving their canoes and chasing the Kololo
into a trap, where they were routed by Sebituane's veteran
regiments.

Sebituane became master of Bulozi after three or four
years of hard campaigning. Only a small part of the Lozi
royal family escaped up the Leambye river and kept their
independence. Here they lived a difficult life in exile, and
bided their time.

The Kololo conquest of Bulozi must also be seen as the
fruit of statesmanship. Sebituane and his advisers soon
realised that the peoples of Bulozi were disunited among
themselves. Not only were the Lozi divided politically between north and south: there were also the other peoples
whom the Lozi had conquered but had not absorbed. All
these peoples, whether Lozi or not, the Kololo called by
the name of Kalaka. Sebituane set about welding the
Kalaka and the Kololo into a new state under his personal
rule. He married wives from various peoples as a sign of
wishing to live at peace with them. He confirmed many
Lozi chiefs in their power, and took them into his royal
council, meanwhile discouraging his own Kololo chiefs
from trying to lord it over the Kalaka. He decreed that

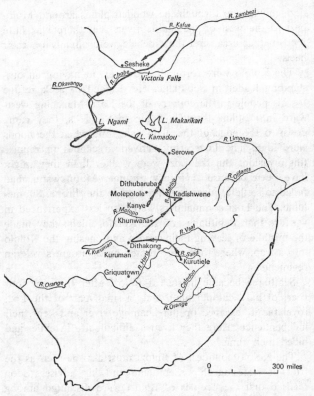

29. Northward movements of the Kololo under Sebituane

all men were "children of the chief," equal in his sight, and to be treated as equal by the laws of his kingdom.

This policy of tolerance and justice was successful and was made still more so by Sebituane's good leadership in wars of defence against the Ndebele and other Ngoni raiders. Three times these attacked Sebituane's kingdom, but each time they were thrown back by skilful tactics. On one occasion, Sebituane trapped the raiding Ngoni by leaving slaughtered oxen in the path of his retreat. Stop-

ping to eat these oxen, the Ngoni were counterattacked
and driven back, while their leader, a renowned general
called Nxaba, was among those killed. On another occasion
Sebituane tricked the Ndebele into crossing the Zambezi
to an island in the middle of the river, with the aid of
Kololo canoes and canoe-men deliberately left behind by
Sebituane. Once the Ndebele were on the island, the Kololo canoe-men quietly paddled away and left them to
starve. Weakened by hunger, these raiders were afterwards
smashed in a Kololo attack. The place is still known as
"the island of the Ndebele."

The Lozi and other Kalaka peoples who fought alongside the Kololo in these battles of defence became understandably proud of their victories, and such pride,
together with Sebituane's care for their equality, made it
easy for them to accept their new ruler. The missionary-
explorer David Livingstone, who became Sebituane's
friend, described him as "the greatest warrior ever heard
of beyond the Colony" (of the Cape of Good Hope). By
the time that Sebituane died, in 1851, the Aluyi had begun to change their name to Lozi and to adopt the language of the Kololo.

But Sebituane's successors were less wise than he.
Sekeletu, who followed him, had neither the intelligence
nor the courage to follow Sebituane's policy. Contracting
leprosy, he blamed his misfortune on the witchcraft of
the Lozi or others whom the Kololo had conquered, and
encouraged the Kololo chiefs to persecute or exploit these
peoples. In the end, Sekeletu's fears even turned him
against his foremost chiefs. His reign ended in the collapse of Kololo authority.

Emerging from their refuge on the Leambye river,
the Lozi who had fled from Sebituane in 1833 now returned to raise rebellion against Kololo rule. They rallied
the Lozi and other Kalaka peoples, and, after 1860,
fought Sekeletu and his successor, Mpololo. In 1865 the
Lozi regained control of their country under the leadership of Litunga Sipopa, although this control was con-

solidated only after difficult years of campaigning by his successor as litunga, Lewanika. Then Lewanika rebuilt the Lozi kingdom, which remained in being even after he had accepted British overlordship at the end of the nineteenth century.

Far to the east, meanwhile, the Ngoni wrote one further chapter in the history of Zambia. Those who came southward from Tanzania, after the death of Zwangendaba in 1845,[13] divided into several groups. One of these, under Mpezeni, moved south-westward into Lubemba, where, in 1856, they were defeated by the Bemba. They moved on south again into Chewa country and settled there. Later, with the establishment of the British Protectorate of North-eastern Rhodesia,[14] British forces overcame their resistance, established farms on Ngoni land, and built a township which they named Fort Jameson.

[13] See Chapter 14.
[14] Soon integrated into the wider Protectorate of Northern Rhodesia.

17. BETWEEN THE CONGO AND
THE ZAMBEZI—2: MALAWI

Historians know little as yet about the early formation of the Malawi people. After 1400, at all events, the mingling of wanderers from Lubaland with local populations, south and south-west of the Lake, gave rise to an increasingly strong group of peoples, who, as was noted in Chapter 4, took different names. The most numerous of them, at least in later times, were the Chewa. But they all thought of themselves as Malawi, or, as the Portuguese of the seventeenth century pronounced the word, Maravi. By 1500 the Malawi were the strongest people in the Shire valley and the lands to the west of it.

They were not, of course, the only people in the territory that is now the Republic of Malawi. Foremost among others were the Yao in the east, as well as several peoples in the north, such as the Ngonde and Nyakyusa who had *ntemi* kingships. Yet it is mainly with the Malawi that history is concerned in this region until after 1800.

The Chiefs grow stronger: Trade and religion

Those ancestors of the Malawi who came from Lubaland seem to have begun their movement towards the Lake before the rise of Kongolo, and the development of what we have called Luba-Lunda methods of government. So the early political history of the Malawi took a different course from that of other peoples, such as the Imbangala, Lozi, and Bemba, who were partly formed by warrior groups of Luba-Lunda origin. Towards 1550, however, the Malawi chiefs began to grow stronger, and there were moves to unify neighboring chiefdoms. Several reasons may account for this, including those already discussed in Chapters 3 and 4, such as the growth of population, production, and trade.

By this time, the Malawi were prosperous farming peoples who were beginning to be interested in trade. They were unusually successful in the production of iron tools and weapons, and their skills in iron-making may explain some of the names they took. Thus Mang'anja seems to have come from the word for a smelting-furnace, while Malawi itself can also mean "the land of flames": that is, of many little smelting operations. No doubt the Malawi did a considerable local trade in iron goods. But they were also interested in the long-distance ivory trade, and their links with the Swahili ports of the Mozambique seaboard, and possibly with Kilwa too, became valuable to them in the sixteenth century. These trading interests strengthened the power of chiefs, and furthered political change.

Another factor reinforcing the power of chiefs, here as elsewhere, was religion. In this respect the chiefs of the Malawi were like many others, including the *ntemi* chiefs of the north, the Luba-Lunda kings, and the rulers of the Shona south of the Zambezi. Their most important leaders, such as those who bore the title of *kalonga,* were believed to have important spiritual powers; these men were thought to be living representatives and spokesmen of the ancestors who had given birth to the Malawi people, and who now, in the spirit-world, watched over the welfare of the Malawi. The title of *kalonga,* as noted in Chapter 4, came from the name of the hero-ancestor who, according to tradition, had led the first group from Lubaland.

Belief in the spiritual power of chiefs, especially as rainmakers and as guardians of important shrines, did much to bind people together in obedience to the laws of the land, to the judgments of their chiefs, and to the latters' decisions on political affairs. Yet the Malawi, unlike their southern neighbors, the Shona, do not seem to have had one supreme chief who was also their supreme religious leader. Only towards the end of the sixteenth century did the *kalonga* begin to unite a number of Malawi chiefdoms, and to form an empire.

The Malawi Empire: Kalonga Mzura

The *kalonga* ruling in the Shire valley in about 1600 was certainly a powerful man. According to the Portuguese, who were then beginning to have a few contacts in the area, his name was Mzura. Like other African rulers, Kalonga Mzura was ready to accept a temporary alliance with Portugal against rival kings. In 1608, for example, he sent 4000 Malawi soldiers to help the Portuguese against a number of Shona (Korekore) chiefs who were resisting their political intrusion into the lands of the Mwanamutapa to the south of Zambezi.

In return the Portuguese gave military aid to Mzura against a powerful nearby rival, Lundu, who ruled another section of the Malawi, possibly the Zimba, as well as the non-Malawi Lolo. At some time not long before 1635 Mzura was able to defeat Lundu, as is shown by a Portuguese report of 1635 which says Mzura was at peace with them, having defeated Lundu with their help, but was beginning to free himself from his tactical alliance.

Mzura, in fact, was in rivalry with the Portuguese for power in the lands of Mwanamutapa where, as will be shown in the next chapter, they were then striving to win control. Having at first allied himself with the Portuguese to get the better of Lundu, Mzura switched alliances and befriended Mwanamutapa Gatsi Rusere. In 1623 he went further and tried to impose his own rule over Gatsi Rusere. In this he failed, and subsequently turned his attention eastward.

The big prize, we should note, was not the conquest of territory but control of the long-distance trade. Any chief who held that control in his own hands could enlarge his power in several ways: he could distribute imported goods such as cotton cloths to his people, make gifts to powerful supporters, and buy useful foreign equipment for himself and his servants. This prize was denied to Mzura along the Zambezi, and increasingly to the *mwanamutapa,* by the intervention of Portuguese soldiers and traders. But Mzura secured control of the other, more northerly, routes to the Coast. By 1635 he had overlordship, even if indirectly, in all the country as far as the port of Quilimane, which his soldiers sometimes raided, and, according to the Portuguese writer Antonio Bocarro, disposed of an army of ten thousand men. From that time Mzura claimed that the Portuguese should address him as emperor, as they did the *mwanamutapa,* and no longer as king.

This Malawi overlordship in the lands between the Shire and the Indian Ocean seaboard of Mozambique continued for more than fifty years. Local peoples such as the Makua and the Lomwe were obliged to accept it, while the Portuguese were too weak to oppose it. Kalonga Mzura soon found himself strong enough to restore peace with the Portuguese, and to try to benefit from any useful services they could render. In the 1640s he welcomed their traders to his capital, and asked them to send Portuguese carpenters to build boats for use in Lake Malawi. There is no evidence, however, that the carpenters ever arrived; the Portuguese in Mozambique could at that point barely help themselves, let alone anyone else. "Technical aid" was the last thing they were likely to concern themselves with.

Mzura's successors do not seem to have possessed his skill in government and warfare, and gradually the empire fell apart. In 1763 a Portuguese reported that it was "more than fifty years since this king (the *kalonga*) had been properly obeyed and respected by all his vassals, and to-day he can scarcely control the districts near his own capital . . ." Here, perhaps, lies the main difference between Mzura's methods of government and those of the Luba-Lunda kings to the westward. The latter used their power to build a strong centralised system which was able

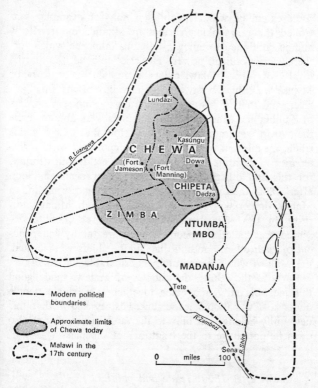

30. Malawi: Chewa and neighbors after AD 1650 (after Marwick)

to hold together even if the king was weak or foolish. Mzura had less control of his subject-chiefs. His personal power was not backed up by political change to bring subjected chiefdoms closely within the central structure. After his death, subject-chiefs reasserted their own independence, especially the line of Chewa chiefs called Undi, who now built a system almost as large as Mzura's had been.

From about 1700 the Portuguese in the Zambezi valley regarded Undi as the leader of the Malawi. And to some extent he was. The ruling Undi, for example, controlled the rain-making shrines in Mzura's old territory, and so continued to enjoy a religious influence which furthered his political power. He also enjoyed the partial loyalty of other Malawi chiefs as far as the territory of Mwase wa Minga westward in the valley of the Luangwa river, and that of Mwase Lundazi on the modern borders of Zambia and Malawi. Yet these chiefs were able to make their own separate arrangements for the long-distance trade; a symptom of and a strong support for their maintenance of separate power. Late in the eighteenth century, for this and other reasons, Undi's power declined. Soon after 1800 there was no longer anything resembling a Malawi imperial system. Marching through Malawi territory in 1831–32, the Portuguese explorer Gamitto observed that "all these peoples today are totally independent of each other," adding that "if the chiefs were united, the Malawi would constitute a considerable nation."

Early in the 1960s, the peoples of Malawi made good this lack of unity and came together as a single people under a new national leadership. History shows that this new unity belongs not only to the modern world, but also owes its parentage to the traditions of the past.

Malawi after 1800: Trade and politics

For the peoples of Malawi, as for their neighbors, the nineteenth century brought years of crisis. Three main factors should be noted: first, the effect of changes in the long-distance trade; secondly, the invasions and settlement of the Ngoni; and thirdly, after 1875, the penetration of the Europeans.

It had been the long-distance trade, back in the sixteenth century and perhaps earlier, which had helped to spur the Malawi chiefs on their drive for power. And trade, as we have noted, was important in the empire founded by Kalonga Mzura. Towards 1850, however, the Malawi lost control of this trade to other peoples: to the Yao in the east, and to the Tumbuka and Ngonde north of the Lake.

The nature of trade was also changing. After 1800 it was increasingly dominated by the demand for captives who could be sold at Kilwa and the ports of Mozambique. As a result, trading peoples were obliged to strengthen their governments, and for three distinct reasons: to protect themselves from other slave-traders and raiders, to ensure the safety of their own caravans to the Coast, and to enable them to seize or buy the captives they needed.

Until now, the Yao had engaged in the long-distance trade without the appointment of political chiefs. Disunited, they suffered in the 1850s from severe internal quarrels, and, at the same time, they lost a war with the Makua. Four groups of Yao now moved westward from their homeland east of the Lake and settled among the Nyanja in southern Malawi. There they united themselves in new chieftainships under leaders skilled in warfare and trade: in fighting for ivory and captives, that is, and in organising caravans to the Coast. The Yao also made other changes in their way of life. After 1860 they began to adopt the beliefs and customs of their Arab and Swahili trading partners. Some of them accepted Islam; their leading men wore Arab-style dress and built houses of the coastal type. By the time of European penetration the Yao had become the strongest people in southern Malawi.

There were parallel developments at the northern end of the Lake. Growing interested in the ivory trade with Kilwa at the end of the eighteenth century, the Tumbuka and their neighbors similarly developed stronger leadership. Around 1800 the Tumbuka were persuaded to form a confederation of clans by a leader who was skilled in trade, Chikulamayembe. At the same time their neighbors, the Ngonde, took much the same path of political change. They were among the northern peoples who had long had an *ntemi* kingship, but their *kyungu*, as they called their king, had been mainly a religious figure. Now the Ngonde *kyungu* emerged as a trading leader as well, securing control of most of the ivory-dealing in Ngondeland, and, in the process, acquiring a new political power.

Another result of changes and expansion in the long-distance trade was the arrival and settlement of Arab and Swahili merchants. Until the 1820s these coastal traders had left the inland trade to the inland peoples. Expansion of the coastal demand, whether for ivory or for slaves, now impelled them westward into Malawi as well as into western Tanzania. Though there were never very many of them, these Arab and Swahili were skilful organisers who knew how to use their trading powers for political advantage. As in western Tanzania, they built up several little trading states of their own, adding new influences, including Islam, to the old civilisation of the peoples round the Lake. Foremost among them was Kota Kota on the Lake, ruled by a Swahili who called himself the Jumbe, a political title long in use on the Mrima Coast. In time these small Muslim states became important centers for the inland slave trade, and were eventually destroyed by the British.

The Ngoni in Malawi

Coming from the far south, after events discussed in Chapter 20, Ngoni regiments crossed the Zambezi near Zumbo in 1835, and moved on northward, taking routes mainly west of the Lake until they arrived in south-western Tanzania. Their senior chief, Zwangendaba, died in 1845, and a new dispersal began. Some Ngoni groups turned south again into Zambia, as already noted in the last chapter. Another, under Zulu Gama, went eastward round the head of the Lake towards the pleasant hills of Songea.

After 1850 these Ngoni groups carved out several homelands in Malawi and eastern Zambia. Those of Mbelwa (Mombera) moved up the Henga valley and destroyed the

power of the Chikulamayembe of the Tumbuka. Others
entered southern Malawi and established themselves in the
Dedza district. Others again, under Chiwere, splitting off
from Mpezeni's group in the Fort Jameson area of modern Zambia, went eastward to the area of Dowa Boma.

Elsewhere they were less successful. After much trouble
the Nyanja managed to keep their raiders out of the Shire
valley, mainly thanks to the defensive power of the Yao,
helped by several military leaders of different origins. One
of these was a Portuguese named Belchior who had served
in the Portuguese army; another was a mulatto called
Mariano; while a handful of Kololo who had been David
Livingstone's companions, and had settled in the Shire
valley, likewise organised defence against Ngoni raids. By
the 1860s most of the warfare caused by Ngoni invasion
was over, and the Ngoni had settled in the homelands they
had found.

These little Ngoni states did not work together, but
nor did they fight each other. They governed themselves
by a simple form of democracy, drawing their strength
not from trade but from their long experience of warfare
during many years of wandering. Each had a paramount
chief. "All the lesser chiefs and headmen," writes an
Ngoni historian, Y. M. Chibambo, "received from him
the leadership of the people . . . (and) they kept their
unity by messengers passing between them. The paramount
chief had power to call gatherings from time to time . . .
In these gatherings the old men and the men of repute
who had a point to make were heard in criticism, and
made suggestions for building up the state. By this means
the paramount and his counsellors heard of and understood the thoughts of their people. It was in such large
gatherings that the laws of the country were delivered to
the people, so that they might hold fast to them and not
be punished unreasonably for breaking them in ignorance . . ."

They were not unlike the Masai, another wandering
people who counted their wealth in cattle. Having found a

homeland in which to settle, they had little interest in enlarging it, but were content to raid the herds of their neighbors. Yet their activities were widely destructive. If they took little part in the slave trade, they were constantly seizing other people in order to swell the size of their own communities, and this caused much suffering, especially to the Chewa, Tonga,[1] and others. Such raids often left hunger and ruin in their wake, and, by driving people from their homes, made things easier for the slave traders. Yet it is also true that the Ngoni arrived in Malawi at a time when the country was already deep in trouble from the slave trade and its warfare, and their own historians have argued that they brought advantage to others as well as to themselves. Another Ngoni historian, I. Mwale, claims that they even did something to help against the slave trade.

"Before the Ngoni came to the country," he writes, "the villages were small and isolated from one another. There was constant pouncing on people to catch them as slaves, and there was no redress . . . Most people never went beyond the boundaries of their own village . . . So no one had any wisdom beyond that of his own village and family. When the Ngoni came, they had one law for all people and they had courts to hear cases where this law was enforced. There was freedom to travel in the land . . . because they had peace within their boundaries." That, of course, is an Ngoni point of view: historians of the Chewa and the Tonga might see things differently. Perhaps the truth lies somewhere in between.[2]

In the 1890s several Ngoni states made armed resistance to European overlordship. But their spears and guns proved vain against the stronger military organisation and better weapons of the invaders.

[1] That is, the Tonga of Malawi and not of Zambia.
[2] See also Chapter 14 for Ngoni political influence in southern Tanzania.

Missionaries from Scotland

The story of Christian missionaries in Malawi belongs really to the colonial period, and lies outside this book. It may be noted, however, that the early missions arrived several years before the colonial period began here, and played a part in developing new trends of thought among the peoples of Malawi, not least because these missionaries were men from Scotland who believed in the value of African people. Two important missionary centers were developed. The famous Livingstonia mission was established in 1875 at Cape Maclear before moving to the north-eastern end of the Lake; another, a year later, was started at Blantyre in the southern highlands.

Coming from a country which gave great importance to education, the Scottish missionaries founded schools, and these were welcomed by peoples who were beginning to see that they faced new and difficult problems as their country was opened to the outside world. Even by 1890 there were more than two thousand Malawians in missionary schools. In that year there arrived the representative of British colonial power, Harry Johnston, and another phase of history began.

18. MWANAMUTAPA AND UROZWI

After about 1400 the lands to the south of the Zambezi, which in 1923 became the British settler-colony of Southern Rhodesia, were the scene of far-reaching developments in central-southern Africa.

A large empire was built, here and in Mozambique, by a Shona people called the Karanga whose center of government was at Great Zimbabwe. This empire, known as Mwanamutapa after the title of its supreme ruler, lasted for about fifty years or perhaps a little more.

Not long before 1500 it split into two. The *mwanamutapa* continued to rule the northerly part of the country, not far from the Zambezi, while the southerly part became independent under another line of *mambos* (kings) whose title was *changamire*. These mambos all belonged to the leading Karanga clan of the Rozwi, so the new empire which they built was Urozwi, the land where the Rozwi ruled. Great Zimbabwe became the capital of Urozwi. Here the changamires lived in a royal dwelling whose walls, rising to a height of more than thirty feet, are still the wonder of all who visit their tall grey ruins today.

Mwanamutapa and Urozwi became well known to the Swahili of the East Coast. These large kingdoms were the inland partners of the long-distance trade of Sofala, Kilwa, and other cities along the Indian Ocean seaboard.

The early empire of Mwanamutapa

Chapter 4 discussed how peoples of the Early Iron Age occupied the country south of the Zambezi more than sixteen centuries ago, and gradually developed farming, metal-working, and the raising of cattle. They were followed by other peoples, also coming from the north, who spoke the Shona language. It is possible that the earliest Shona-speaking groups arrived as early as 1100 or before. Others seem to have come in about 1300. Their traditions indicate that they came from a dispersal area in southern Tanzania, or Katanga, and were related to the ancestors of the Malawi. They settled in these healthy upland plains, grew in numbers, and evolved new states.

Towards 1400 the Shona came under two different kinds of pressure, both of which pushed them towards political change. One was the steady growth of East Coast demand for ivory and gold. Swahili traders came from ports like Sofala, settled among the Shona, and greatly expanded the earlier gold and ivory trade across Mozambique to the sea. The requirements of this trade increased the power of Shona chiefs, just as it did with the rulers of other peoples who embarked on long-distance commerce.

A second pressure seems to have been exerted by Tswana people, in the south-west, who tried to expand into Shona territory from their dry country on the edge of the Kalahari desert. It may be this that impelled the Shona to improve their methods of self-defence, and to extend the power of their chiefs.

In about 1425 a branch of the Shona, the Karanga who lived in the south-western part of the country, set forth to build an empire which could make them both secure and prosperous. This they did under chiefs of the Rozwi clan, who, like other African rulers, were initially religious leaders. They it was who provided the priests of Mwari, the name by which the Shona call God; and it was the priests who presided over the shrines of great ancestors who, the traditions taught, had led the Shona into this fertile homeland and given them the skills of farming and metal-working. Whenever the Shona wished to ask favors of these ancestors, it was through the Rozwi priests that they addressed their prayers; out of this spiritual authority, the Rozwi now acquired a new political power.

Their leader in the early part of the fifteenth century was Mutota, who embarked upon a campaign of military unification. He called up armies from the Karanga and marched northward to the Zambezi, where the Tonga and Tavara gave him the name of *mwana mutapa*, "lord of the plundered lands"; and this became his royal title. When Mutota died in about 1450, he was ruling most of

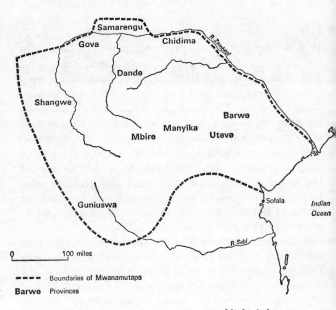

31. Empire of Mwanamutapa as established between AD *1440 and 1490, before the break between Mwanamutapa and Changamire*

the country which later became Rhodesia, except for its eastern highlands. His son Matope followed where he had led, and went much further. Matope brought under Karanga overlordship the eastern highlands and the greater part of central Mozambique. His power ranged as far as the outskirts of ports such as Sofala, where the Swahili were left in control.[1]

This vast empire, reaching from the neighborhood of modern Bulawayo to the borders of the Indian Ocean, was ruled by Matope in much the same way as other large states in Africa, such as Bunyoro-Kitara in Uganda, or Songhay and Kanem-Bornu in the Western Sudan. The mwanamutapa stood at the peak of the pyramid of power. Under him were many lesser kings and chiefs whom he had conquered and who paid him tribute. Outside the Karanga homeland the most important of these were the kings of Uteve, Manyika, and Barwe in western Mozambique. Within the borders of the homeland the biggest chiefs under the mwanamutapa were Togwa, lord of Mbire (now the region of modern Salisbury), and Changa, who ruled over Guniuswa, the country between Mbire and the Limpopo river. By the time he died around 1480, Matope was the strongest ruler in central-southern Africa.

But this structure failed to survive his death. As in all such kingdoms, powerful lords challenged the authority of the emperor, and strove for independence; Changa of Guniuswa did so, and won the backing of Togwa of Mbire. When Matope died and was succeeded as mwanamutapa by his son Nyahuma, Changa and Togwa rebelled. The two armies clashed in about 1490. Nyahuma died in battle, and Changa seized the power. By this time he had taken the name or title of Changamire.

Here can be seen the influence of the long-distance Swahili traders. They had long been trafficking in Mwanamutapa, bringing cotton goods from India, pottery and porcelain from Persia and China, and other luxury items

---

[1] Here I am broadly following the pioneering research of D. P. Abraham: cf. his "The Monomotapa Dynasty" in NADA, Salisbury, 1959, p. 58, and his "Early Political History of the Kingdom of Mwene Mutapa, 850–1589," in *Historians in Tropical Africa*, Salisbury, 1960. What we still greatly need, however, is research into oral traditions by Shona scholars themselves—a development sadly hampered by the political repression and cultural discrimination suffered today by all Africans in Rhodesia.

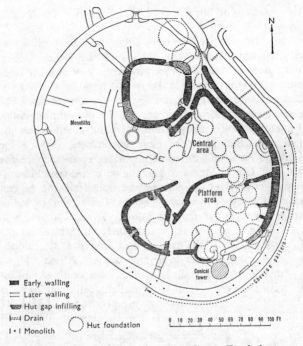

N

Monoliths

Central area

Platform area

Conical tower

Chevron pattern

Early walling
Later walling
Hut gap infilling
Drain
Monolith
Hut foundation

0 10 20 30 40 50 60 70 80 90 100 Ft

Plan of the royal residence at Great Zimbabwe

in exchange for Central African gold and ivory. This trade had greatly enlarged the wealth of Guniuswa, where many gold-mines were situated. The Swahili traders recognised the power of Changa, supreme lord of Guniuswa under the distant mwanamutapa, and it may be that they encouraged him to set up a separate kingdom so as to improve their trading positions in the inland country.

The first changamire managed to keep some control over the northerly regions for four years. But Chikuyo, son of the dead Mwanamutapa Nyahuma, gathered an army and killed Changamire in his turn. Chikuyo then took control of the northerly regions, established himself in a zimbabwe or royal dwelling near the modern Mount Darwin, and ruled the area near the Zambezi. This was the northern country which the Portuguese now began to call Monomotapa, a corruption of the king's title. Chikuyo failed, however, to bring the southern country under his command. Mbire and Guniuswa remained in successful revolt, and Changa's son, the second changamire, became ruler of the southern provinces of the old empire, thus forming the new political system of Urozwi, with his seat of government probably at Great Zimbabwe.

It is not exactly known when the high walls of Great Zimbabwe were built, but probably they were raised during the early fifteenth-century expansion of the Karanga. Here, in any case, the lord of Urozwi lived as a great political and spiritual leader. Here it was, in a large stone structure on a nearby hillside, that the priest of Chaminuka, the senior Karanga spirit, presided and gave judgment on problems that were brought to him. One of his duties was to interpret the cries of the fish-eagle, Hungwe, whose titles were also *Shirichena,* the Bird of Bright Plumage, and *Shiri ya Mwari,* the Bird of God. When Europeans first came here at the end of the nineteenth century, long after Great Zimbabwe had fallen to Ngoni destruction in the 1830s, they found a number of tall bird-figures, elegantly carved in soapstone, standing on the walls. They did not know what these sculptures of *Shiri ya Mwari* signified, but they pulled them down and took them to museums.

Mwanamutapa and the Portuguese: Three periods

Much of the history of Mwanamutapa after the break with Changa can be studied in Portuguese documents, for it was towards Mwanamutapa, with its promise of gold and silver, that the Portuguese turned their main inland effort. They had their first direct report of the empire from a

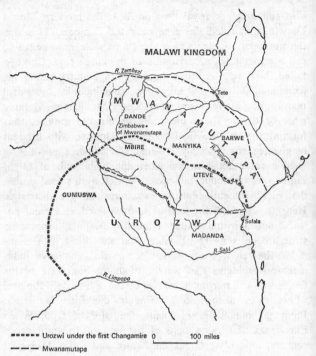

32. South of the Zambezi soon after AD *1500*

traveller, Antonio Fernandes in 1516;[2] and from then onwards they never lost interest. They established small trading settlements at Sena and Tete on the Middle Zambezi, and used them as bases for inland exploration, trade, and conquest. Gradually, their influence grew, and as it did so, the independence and welfare of Mwanamutapa increasingly suffered. This long process of foreign interference can be divided into three periods.

[2] In a report published in that year by Gaspar Veloso. The exact dates of Fernandes' wanderings in the lands of Mwanamutapa are not known, but they were probably the years 1509–12.

In the first, up to 1628, the Mwanamutapa Chikuyo and his successors accepted the Portuguese as friends, trading partners, and, later on, even as military allies. Little by little, the Portuguese strengthened their positions inside the country. In 1628–29 they sent in troops and killed many of the senior chiefs. By 1628 they had greatly undermined the independence of the mwanamutapa. There followed a second period, nearly two centuries long, of Portuguese infiltration and disturbance, and of many fruitless attempts by the mwanamutapas to regain their independence. Both sides became weaker, but the reigning mwanamutapa retained little power after about 1700, while the Portuguese, who had meanwhile gone far to ruin the country, continued to cling to their Zambezi settlements.

After 1800, in a final phase, the chaos of the slave trade spread to Mwanamutapa. Now the great days of the past were only faint memories in the minds of men; and while a mwanamutapa remained in the land until early in the present century, his power had long since vanished. In 1917 the last of the long line of mwanamutapas was deposed by the Portuguese after another vain revolt, and five centuries of dynastic history came to an end.

1500–1627: Trade and friendship

Mwanamutapa Chikuyo, coming to power in about 1494 after the loss of the southern provinces, which by then formed the heart of Urozwi, built himself a stone fort in Mbire near the Musengezi river, and set about defending the still considerable empire that was left to him after Changa's breakaway.

Four factors dominated the politics of this northern system of the Karanga, who were now known to their neighbors as the Korekore, during these centuries. First, there was a successful attempt by the mwanamutapas to maintain their rule in all the country between the Zambezi and the area of modern Salisbury, and far eastward into

Mozambique. Of these mwanamutapas the most important were Chikuyo (about 1494–1530), Nogomo (about 1560–89), and Gatsi Rusere (about 1596–1628).

The second factor consisted in wars and rivalries between the mwanamutapas and the changamires, with vassals of the old empire taking now one side and now the other. Of these vassals the most important were the kings of Uteve, Madanda, Barwe and Manyika, all of whom ruled over countries astride the Mozambique-Rhodesian border and in western Mozambique.

Thirdly, there was bitter rivalry between Portuguese traders or royal agents in the Interior and Swahili merchants who had long been active in the trade with the Coast. In these rivalries the Portuguese rapidly gained the upper hand because of their seizure of the seaboard city-states, such as Kilwa, and of southern ports such as Sofala.

Fourthly, the mwanamutapas had increasing trouble with their normally loyal chiefs, who, often enough, began to act on their own, sometimes weakening the unity of the state. On the other side it was much the same with the Portuguese. While Portuguese official policy was to stay on good terms with the ruling mwanamutapa, local Portuguese traders and settlers soon preferred to push their own private interests, even when these came into conflict with official policy. As will be seen when we come to the nineteenth century, the breakdown of this once great kingdom left Portuguese settlers and local chiefs to find agreement with each other, and the result, more often than not, proved to be chaos.

Having killed Changa and recovered the throne of his dead father, Nyahuma, Chikuyo now faced new difficulties. These came partly from the hostility of the king of Uteve, who, in alliance with the second changamire of Urozwi, succeeded for a time in severing the trade routes between Mwanamutapa and the Coast. In this the king of Uteve was helped by the first guns to be used in the inland country; these were given him by Portuguese traders in return for permits by which the king allowed them to reside in Uteve. The traditions also say that the Portuguese provided some cannon as well.

Under Neshangwe Munembire (about 1630–50) and Nogomo (about 1560–89), the Portuguese were able to deepen their penetration of the inland country, both in the vassal kingdoms and in the homeland of Mwanamutapa, and to set up permanent trading stations along the Middle Zambezi. They became strong enough to take over much of the trade of the Swahili merchants. But the mwanamutapas were still in firm control.

At this time the principal Portuguese base was Mozambique Island, which they had occupied in 1507. In 1558 they built a castle there, Fort Saint Sebastian, and, as mentioned above, held it against the Dutch in later years. For entry into the southern lands, such as Manyika and Uteve, they based themselves on Sofala, which they had occupied in 1505 and where they had a smaller fort. Elsewhere, at Delagoa Bay in the south and Quilimane in the north, they had trading outposts.

After 1550, desiring stronger footholds in the interior, the Portuguese settled at Sena and Tete up the Zambezi. Sena lies 160 miles from the sea, and here the Portuguese built a small stone fort. By 1600, Sena had about fifty Portuguese and some eight hundred Africans and a few Indians. Tete lies 320 miles from the sea, and here too they built a small stone fort and equipped it with half a dozen cannon. By 1600, Tete had about forty Portuguese settlers and soldiers, and perhaps 600 other Christians of various origins.

From Sena and Tete they established outlying trading posts in neighboring kingdoms south of the Zambezi. Of these posts the most important were Masapa near the foot of Mount Fura (Mount Darwin), where the mwanamutapa had his principal zimbabwe; Luanze, about 110 miles south of Tete; and Bokoto and Dambarare, both of which were deep into Mwanamutapa, although their exact positions are not known. All these inland bases, including Sena and Tete, were occupied by permission of the mwanamutapa in exchange for payment of an annual tax by the Portuguese commander at Mozambique Island. As long as this tax was paid, Portuguese traders were allowed to travel freely in Mwanamutapa and its vassal kingdoms. Such was the strength of the mwanamutapa's rule of law that a Portuguese missionary, after visiting these lands in the 1590s, declared that travel there was safer than in Portugal.

In 1573, because of various quarrels and disturbances, the Portuguese were able to improve their positions. They persuaded Nogomo to sign a treaty which gave them possession of a number of gold mines, and allowed them to look for silver mines which they believed, wrongly, to exist somewhere in Mwanamutapa. More important, Nogomo also gave them the permanent ownership of a strip of territory along the south bank of the Zambezi from Tete to the sea. And he accepted a small Portuguese garrison at Masapa, near his capital, as a means of strengthening his own army against disloyal vassals.

The Portuguese had thus inserted the thin end of their wedge. They steadily hammered it further in, and soon they had thrust open the door for their own settlers and adventurers to flood across these lands. Many Portuguese cleared land for plantations, using African captives whom they bought or seized, treating them as slaves. Several of these settlers built up private armies, increasingly challenging the authority of the mwanamutapa and his senior chiefs.

Nogomo's action was not as foolish as it may seem. His aim was to secure regular trade with the Coast, and in this he succeeded. Large supplies of cotton cloth and other imported goods came up the trails along the Zambezi, or by canoe upon its waters. At the same time Nogomo increased his revenue by placing an export tax on gold. But events were to show that Mwanamutapa would have to pay a heavy price for these advantages.

1628–1800: Interference

Under Gatsi Rusere (about 1596–1627), relations with the Portuguese became steadily more violent or difficult. The trouble came mostly from the weakness of the control which the Portuguese commander at Mozambique Island could exert over Portuguese agents, traders, and settlers in the inland country. The commander might wish for peace, but the Portuguese in the inland country obeyed or ignored him as best suited their private interest. There was a corresponding disunity on the African side. The last chapter noted that Kalonga Mzura of the Malawi, across the Zambezi, at first sided with the Portuguese against Mwanamutapa Gatsi Rusere, and then switched his alliances with the idea of bringing Gatsi Rusere under his own overlordship. Such disunity was a constant source of weakness in African resistance to the Portuguese.

Trouble also came from the kind of Portuguese who were now in the inland country. More and more, these men lived and fought as petty despots who cared nothing for the people of Mwanamutapa. They enslaved and pillaged and stole. Many had forts and armies of their own, "greatly harming our people," as Mwanamutapa Mavura wrote to Mozambique Island in the 1640s, "killing some and wounding others, stealing their sons and daughters and the cows of their herds, so that every day I have complaints at my zimbabwe."

Relations were not always bad. More than once the mwanamutapas received military aid from the Portuguese in putting down revolts. After one of these, in 1607, Gatsi Rusere agreed, as Nogomo had done before him, to give the Europeans gold and silver mines. Yet the settlers repeatedly destroyed the peace. Matters came to a head in 1628. Faced with a Portuguese refusal to pay the annual tax, the mwanamutapa took punitive action, and the Portuguese settlers called for aid from Mozambique Island. They

got little, but they combined their own forces, called up a
large number of African warriors who were willing to
serve them, and formed a joint army of 250 Portuguese
and, it is said, 30,000 Africans. With this army they made
war on Kaparidze, who had succeeded Gatsi Rusere; and
in two campaigns, in 1628 and 1629, went far to destroy
the mwanamutapa's military power. In a major battle in
1629 they killed many senior chiefs, deposed Kaparidze,
and placed their own nominee, Mavura, on the throne.

On Mavura they imposed a new treaty, which sounded
the knell of Mwanamutapa's independence. Some of its
terms repeated earlier treaties, but the whole document
went much further. Signed by Mavura and the Portuguese
on May 24, 1629, it provided that:

First, this kingdom is delivered to his (Mavura's) rule in the
name of the king of Portugal. From now onwards Mavura
agrees to be the vassal of the king of Portugal . . .
He (Mavura) agrees to allow every religious order (of the
Christians) to build churches at his capital and anywhere else
in his country.
Ambassadors (of Portugal) who visit him shall be allowed to
enter his zimbabwe with their shoes and hats on, and wearing
their arms . . . and he shall give them chairs to sit on without
their having to clap hands (in respect) . . . And all other
Portuguese shall be allowed to speak to him in this way . . .
He shall open his lands freely to the Portuguese . . .
Through all his country he shall allow the Portuguese to search
for and dig as many mines as they please . . .
Within one year he shall expel all the Moors (the Swahili long-
distance traders) from his kingdom. Any of these who may be
found here, after this date, shall be killed by the Portuguese,
and their property shall be handed to the agents of the king of
Portugal . . .

After this the Portuguese had increasingly the upper
hand. Officially, the king of Portugal continued for a time
to treat Mavura with respect. Two years later, hearing of
these distant events in his palace at Lisbon, he wrote
Mavura a polite letter. Its terms are worth quoting if only

because they show the respect with which European kings had been accustomed to treat their distant African allies:

Most noble and powerful king of Monomotapa, (wrote the king of Portugal, tacking on to his own title a string of claims which he could certainly not have made good) I, Dom Philipe, by the grace of God king of Portugal, of the Algarves, and of the sea on both sides of Africa, lord of Guinea and of the conquest, navigation, and commerce of Ethiopia, Arabia, Persia and India, etc., greet you well, as one whom I love and esteem as a brother.
I have seen the letter which you wrote to me by the ships of last year (1630), and having understood from it, as my Viceroy of the State of India also wrote to me, how the wars and disturbances in your kingdom have ended, and how my captains have given you the government and possession of your kingdom . . . I think right to inform you that I have received much satisfaction from all this . . .

But the polite words were empty. They might sweeten for Mavura the bitterness of defeat; all the same, the defeat was a real one. Little by little the country fell apart. More and more the settlers had their way. Lording it over the Africans from their inland bases as far as Dambarare, they did as they pleased, plundering and killing, until even the mwanamutapa himself could not challenge them.

Only the European settlers gained from this. African chiefs went in fear of their lives. Many people were reduced to slavery, and even the Portuguese in distant Europe grew alarmed, if only because the greed and violence of the settlers had brought chaos to the long-distance trade. Inquiring into this deplorable state of affairs in 1667, an honest Portuguese official named Manoel Barreto reported three reasons for the decline of the gold trade:

First there is the unwillingness of the (African) chiefs. These will allow no digging in the Monomotapa's lands, because they fear that the Portuguese living there will then take these lands by force . . .
Secondly, there is a lack of population (to do the digging) . . .

But the principal cause of the lack of population is the bad behaviour of the Portuguese, from whose violence the Africans take refuge in other lands . . .

This was not to be the last time that Portuguese violence would drive Africans from home. It was to do so a few years later in the western kingdoms of Kongo and Ndongo,[3] and again during the Portuguese colonial invasions of the nineteenth century. Even in the 1960s the same flight from Portuguese violence was continuing across the modern frontiers of Angola and Mozambique.

Ruin for Africans followed in the trails of the settlers; and these trails spread ever more widely. The country declined into chaos. "That vast empire (of Mwanamutapa) is in such decay," the king of Portugal was complaining to his viceroy at Goa in 1719, "that no one rules over it, because everyone (among the Portuguese) has power there . . ."

After 1800: Disaster

Now came the misery of the slave trade, stretching its cruel fingers far into the reduced lands of Mwanamutapa. The plague of slaving sickened wide regions. Many years later, when passing through these lands in the 1850s, David Livingstone noted that Portuguese plantation-owners along the Zambezi were even selling off their farm-slaves, because they found they could make more money by shipping men to Brazil than by cultivating the soil. The old might and majesty of the mwanamutapa were altogether gone; Livingstone heard of him as a small chief "of no great power." There were many wars and troubles. New settler-adventurers, such as Gouveia,[4] became active on the scene. Finally in 1917 after another vain revolt, the

---

[3] See Chapter 19.
[4] See later in this chapter.

last mwanamutapa, Chioko, was deposed by the Portuguese, and the long dynasty came to an end.

Yet if the glories of the past had vanished, they continued to live in the memories of men whose country was now divided between the colonies of Rhodesia and Mozambique. Even in the 1950s there were elders who could relate the traditions of a great history, and still thought of the hill of Chitako-Changonya, where Mutota, the first mwanamutapa was buried in about 1450, as the heartland of their people, although "we no longer talk about these matters very much, now that the Europeans have taken the place of Mutota's sons." But "there are old folk who say that, if you listen carefully, you can still hear the roll of Kagarukate, the great drum of Mutota, at the time of the new moon, as you stand looking down on the river Dande, beside the lofty grave."

Urozwi and the Changamires

After 1600 the Portuguese were able to establish trading posts in the kingdoms lying along the western frontier of Mozambique, and notably in Uteve and Manyika. Here they had two principal settlements, at Chipangura and Matuka, and developed the same system of large plantations worked by African slaves, private armies, and violent interference in African affairs.

They failed, however, to push this system westward into Urozwi. Occasional Portuguese traders no doubt passed through Urozwi during the seventeenth century, and perhaps even visited Great Zimbabwe, its capital; but they have left no records of having done so. In any case they won no battles there, and established no settlers.

For more than three hundred years, until the invasions of the Ngoni, the great kingdom of Urozwi stood firm, one of the largest and most stable systems of government that the history of any part of Africa can show. The changamire ruled from his majestic dwelling at Great Zimbabwe. Lesser chiefs and vassals built stone dwellings elsewhere, notably at Khami, Naletale, and Dhlo-Dhlo. All bore witness to the spiritual and political powers of the Rozwi lords, but none of their many ruins show any sign of military defence or fortification. Clearly, the country was at peace with itself, and feared no enemy from outside. When the Ngoni fell upon them in the 1830s, the Shona were completely unprepared for this ruthless onslaught.

The northern borders with Mwanamutapa were more or less firmly established by 1550 after several years of warfare. The ruling changamire was obliged to abandon Mbire province (south of modern Salisbury) by Mwanamutapa Neshangwe who then took the epithet Munembire, Owner of Mbire. The eastern borders marched with the lesser states of Manyika and Uteve, which were often in alliance with the changamire. The western borders sifted away into the sands of the Kalahari, while the southern borders were along the Limpopo river.

Keeping the few traders who came from the East Coast under strict control, the changamires had little trouble from the Portuguese. Here their actions were sharp and resolute. In the 1680s the changamire grew tired of Portuguese violence on his frontiers and decided to retaliate. In 1684 he sent a force to harry the Portuguese at Sena, and there followed a fierce day-long battle at Maungo, in the country south of Sena. Though armed with guns, the Portuguese were outnumbered and outfought, and fled after nightfall.

African disunity again helped the Portuguese. The mwanamutapa, seeing his rival, the changamire, kept busy in the eastern districts, invaded the western districts of Urozwi. The invasion was repelled after a battle in which the changamire's army is said to have killed five thousand of the mwanamutapa's soldiers. But the Portuguese were given time to prepare for further attacks; they added to the defences of Sena and Tete, and tried to bring more soldiers from Portugal. In Dambarare, near the middle of

Mwanamutapa where gold was being mined in some quantity, they stationed forty soldiers, and made ready to defend themselves.

The blow fell nine years later in 1693. This time things went differently. The Portuguese had to face the combined forces of Mwanamutapa and Urozwi, for a new mwanamutapa, Kamharapasu Mukumbwe, had invited the Urozwi ruler, Changamire Dombo, to attack the Portuguese garrisons at Dambarare and elsewhere. Dombo lost no time. His regiments swept down on the Portuguese, utterly surprising them. They killed all the Portuguese soldiers and settlers they found at Dambarare, as well as some Indian traders, flayed two Dominican priests alive, and marched on the remaining Portuguese outposts. The inhabitants of these fled to Tete and Sena while the changamire's armies ranged through Mwanamutapa. The Portuguese viceroy in Goa, after reading the reports of the defeat, wrote to the king in Lisbon, echoing what Barreto had explained thirty years earlier. "These wars," the viceroy told his employer, "are caused by the arrogance of our own people who have many Africans (as slaves) and commit excesses which drive the (African) kings and princes to revolt . . . Everybody (amongst the Portuguese) wants to rule, and they say that if there cannot be somebody to tame and rule these kings and princes, then everything will be lost."

The taming was attempted by another Portuguese military expedition, but again Changamire Dombo proved too strong. This time he counterattacked the Portuguese in Manyika, drove them out or killed them, and pursued for many miles those who managed to escape. Later, the Portuguese succeeded in regaining control of the lands of Mwanamutapa along the south bank of the Zambezi, but never again did they try to invade Urozwi. Nor were any Portuguese traders able to regain the right of entry to Urozwi after Dombo had thrown them out.

But while Urozwi lay safely beyond the reach of troubles from outside, the peoples of the Mozambique kingdoms fared less well. Here the Portuguese, as we have seen, gained several footholds, and there were many wars between Africans. This explains the defensive nature of the stone settlements which local peoples built in the Inyanga highlands, along the modern Mozambique-Rhodesian border, after the sixteenth century.

The Ngoni, Gouveia, the British

By 1800 Urozwi had long been a land of peace and plenty, content with itself, a country of prosperous villages, big herds of cattle, many farms. No danger from outside had threatened there for as long as any living man could remember. Now, with a sudden and terrible violence, everything changed.

Eastward in Mozambique, during the 1820s, the Ngoni leader Soshengane and his people, known as the Gaza, had conquered much land and built a new state. Soshengane defeated his Ngoni rivals, Zwangendaba and Nxaba who, with their warriors, turned westward. Zwangendaba's Ngoni broke recklessly into the peaceful lands of Urozwi, attacked and ruined the great centers of Zimbabwe and Khami, and ended the last Rozwi resistance on the hill of Thaba zi ka Mambo.

Long afterwards, in 1898, a survivor of Zwangendaba's regiments described this last fight of the lords of Urozwi. After a stiff resistance, they fled to the hills where it was hard for the Ngoni to get at them. From the top of Thaba zi ka Mambo "they threw down beads and skins and hoes and offered us cattle and sheep, to go away and leave them in peace . . ." The Ngoni refused these offers. "The next day they came out again on the rocks and directed us to stand below a certain strange overhanging rock. It looked like a big balcony giving standing room for three hundred men. Here on this were gathered the Mambo and his counsellors . . . about a hundred feet above where we were standing in a sheer drop, and it is here that the

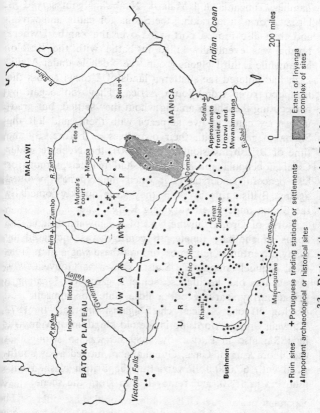

33. *Distribution of ruins in Rhodesia*

MALAWI

Indian Ocean

R. Shire

Sena +

Tete +

+ Masapa

R. Zambezi

Feira + Zumbo

+ Mutota's court ▲

MANICA

Sofala +

Approximate
frontier of
Urozwi and
Mwanamutapa

R. Sabi

Dombo

M W A N A M U T A P A

U R O Z W I

Great
Zimbabwe ▲

Dhlo Dhlo ▲

Khami ▲

R. Limpopo

Mapungubwe ▲

Bushmen

Batoka Plateau

Ingombe Ilede ▲

R. Kafue

Gwembe Valley

Victoria Falls

Extent of Inyanga
complex of sites

0   200 miles

• Ruin sites   + Portuguese trading stations or settlements
▲ Important archaeological or historical sites

Mambo threw himself down in our midst to fall dead at our feet . . ."

Zwangendaba's Ngoni continued northward to the Zambezi, crossing it in 1835 and moving into the lands of Zambia, Tanzania and Malawi. Nxaba's Ngoni stayed in Urozwi for a time, raiding the Shona for cattle and wives, and then also moved northward over the Zambezi where Nxaba was eventually killed in battle with the Kololo. Meanwhile a third Ngoni group, the Ndebele under Mzilikazi, had entered the shattered lands of Urozwi across the Limpopo river from South Africa. They too began by persecuting the Shona among whom they settled, but gradually they came to live at peace with them, and left the Shona to get on with their own lives as before. By the time of British invasion, in the 1890s, the Ndebele under Chief Lobengula and the Shona had reached a more or less peaceful understanding; when the Ndebele revolted against British rule in 1896, they were quickly joined by the Shona under their surviving Rozwi leaders.

North of Urozwi, in the land of the mwanamutapa, the chaos of the late nineteenth century was increased by many adventurers. Foremost among these was a man from Goa, Manoel Antonio de Sousa, known as Gouveia, who played the old Portuguese settler's game of forming a private army, carving out a little state for himself, and playing off one African chief against another. In 1873 Gouveia won overlordship in the old kingdom of Manyika; in 1883, also in Barwe; by 1889 he was so strong that the Ngoni king of Gaza, Gungunhana, moved away southward with 60,000 followers. But the British clashed with Gouveia in 1890, and removed him from the scene.

19. WESTERN CONGO
AND ANGOLA

The modern republics of the Western Congo took shape within the colonial frontiers of French and Belgian empires which were dissolved in 1960. Thus the French colonial territories of Middle Congo and Ubangui-Shari became Congo-Brazzaville and Central Africa, while the Belgian Congo became Congo-Kinshasa. The history of these countries offers interesting parallels with that of Central and East Africa, and calls for brief attention here.

A few important points should be noted.

The first is that the peoples along the western reaches of the Congo river, and south in Angola, had a history similar to that of their eastern neighbors. As noted in Chapter 4, they evolved farming and metal-working communities which gradually became larger in population, and developed similar forms of self-rule. After 1550 they were all affected by the spread of what have been called Luba-Lunda methods of government and unification. Their neighbors to the north and north-west, living for the most part in dense forest country, had a different development. These forest peoples, such as the Fang and Kota, were linked not with central and eastern Africa but with their forest neighbors in West Africa.

A second point is that the peoples of the western Congo and Angola—notably the Kongo, Mbundu, and their neighbors—were deeply affected by the arrival and activities of the Portuguese, and in ways that closely resembled the course of events in Mwanamutapa.

Thirdly, these peoples were also connected with Central Africa, as already noted, by Luba-Lunda enterprise in trans-African trade. They gained and lost by this inland trade, especially after 1800, in much the same measure of good and bad as the peoples of Central and East Africa.

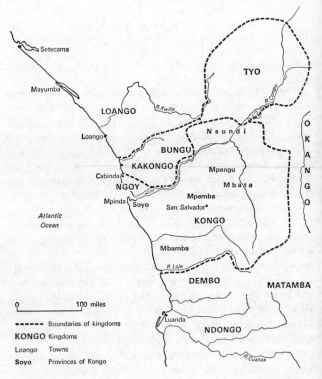

34. The Western Congo kingdoms in AD *1500–1600*

Kongo: Alliance with Portugal

Portuguese ships first reached the mouth of the Congo river in 1483. Within a few years the emissaries of other Portuguese expeditions were welcomed at the court of the king of Kongo, Mani Nzinga a Nkuwa, who was impressed by the chance to buy European cottons, metalware and other goods, and agreed to accept Christianity as one of his state religions. He himself was baptised as John I of

Kongo. He was succeeded in 1506 by the renowned Nzinga Mbemba, whose baptismal name was Affonso I, and who formed a regular alliance with the Portuguese king. In this Affonso followed the same course, which must have appeared perfectly sensible at the time, as the mwanamutapas of the late sixteenth century, notably Nogomo; although Affonso, unlike Ngomo, did not give the Portuguese a strip of his territory.

Like other kings, Affonso claimed the monopoly of foreign trade and tried to exercise it by channelling all of his trade through his port of Mpinda on the estuary of the Congo river. Almost from the first the Portuguese began buying captives for enslavement in the islands of São Thomé and Principe, where they had opened sugar plantations, and afterwards for transport to the Americas. Again like other kings, Affonso agreed to sell them captives, though not from his own people, in exchange for European goods and military or other aid.

He lived to regret this bargain. Having opened his country to the slave trade, he found that he could not limit the damage. In 1526 he complained to his royal ally in Lisbon that Portuguese traders along the coast were evading his monopoly, trading separately with his coastal chiefs, and undermining his authority among them. They were also, he wrote, spreading confusion in other ways "and so great is the evil-dealing and greed of these traders that our country is being utterly depopulated." This was an exaggeration, but there is no doubt that the damage was serious. Affonso declared that the slave trade should be ended, and told the Portuguese king that all he wanted from Portugal were "priests and people to teach in schools, and no other goods but wine and flour for the Holy Sacrament."

He was finding, in short, what the mwanamutapas would also find a little later: that foreign aid could exact a bitter price in terms of foreign interference. As in Mwanamutapa, his efforts were vain. The slave trade continued, and so did the alliance. It was reinforced in 1569 when Kongo was invaded by a Lunda people, the Yaga, and the Portuguese, at the king's request, sent a military expedition which helped to expel them. After that the local power of the Portuguese, whether as agents of Lisbon or as settlers and traders, continually expanded.

In 1641 the Dutch appeared as rivals to the Portuguese, and the reigning king of Kongo, Garcia II, made some attempt to use them as a counterweight to Portuguese influence. He, too, regretted the slave trade, now continually growing larger in step with the transatlantic demand. In a letter to the Dutch, he wrote that the trade should be stopped. It was, he told them, "our disgrace, and that of our predecessors, that we, in our simplicity, have opened the way for many evils in our kingdom . . ."

But the evils were too great to be checked, let alone stopped. Soon the Dutch withdrew, having more important interests in the Indian Ocean; and in 1665 a Portuguese army, invading Kongo, smashed the king's armies in a decisive battle. From that time onwards, as in Mwanamutapa after 1629, the kings were seldom more than Portuguese puppets, and the Kongo kingdom fell apart in conflict and confusion. In the second half of the nineteenth century it became fully part of the Portuguese colonial empire. Many revolts followed. The latest of these, still in progress when this book was written, began in 1961.

Ndongo and Matamba: Resistance to Portugal

When Kongo first began supplying captives to the Portuguese, in 1500, they took them mainly from their southern neighbors, including the Mbundu kingdom of the *ngola*, Ndongo. This gave the Mbundu full warning of what they had to expect from the Portuguese, and the latter, when they first made official contact with Ndongo in the 1520s, were accordingly treated as enemies. The ngola seized the Portuguese captain, Balthasar de Castro, and held him prisoner for six years.

Subsequently the ngola tried for peaceful relations with

the Portuguese, but without success. In the end the Portuguese decided to invade Ndongo and take by force what they could not get by infiltration, being lured on further by a false report that the area contained rich silver mines. In 1575 they sent out a commander, Paulo Dias de Novais, with four hundred soldiers; and four years later Dias marched inland from his coastal base at Luanda. There now opened nearly a century of destructive warfare. When the wars at last ceased, Ndongo lay in ruins, ravaged, emptied of people, and incapable of self-defence.

These wars began with small raids by the Portuguese, which continued until 1605. Then the Portuguese sent larger armies and invaded more deeply into Ndongo. After 1640 they gradually gained the upper hand and were able, by 1683, with some help from Kongo, to disperse the last remnants of Mbundu resistance.

Famous among Mbundu leaders was their heroic queen Nzinga, who, withdrawing from Ndongo under Portuguese pressure, continued her resistance from Matamba, a neighboring kingdom. Born in 1580, Queen Nzinga died in 1663 after a lifetime of wrestling with the Portuguese, whether by peaceful negotiation, by alliance with the Dutch, or by wars of self-defence.

The bitter years in Angola

After 1700 Angola and the Western Congo became little more than a reservoir for captives whom the Portuguese enslaved and carried chiefly to Brazil, where, by 1800, about half the population was of African origin. Increasingly, too, the situation deteriorated because of the arrival of Portuguese settlers who opened plantations in Angola and worked them with enslaved Africans.

All this affected the inland country. Slave trading penetrated beyond Ndongo, Matamba, and Kongo into the eastern lands where the Ovimbundu and Imbangala held sway. These in turn were caught up in the trade, and extended it through the Congo grasslands. And here, as elsewhere, the peoples who were strong gained by the trade, while those who were weak suffered raiding and enslavement.

Arriving in the name of Christian civilisation, the Portuguese had brought misery and ruin, whether by their ceaseless demand for captives or by their many wars of conquest. Disunited, with the strong among them preying on the weak, African states lost their independence and, with it, much of the vigor of their own civilisation.

20. SOUTH OF THE LIMPOPO

Two powerful pressures from the far south took effect after 1800, and each, in different ways, did much to enlarge the crisis of the nineteenth century in parts of Central and East Africa. One was the northward spread of European settlers from the Cape of Good Hope; the other was the invasion of Urozwi and neighboring lands by the Ngoni. This chapter will consider why and how these pressures took shape.

The roots of apartheid

In 1652 the Dutch settled a handful of their countrymen, under Jan van Riebeeck, at the Cape of Good Hope, in order to provide a refreshment station for crews sailing to and from the Indian Ocean. Riebeeck's orders were to grow vegetables, raise cattle, and supply food for Dutch sailors.

These settlers were at first very few, and their affairs failed to prosper. But gradually they began to clear farms on fertile soil near the Cape, and by 1688 there were as many as six hundred farmers, or Boers as they now began to be known after the Dutch word for farmers. They treated the Africans they found—little groups of Khoisan (Bushmen and Nama)—with savage contempt, enslaving them for labor on farms or driving them away. Thus the roots of *apartheid*[1] were planted by the Boers—the Afrikaners or "Africans" as they later called themselves—during the earliest years of their settlement.

They took more land—each settler claiming an enormous

[1] The Afrikaans word for the White South African policy of so-called "separate development," a term which conceals the systematic oppression of blacks by whites in every field of life.

farm which he appropriated to himself "for ever," and where he could run large herds of cattle—and hunted far to the northward. In 1760 one of them, Jacobus Coetsee, crossed the river which they named Orange after the dynastic title of the Dutch royal family.

Soon they were in violent collision with Bantu Africans, notably the Xhosa and their neighbors who lived to the east of the Cape of Good Hope. If the Boers had found it easy to bully Bushmen and Hottentots, who lived in small

35. Outline distribution of main South African peoples in about AD *1800*

groups and had no iron-pointed spears, they found the Xhosa a different matter. These were far stronger in numbers and military organisation. Boers and Bantu fought many small battles as the Boers tried to seize more land. These battles grew into wars; between 1779 and 1846 European history counts no fewer than seven "kaffir[2]

---

[2] The word "kaffir," a term of contempt, comes from the Arabic name for a non-Muslim African.

wars" along the shifting boundary between the settlers and the Bantu.

After 1814 Boer penetration increased. In that year the British, having defeated the French who had previously controlled the Cape of Good Hope, became rulers of the southernmost part of Africa. By then the British were against slavery and condemned Boer enslavement of Africans. To escape from British control, therefore, Boer farmers moved further inland, especially in the 1830s and 1840s. By the 1840s they had penetrated far into the interior of South Africa, where they sought land for their cattle and used their skill with guns to defeat the African inhabitants. Dr. David Livingstone was among those who described their methods. "I have myself been an eyewitness of Boers coming to a village," he wrote, "and, according to their usual custom, demanding twenty or thirty women to weed their gardens, and have seen these women proceed to the scene of unrequited toil, carrying their own food on their heads, their children on their backs, and instruments of labour on their shoulders. Nor have the Boers any wish to conceal the meanness of thus employing unpaid labour: on the contrary, every one of them . . . lauded his own humanity and justice . . . 'We make the people work for us (they told Livingstone) in consideration of allowing them to live in our country'": in the country, that is, which they were then taking by force from its own people.

One indirect result of this steady Boer penetration of South Africa was to increase the scarcity of farming land among the Ngoni peoples, and so contribute to the "wars of wandering" which we shall consider in the next section. Another result, later on, was that the Boers opened the road for the British to go northward over the Limpopo, and establish their territories of Southern and Northern Rhodesia.

Shaka and the Wars of Wandering

South-eastern Africa—Zululand and Natal—were shaken, in 1800 and after, by many desperate upheavals known as the "wars of wandering"[3] because of the migrations which they set in motion. They had profound consequences for many African lands, including the kingdoms of Urozwi and of western Mozambique, and parts of Zambia, Malawi and Tanzania.

One cause of them was pressure on land. By the eighteenth century, farming peoples of the Nguni language group had filled up all the land between the Indian Ocean and the steep cliffs of the Drakensberg Mountains as far as the southern coast of what is now the Cape Province of South Africa. Further on, beyond the Great Fish River, they were already being attacked by incoming Boer settlers. The need for farming land brought deepening rivalries among the Ngoni. Those who eventually took the lead were the Mtetwa living between the Mfolozi and Tugela rivers. Here again the changing times produced a stronger form of chieftainship, and eventually a large empire.

In about 1790 an Mtetwa chief, Dingiswayo, began to unite a number of clans and to strengthen Mtetwa military methods. He explained, according to one account, that "he wanted to do away with the ceaseless quarrels that occurred between the tribes, because they had no supreme head over them to say what was right and what was wrong." In building a new Mtetwa state, however, Dingiswayo clashed with a powerful rival, Chief Zwide of the neighboring Ndwandwe, another branch of the Ngoni. In 1817 or early 1818 the Ndwandwe defeated Dingiswayo's warriors and killed Dingiswayo himself.

Their triumph was brief. Unexpectedly, they were at once challenged by one of the Mtetwa sub-chiefs, a young

[3] *Mfecane* in seZulu, *Lifaquane* in seSotho.

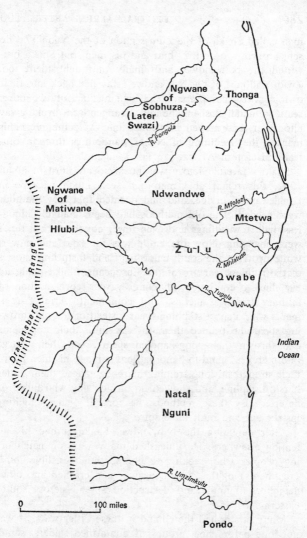

36. South-east Africa (Zululand and Natal) when Shaka rose to power, showing the homelands of the main peoples living there

man called Shaka of the Zulu section of the Ngoni. Zwide
sent an army to destroy him and his men, but Shaka out-
witted the Ndwandwe, and finally outfought them too.
Zwide and part of the Ndwandwe army fled back into their
own country and prepared to fight again, but two other
sections, under Soshengane and Zwangendaba, broke away
altogether, and moved northward into Mozambique. This
marked the beginning of Ngoni wanderings through central and eastern Africa.

Shaka's fateful victory was no accident. Born in about
1787, this remarkable man had seen much warfare in
Dingiswayo's service, and had decided that new methods
were needed. The old methods had been relatively blood-
less, with few killings and even fewer conquests, but times
were changing. Now the battle was for land and power,
while up from the south came ugly and disturbing stories
of the ruthless warfare of the Europeans. Shaka made up
his mind to continue with Dingiswayo's reorganisation of
military training, tactics, and equipment. Arming regiments with a short stabbing-spear instead of the old throwing spear, he trained them to wait until their opponents
had thrown their long-handled spears, and then charge
into merciless hand-to-hand battle. He made his men prove
their strength in long training marches, placed them under
harsh discipline, and showed no pity on any who failed or
deserted. By these methods, he forged a sharp fighting
instrument and built an empire.

After defeating the Ndwandwe, Shaka turned his attention elsewhere. He unleashed many wars on neighboring peoples who, seeking to escape the irresistible *impis*
(regiments) of the Zulu, fled away and crashed into other
neighbors. Tumult and destruction spread across south-
eastern Africa.

Many others had their hand in these bitter wars. It was
not long before new groups of gun-armed raiders, sometimes led by men of mixed Nama and European parentage,
appeared from the south. Among these were the Griquas
and Koranas, splintered Nama peoples who had come

together in desperate bands after European attack, and had moved northward in search of peace or plunder. Hard on their heels, and moving among peoples ravaged by warfare, armed Boer farmers with their trek-wagons also came northward for land.

Some consequences

By 1833, when the worst of the wars of wandering were over, the overall picture had been drastically changed. Shaka ruled a large empire east of the Drakensberg Mountains. North of him there were the Swazi, another Ngoni people, who had saved their independence by staying in their hill country and fighting only when attacked: in colonial times, this area was to become Swaziland. North of the Swazi was Soshengane's empire of Gaza in what is now southern and central Mozambique.

Westward of Shaka's empire, in the hills of the Drakensberg and in the plains immediately to the west of those mountains, a new state had come into existence. This was the work of an outstanding leader called Mosheshwe, who, by skill and courage, had rallied the broken fragments of several peoples and was now in course of forming the Basuto nation. In later years the Europeans called their country Basutoland. But the Basuto knew it as Lesotho, and this is the name they gave it when they ceased to be part of the British colonial system in 1966.

Elsewhere the tides of the *Mfecane* swept the Ngoni far across Africa. North of the Limpopo river Zwangendaba ruined Urozwi, much of which was afterwards occupied by the Ndebele, while other Ngoni groups raided and settled still farther northward. South of the Limpopo, the plains which have now become the Republic of Botswana were also engulfed in the wars of wandering and invaded by the Boers. It was from there that the Tswana people who became known as the Kololo set forth upon the march that took them into western Zambia.

21. EVERYDAY LIFE—
1: NOTES ON ECONOMIC HISTORY

The peoples of East and Central Africa have a long history of growth, change, and development, as this book has shown. From few peoples they have become many. They have mastered their plains, hills and forests, invented and adapted a wide range of political and other skills, and built a civilisation whose underlying unity of spiritual values has been continually diversified by a wealth of local differences and contrasts.

Yet political history, however varied and exciting, can give only a part of the picture of the past. The formation of great communities such as those of the Kikuyu, Kalenjin, and Luo; the steady expansion in the power of chiefs and the founding of states such as Lubemba and Ugweno, Unyamwezi and Uhehe; the emergence of centralised imperial systems such as Kilwa and Bunyoro and Buganda, Mwanamutapa and Urozwi, Kazembe and Bulozi and Malawi: all these and similar developments tell us about the directions of growth, the lines of expansion, the patterns of change: in a phrase, about the movement of history. They open a vision of the power and dignity of men's efforts and achievements; they illustrate the drama of success as well as the tragedy of failure.

But it must be remembered that these events were always the fruit of a multitude of small events in the everyday life of ordinary people. And in order to understand Africa's political history, we have to look beyond the big events, beyond the high traditions and the rulers of magnificence and power. We have to listen behind the deep drum-beats of history, behind the din of armies on the march and the bitter crash of battles. We have to observe, if we can, how ordinary people lived and worked and organised their lives. It is the business of economic and social history to ask and try to answer the kind of historical questions posed in a well-known poem of Brecht's:

Who built Thebes of the seven gates?
In the books there stand the names of kings.
Was it the kings who hauled and heaved those lumps of stone?
And in Babylon so many times destroyed,
Who was it raised those walls again?
Which were the houses of gold-beaming Lima
Where the masons dwelt? And where,
When the Chinese Wall was finished,
Did the builders go at the evening bell?[1]

Those who want to grasp the fuller meaning of history in Africa must also ask and try to answer questions like these. They must manage to catch the clink of the farmer's hoe, the thump of the housewife's pounding stick, the hiss of the iron-smelter's bellows. They must somehow watch the trading caravans on their toiling march across the hills and plains, and contrive to hear the creak of mast and canvas, the splash of paddles, the sailors' voices echoing on distant waters. And behind these sounds and sights of everyday life they must imagine the farmers and their wives, the miners and the traders and the seamen, who were the true makers of history and the real creators of wealth and power.

Such matters have been touched on here and there in these chapters. What follows now are a few suggestions for further thought.

The householding system

When compared with the ancient civilisations of Egypt and China, or the civilisation of Europe after the rise of modern science in the seventeenth century, that of tropical

[1] Bertolt Brecht, *Fragen eines Lesenden Arbeiters,* here in partial translation by B.D.

Africa in pre-colonial times was, in ways already noted, technologically primitive. It was non-literate except along the Coast after the coming of Islam. It had no advanced machines, no exact mathematics, no wheeled transport, not even any potter's wheels.

Yet in other ways, as we have also noted, this civilisation was far from primitive. It enabled Africans to survive and prosper. It gave them the power to produce much besides food, including many thousands of tons of gold, copper, iron and other metals. It inspired them to resist conquest from outside, and proved strong enough in its values and beliefs to live on even after they were militarily and politically subjugated.

This was a rural or village civilisation that was modified by a certain amount of production for trade, and by social divisions which gradually enlarged the power of rulers, and gave rise, at certain points, to towns and city-states. Simplifying a complex matter, it can be said that the basis of this village civilisation was the householding system. The essential unit was the extended family, which usually included three or four generations, and aimed at producing most of the goods its members needed. Among some peoples, families lived far from their neighbors. But more usually they lived in a community of other families in a village. There were many variations: a few peoples, for example, divided all their menfolk into different villages according to their ages.

While each family aimed in principle at being self-sufficient, there were important exceptions. Where much labor was needed, forms of interfamilial cooperation developed. There were many kinds of such mutual aid. In kiSwahili this was called *ujamaa*.

As time went by, the system became more complicated as a division of labor evolved. In practice, few families tried to be completely self-sufficient: the villages became the basic unit in that sense.

Families came to specialise and develop a wide range of skills. They learned, for example, how to prospect for mineral ores, how to extract metal from these ores, how to forge and work it, how to make fine ornaments. When archaeologists uncovered the graves of chiefs on the hill of Mapungubwe, they were surprised by the refinement of the gold ornaments they found. Some of these were small rhinoceros figures made of gold plate beaten to a thickness of only four-thousandths of an inch, a remarkable achievement for men who had worked without modern tools. Other specialists evolved impressive skills in irrigation, in medicine, in building in stone, and in the arts of government.

Markets were opened for the exchange of goods: of hoes for yams, of pots for bananas, of cotton cloth for cassava, and other everyday things. Currencies were evolved of many kinds. Gradually, with political change and the expansion of populations, they grew in size and use. Trade moved across longer distances. People began to produce goods for the purchase of foreign articles: for the brilliant wheel-made pottery of Persia and porcelain of China, for the many-colored beads and cotton cloths of India, and, later on, for the guns of Europe.

As markets widened and specialists became more skilled, there came into existence towns which produced little food of their own, but lived on the produce of neighboring villages. Kings and ruling groups took over an increasing amount of the available wealth. Yet with some exceptions it was still the householding system, the relative self-sufficiency of family or village groups, by which most people continued to live.

Limits on growth

One may imagine that in many ways this quiet old civilisation, or group of related civilisations, was happier than the restless life of today, and that *ujamaa*, mutual aid and all it meant, offered a preferable way of life to the majority of men. There was here a rustic easiness, a sense of individual value, a certain dignity, that the modern world has all too often lost. Yet there was also a singular weakness. These cultures could survive only so long as they were not challenged by others standing on a more advanced level of technology. Once that happened, they were lost. For they could not provide the progress in science and machinery, in organisation and production, that were needed to meet such a challenge.

Content with handicraft methods of production in very small units, the householding system never called for radical changes. These methods had long provided a sufficiency; and all the teachings of tradition were against their modification or enlargement. Most African religions taught that one should tread in the steps of the ancestors. The morals of a good man were aimed at ensuring that he should live as his neighbors lived, not worse but also not much better, eschewing personal ambition, never trying to win more than his accustomed share. Of course there were exceptions; but the whole morality of traditional life stood against them. So that while there was steady evolution within the householding system, there was little or none that could transform its basic methods and relations of production.

This goes far to explain the helplessness of Africans in the face of invasions of the late nineteenth century, invasions propelled by systems of production far in advance of those of Africa. The Africans fought back, doggedly persistently, and in a great variety of ways: in the end their technological weakness always defeated them. Only a far-reaching revolution in methods and relations of production, the revolution into which Africa is now passing, could have given them the necessary power of self-defence. But the colonial system, once installed, by its nature obstructed this kind of revolution. Not till the 1960s, in the wake of direct colonial control, did the opportunity for radical change once again become a real one. Seen in this light, therefore, the real problem for the Africans of today is to know how to remain true to their own historical de velopment while embarking on an entirely new phase of social growth: to know how to keep the best of their past, the spirit of *ujamaa*, of neighborliness, of respect for human values, while combining these with modern systems of organisation and production.

22. EVERYDAY LIFE—
2: NOTES ON SOCIAL HISTORY

One could often hear it said, not so many years ago, that the Africans and their cultures were primitive or savage. One can sometimes hear it said today. This was the common "outside" judgment of the nineteenth century, prolonged through most of the colonial period of the twentieth. In so far as it did not rest on mere prejudice, it was an opinion which arose from a misunderstanding bred of ignorance. This misunderstanding chiefly consisted in thinking that because the material technologies of the Africans were simple, rustic and mechanically backward, it must follow that their arts and religions, social customs and patterns of life were likewise "undeveloped." The Europeans of a century ago went into Africa and found people living in grass huts and wearing few clothes, possessing no machinery, knowing no modern science. They jumped to the conclusion that these peoples were either primitives or fools.

This spiritual arrogance of the conquerors, wielding their superior weapons of destruction as though these were certificates of a higher morality, can only seem deplorable today. Consider, for example, the attitude of the first governor of the British East Africa Protectorate, Sir Charles Eliot. This man was called to rule over many of the peoples whose long and complex history has been sketched in this book: over peoples who, as we have seen, had passed through many stages of socio-political growth, evolved subtle and enduring systems of power-distribution and decision-making, and acquired cultures of resonance and depth. Sir Charles Eliot may be excused for not knowing what we know today. Harder to excuse, if very revealing, is the fact that he was convinced there was nothing to know. "We have in East Africa," he declared without further ado, "the rare experience of dealing with a *tabula rasa*, an almost untouched . . . country where we can do as we will." The true *tabula rasa* was clearly in his own mind.

We have learned much since then, and today a thorough reappraisal of the cultural ideas, beliefs and structures of traditional Africa is long overdue. Especially in the last twenty years, the labor of historians, social anthropologists and others has gone far to elucidate the apparently inexplicable or perverse, so that the African materials are now to hand for a rewriting of cultural as well as political history. This process of learning has of course applied to Africans as well as non-Africans. Some seventy years ago, the Luo of western Kenya were told by their priests to welcome Europeans because these were believed to have come, as long-promised "red strangers from the sea," with the good will of the ancestors of the Luo; while the Hima of Uganda are said to have greeted the first Europeans to reach them as the descendants of their Chwezi kings of the fifteenth century, returned now to "set the world in order." Africans have also learned to measure the myth against the truth.

African civilisations of the past can now be seen, in fact, to have possessed and been moved by a logic of understanding and development that were in no essential way different from those of the Europeans, but whose forms and rate of change were extremely different because their circumstances, their possibilities, their actual problems and solutions, were not at all the same. The specificity of African history lies not, accordingly, in any fundamental human oddity about the Africans—not, as the racist theories of the past have held, in some "natural inferiority," some fatal deficiency in the size or shape of the brain, some "inherent childishness"—but in the specificity of African conditions. This truism would not be worth repeating were it not for the tenacity of survival which certain racist theories have shown.

By social systems of their own evolving, the Africans

populated their vast and difficult continent with an out-standing success, doubling and redoubling their numbers, spreading to every land that could sustain human life, inventing and repeatedly elaborating new techniques and patterns of growth. In so doing they constantly developed fresh variations of social structure. From the vertical divisions of kinship organisation they evolved horizontal divisions of society as the specialisation of labor grew more complex with the rise of craftsman groups, with the crystallisation of states governed by chiefs or other instruments of centralised rule, and with the whole long process of incipient class formation.

Here the main point to keep in mind is the word "incipient." For their chief differentiation from Europe and the "advanced world," in respect of social structure, lay in the fact that the Africans did not develop systems fractured into sharply defined classes. They did not have, in short, those forms of structure which gave the "advanced world" its characteristic if painful means of material progress: its early entrepreneurs, its masses of hungry wage-earners, its cash economies with their relentless dynamic of employer and employed. They conserved in these respects an underlying egalitarianism.

This did not mean, as their history shows, that their systems were therefore static or incapable of change. Elaboration of social structure gave rise, at one extreme, to the emergence of ruling groups whose powers were greatly increasing by the nineteenth century. At the other extreme, this elaboration began to produce a reservoir of men and women who were more or less bereft of social power. These developments may be interpreted as the forerunners of a far sharper social stratification than had existed before, and were productive of new relations and methods of accumulating wealth and using labor. How far these societies might have gone in this direction remains a matter for guessing, since the Europeans, claiming or seizing all effective social and economic power, arrived instead.

Yet the underlying unity of these societies generally held firm in spite of deepening horizontal divisions. This was because the traditional socio-economic fabric, woven through centuries of trial and error, proved strong enough to contain and resolve the conflicts of community life which these divisions set in train. As an epilogue to political history it may be useful here to discuss, if briefly, the nature and origin of this cohesive strength. For this was the strength of conservation that both protected these societies from decay or dissolution, and at the same time limited their scope for radical change.

It took forms that are usually called religious, although religion in this context is hard to separate from politics and economics. Like medieval Europeans, Africans lived in an age of faith where moral rules were not only seen, but generally accepted, as the all-embracing arbiters of every man's behavior. These rules were generally concerned, above all, with the good of a given group in a given locality. In other words, each group evolved its own distinctive religion. Yet most of these religions, although with countless variations, followed the same pattern. This pattern consisted in a belief that the power and will of God, known under different names and forms, was transmitted to living men through a line of chosen ancestors. These ancestors were accordingly seen as the guardians of the living and the yet unborn. They it was who knew what men should do and not do, who could intervene in the workings of the world for the benefit of the good and the discomfiture of the evil, and whose favor and protection were necessary to survival.

In practical terms one may interpret these beliefs as the principal safeguard and sanction of a given way of life, in a given locality, that was the fruit of long experiment. Thus the Shona of Urozwi had built, by the sixteenth century, a strong and stable culture which rested on cattle-raising, crop-growing and metal-mining which were certainly the outcome of much local adaptation and invention through many generations. But the Shona saw this way of life not as man-given, but as God-given. They held that it was their principal ancestors, the *mhondoro,* who had brought them into the good land of Urozwi, shown them how to raise cattle and grow crops, and taught them the use of metals. And the mhondoro had been able to do this because they drew their power and knowledge from Mwari, as the Shona called God.

So it followed for the Shona that the continued success of their way of life depended on continued protection by the mhondoro who spoke for Mwari. This protection could be assured only if living men constantly applied to the mhondoro for help and guidance. In the case of the "great mhondoro"—of Chaminuka and Nehanda and others who were, as we might say, the national ancestors of the Shona—this application was made at central shrines of which the most important, at least in early times, was probably at Great Zimbabwe. For smaller matters, family matters, each Shona unit had its own local or family shrine at which application for help or guidance could be made to family ancestors (*vadzimu*).

Hence the highly conservative nature of African religion, or at least of most African religions. What was important was to follow in the footsteps of the ancestors as interpreted by the priestly guardians of ancestral shrines. To do this, however, it was necessary to conserve the traditional balance of society: to discourage men from forms of individual enterprise such as might raise individuals to a wealth or power much above their fellows, and to preach the virtues of traditional equality. So it came about that the good man in Shona society would be one who rejected personal ambition, distrusted individual enterprise, and tried to live "the average life." Anyone who lived like this could reasonably expect the blessings of the chosen ancestors, and thus of Mwari; while anyone who did not could certainly expect the reverse. Certainly there were sceptics, but the sceptics were exceptions who only proved the rule.

Yet the Shona, like other Africans, were practical

countryfolk who viewed these matters with an obstinate realism. They believed that those who broke the rules would incur the ill will of the ancestors in perfectly obvious and painful ways. They believed that the world also contained a negative power, likewise deriving from the spirits, which punished wrong behavior. This power was what is known as witchcraft. Here we are into difficult questions which cannot be examined here. Broadly, though, it is right to see in witchcraft the regulating force of Evil which became operative whenever men and women broke the rules, voluntarily or not, or otherwise offended against the power of Good as represented by the will of God-endowed ancestors. This power could become operative—could, as it were, be unleashed against someone—as a result of a deliberate breaking of the rules or even of what we should call sheer bad luck. Thus the Bemba of Zambia, who also believe that a good man should never be much wealthier or more fortunate than his fellows, have a saying which declares that it is good luck to find two wild-bee hives full of honey, but to find three is witchcraft.

Here again one sees, in the workings of this negative power, the strongly conservative bias of traditional belief. There was continual experiment and change because it was almost always possible to select among a member of "right choices"; and this flexibility of selection—this "optation" between justified alternatives—had persistently innovating consequences. But change or innovation had always to assure itself of appropriate spiritual sanction and protection. All these cultures display this in a rich variety of ways.

Rites affecting individuals help to illustrate these aspects of African society. At each main stage of an individual's life there were rituals at which one status within society was ceremonially abandoned for another. The most important of these rituals of change—of these *rites de passage*, as anthropologists since Gennep have called them—were occasions for more or less profound social education. Boys and girls, reaching puberty, were launched upon adult life after long instruction in the beliefs and customs of their people, an education that was often accompanied by the "status symbol" of circumcision. In something of the same way, societies also changed and embarked on new patterns and attitudes. A people who became too numerous for its local means of livelihood would have to detach some of its younger folk, and send them off in search of fresh land elsewhere. This too required its appropriate ceremonies so as to ensure that the ancestors agreed, and would continue to protect the migrant group, now becoming a new people on its own, as well as the parent group who had let them go or sent them away.

Following through this approach, one can grasp how religious beliefs were adjusted to allow for the emergence of chiefs or kings whose social power was clearly far greater than the average. In the case of the Shona, for example, intercession with the great mhondoro was impossible for ordinary people: they believed that leading priests had to do this for them. These priests, generally, were of a special priestly clan known as the Rozwi; and it was the leaders of the Rozwi, adding political power to spiritual power, who emerged as their kings in the fifteenth century. Such kings, like other African rulers with comparable powers, were not thought of as "divine," as gods, but as the necessary spokesmen of divine authority. They were held in much awe and respect, and were expected to live apart from ordinary men. And it is no doubt true that kings such as these, as time went by, successfully added to their power by extending their claim to spiritual authority. By the nineteenth century, for example, the kings of the Buganda had managed to acquire practically despotic powers which they had certainly not possessed in earlier times. Religion, in short, was manipulated in Africa as elsewhere in the world.

This subtle matrix of social belief took shape in artistic and legal as well as religious forms. The traditional arts of Africa were often of great aesthetic and dramatic value, notably in the forms of dancing, drumming and the carving of wood or other materials. Often they were arts for pleasure, for amusement, for decoration, for the sheer love of life. But always they were arts conceived within the embrace of spiritual belief of one kind or another. Even when they were most enjoyed, they constantly referred men back to the landmarks of the good life as laid down by the ancestors.

Legal wisdom did the same, whether in maxims of the courts or in popular sayings. *Lenstwe lakgosi kemaloa,* say the Tswana of Bostwana in their courts: "the chief's word is law"; or *lentswe lakgosi lealgelwa lesaka,* "a village is built round the chief's word." But also, lest chiefs abuse their legal power, *garelebo motho, releba molato,* "we do not look at the person, but at the offence;" or again, *molau sefofo, obile otle oje mong waone,* "the law is blind, it even eats its owner," meaning that not even judges can be above the reach of the law. Other such maxims recommend moderation in judging offenders. When a Tswana judge is appointed he is told: *motse obokwa, kaletlhare, gaotsewa kamolamu,* "a village is gathered with a twig, it is not taken with a club." A new judge, that is, should establish his authority by displaying wisdom, not force.[1]

These few notes may serve to whet the appetite for further reading into the nature of these civilisations in Africa. It is in any case this kind of approach that will alone reveal their strength and weakness. They achieved much. By continual experiment through centuries they peopled their continent and produced long-enduring systems of law and order, morality and social cohesiveness. But they became, in another large sense, the victims of their own achievement. Having found their balance with nature, their compromise with ecology, their means of survival and increase, they defended their systems with beliefs which often laid an overwhelming value on con-

---

[1] I take these sayings from I. Schapera, "Tswana Legal Maxims," in *Africa,* 2 of 1966, p. 121.

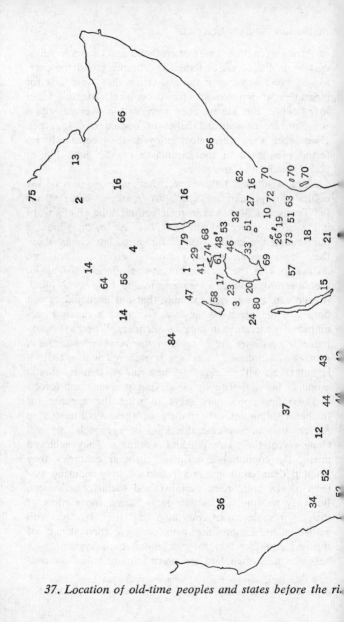

37. *Location of old-time peoples and states before the ri.*

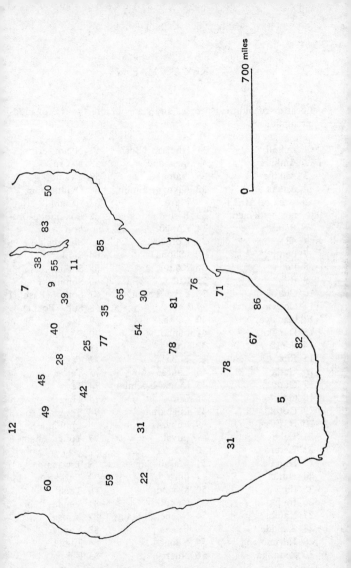

of modern nations. (See page 304 for the key to this map.)

KEY TO MAP 37

Location of old-time peoples and states before the rise of modern nations.

1 Acholi
2 Amhara
3 Ankole
4 Anuak
5 Area of Afrikaner settlement
6 Baluhia (see 48)
7 Bemba
8 Bena
9 Bisa
10 Chaga
11 Chewa
12 Chokwe
13 Danakil
14 Dinka
15 Fipa
16 Galla
17 Ganda
18 Gogo
19 Goroa
20 Haya
21 Hehe
22 Herero
23 Hima
24 Hutu
25 Ila
26 Iraqw
27 Kamba
28 Kaonde
29 Karimojong
30 Karanga

31 Khoisan (Bushmen and Nama)
32 Kikuyu, Embu, Meru
33 Kisii
34 Kongo
35 Korekore (Shona)
36 Kota
37 Kuba
38 Lake Tonga
39 Lala
40 Lamba
41 Lango
42 Lozi
43 Luba
44 Lunda
45 Lunda-Ndembu
46 Luo
47 Lugbara
48 Luhya
49 Luvale
50 Makua
51 Masai, Samburu
52 Mbundu
53 Nandi
54 Ndebele (Matabele)
55 Ngoni
56 Nuer

57 Nyamwezi
58 Nyoro
59 Ovambo
60 Ovimbundu
61 Padhola
62 Pokomo, Korokoro
63 Shambala
64 Shilluk
65 Shona
66 Somali
67 Sotho (Basuto)
68 Suk (Pokot)
69 Sukuma
70 Swahili
71 Swazi
72 Taita
73 Tatog
74 Teso
75 Tigre
76 Tonga (Mozambique)
77 Tonga (Zambia)
78 Tswana
79 Turkana
80 Tutsi
81 Venda
82 Xhosa
83 Yao
84 Zande
85 Zimba
86 Zulu

servation rather than constructive change. And when the violent upheavals of the late nineteenth century and colonial years at last broke through and levelled their defences, opening them to the full impact of the industrialised world, they were left to grope their way painfully towards new beliefs, new landmarks, new means of regaining their equality with the rest of mankind. A difficult transition became necessary. It is this transition with which the whole of Africa, in one degree or other of intensity, is now at grips.

TIME CHARTS (approximate dating)

	EAST AFRICA	CENTRAL AFRICA	ELSEWHERE IN AFRICA	OUTSIDE AFRICA
BC 500		Late Stone Age. Little groups of hunters and food-gatherers are living in wooded uplands and river valleys. Skilled in fishing and trapping game, they have tools and weapons only of stone, wood and bone. Their total number is very small when compared with the size of populations even a thousand years later.	Rise of Kushite kingdom of Meroe on the Middle Nile, in the northern part of the modern Republic of Sudan.	Greek civilisation at height of its brilliance. Iron Age in Britain and northern Europe.
			Sabaeans from southern Arabia have settled in northern Ethiopia, and, together with the local peoples, have begun to build a new civilisation there. This will be the parent-civilisation of Axum.	Sailors in the northern waters of the Indian Ocean have begun to understand how to use the monsoon winds to drive their sailing ships, which are still very small and primitive.
AD 0	Around this date, the skills of metal-working begin to be understood and practised for the first time, perhaps		Kush still rich and powerful.	Roman power dominates the Mediterranean world.

beginning with copper in the regions of modern Katanga and northern Zambia, but soon going on to iron. Populations still very small, and primitive in their skills. Signs of early farming of millet.

Sailors from Egypt and Arabia have begun to visit the East Coast villages, with whom they trade, buying African ivory, tortoise-shell and other products.

Axum, in northern Ethiopia, becomes center of a trading kingdom which will grow rapidly. Its main port, Adulis in the Red Sea, is visited by ships from Egypt and India.

China, ruled by Han emperors, is in great period of civilisation.

Large states in India have appeared with the Maurya Dynasty after 322 BC

AD 100	Gradual spread of early techniques of metal-working across the wooded uplands of Central Africa, and probably into East Africa. In both regions the Late Stone Age continues for several centuries more.	A Greek merchant of Egypt writes a guide to the Indian Ocean trade, the *Periplus of the Erythraean Sea* (about AD 120). This includes our earliest description of life along the East African Coast between the Horn and Southern Tanzania.	
		Romans rule Egypt.	Most of British Isles ruled by Romans.
320	Earliest Iron Age settlements at Zimbabwe at about this time, but no	Axum completes destruction of Kingdom of Kush	Foundation of empire of the Gupta rulers in north-

	EAST AFRICA	CENTRAL AFRICA	ELSEWHERE IN AFRICA	OUTSIDE AFRICA
		building in stone as yet. Gradual spread of Early Iron Age 'Leopard's Kopje' culture across central plateau south of Zambezi, and of Early Iron Age 'Ziwa' culture across eastern plateau.	(Meroe). King Ezana of Axum accepts Christianity. Axumite port of Adulis continues as important center for the western trade of the Indian Ocean.	ern India. Beginning of new era of Indian progress in many fields.
400	At about this time seafaring Indonesians from Java and Sumatra have arrived in Madagascar, settled there, and also visited the East Coast. They introduce a new kind of banana from Asia, which will be widely accepted in Africa.		Rise of new 'X-Group' culture in land of Kush. This will be the parent of a brilliant Christian civilisation in Nubia between AD 600 and 1200.	
700	There are now more people in these countries than in earlier times. Early Iron Age peoples of the Bantu language family are settled in small villages in many parts of East as well as Central Africa.		Rapid rise of Islam in North Africa after the Hijra in 622.	Expansion of Indian Ocean trade as Muslim Arabs establish trading stations in N.W. India, Ceylon, S.E. Asia, south-

across the Limpopo river. They carry the Iron Age into South Africa.

With this spread and dispersal there is the development of many different Bantu languages in the lands to the south of the equator.

Early origins along the East Coast of Swahili culture, and of the Swahili language, a Bantu language much influenced by Arabic. This goes hand in hand with some development of coastal trade, and with more permanent settlements along the coast, including that of Unguja Ukuu on Zanzibar.

850

Development of Iron Age 'Kisale' culture in Katanga, and increase in importance of copper-mining. Some long-range trade in copper now develops.

Now, or soon afterwards, people of Ingombe Ilede, m southern Zambia, are wealthy enough to bury their chiefs with many gold ornaments.

civilisation in Nubia (Northern Sudan) since middle of 6th century. Three kingdoms appear.

Rise of trading state of Ghana in western part of Western Sudan. More trade across the Sahara.

rica.

Beginning of European Middle Ages. Foundation of the Empire of the Franks.

	EAST AFRICA	CENTRAL AFRICA	ELSEWHERE IN AFRICA	OUTSIDE AFRICA
916	Al-Mas'udi visits East Coast, and afterwards (in about 943) writes about an important African kingdom which was perhaps the mouth of the Zambezi.	Continued spread of Iron Age. 'Kalomo' culture in this period in southern Zambia (middle and later stages: 900–1200). Early Iron Age in Malawi.	Egypt ruled by Fatimid caliphs (969–1171). Cairo becomes a vital center for linking the trade of the Indian Ocean with that of the Mediterranean.	
1000	Many more trading settlements. Most important now include Zanzibar, Pemba, Kilwa, and those of the Banadir Coast (later, Somali coast).	Central African ivory and gold trade with East Coast is already in existence. Imports of Indian cottons, beads, and other goods.	Period of great age of Islam, which continues for three more centuries. In West Africa, Ghana at height of its power as a trading empire. Other important states, including Kanem, have appeared. Almoravid invasion of Ghana.	Rise of Norman power in France. In 1066 Normans conquer Anglo-Saxon England. China ruled by emperors of Sung Dynasty (960–1279).

coast. End, about now, of the Daybuli period; and the Shirazi movement southward from Banadir coast.	plateau south of Zambezi associated with Shona peoples. First stone buildings at Great Zimbabwe.	Egypt ruled by Ayyubid kings (1171–1250). They attack and undermine the Nubian Christian kingdoms, which now begin to disappear.	flourish there (1071–1147). They are followed by the Almohad line of rulers (1147–1289).
	Continued growth of Iron Age populations in many parts of the inland country. These are now moving out of the Early Iron Age, and are beginning to form larger units of self-rule.		In England, Magna Carta (1215).
1200 Rise of Kilwa to commercial wealth and political power along the southern coast. King Ali bin al-Hasan of Kilwa begins to mint coins. Trading city of Kisimani on Mafia Island is as important as Kilwa, and may be the seat of King Ali bin al-Hasan.	Continued expansion of gold and ivory trade with the East Coast, and mainly with the (Mozambique) trading city of Sofala.	Ghana collapses under Almoravid and other attacks. Rise of Mali after about 1230. Mali becomes an even larger trading empire than Ghana had been, and flourishes for about 150 years.	In India, new Muslim states.
Groups of villages begin forming themselves into	Ancestors of Chewa are established in village groups in Malawi.		China ruled by Yuan (Mongol) Dynasty (1260–1363).

	EAST AFRICA	CENTRAL AFRICA	ELSEWHERE IN AFRICA	OUTSIDE AFRICA
	small states in southern Uganda and regions to the south.			
1331	Moroccan traveller Ibn Battuta visits Mogadishu, Mombasa and Kilwa. Latter ruled by King Hasan bin-Suleiman II City now has several fine stone buildings, including the great palace of Husuni.	Development of early chieftainships in Malawi, ancestral to Undi and others. Tonga spread across southern Zambia.	Christian Ethiopians survive many wars against Muslims and pagans. They begin to build foundations of later Ethiopian Empire. Egypt ruled by Mamluk sultans (1250–1517). In West Africa, empire of Mali at height of its power.	Decline and fall of Sultanate of Delhi in period 1340–1526. Indian states of Deccan, under Bahmanid rulers, at height of their power. China ruled by Ming Dynasty (1368–1644).
1400	Much of southern Uganda ruled by Chwezi Dynasty, with new methods of central government.	Development of strong chieftainship among the Karanga of south-western country south of Zambezi. Soon the Karanga will build an empire.	In West Africa, rise of empire of Songhay, and of new city-states in Hausaland (northern Nigeria) and in Yorubaland and Benin (southern Ni-	Hundred Years' War between England and France (1337–1453).

spreading through western Tanzania.

Coastal states flourish. Older cities become richer. Newer cities, such as Gedi, acquire fine stone buildings.

1415 Malindi sends a giraffe to the emperor of China. Two Chinese fleets visit Banadir and Kenya coast (1417–21).

1425 Troubled period begins in government of Kilwa: conflicts between rulers and senior governors (amirs).

Approximate date of foundation of early empire of Mwanamutapa under Mutota, who dies in about 1450 and is succeeded by Matope.

Greatest expansion of early empire of Mwana-

Portuguese begin sailing down the Atlantic coast of Africa. In 1483 they make contact with the (Angolan) kingdom of the Kongo people (Bakongo).

Askia Muhammad becomes powerful emperor

In England, Henry Tudor puts an end to the Wars

	EAST AFRICA	CENTRAL AFRICA	ELSEWHERE IN AFRICA	OUTSIDE AFRICA
		mutapa. Matope dies c. 1480. Some years later, c. 1490, the Karanga (Rozwi) chief Changa of Guniuswa (Butua) breaks away from overlordship of Mwanamutapa, and begins forming new state (Urozwi).	of Songhay in West Africa (1493).	of the Roses (1485), and founds the Tudor line of rulers.
1498	Vasco da Gama arrives with 3 ships, sails from Malindi to India, and returns in 1499 to Portugal. Beginning of Portuguese presence on East Coast.	Great Zimbabwe becomes capital of the Karanga kingdom of Urozwi, ruled by kings (mambos) who take the dynastic title of Changamire.	Expansion of Songhay under Askia Muhammad. Growth of trading cities of Timbuktu and Jenne. Expansion of new gold trade between these cities and central region of modern Ghana (Asante).	First voyage of Columbus (1492).
	From southern Sudan, Luo migrations in progress. New rulers in southern Uganda. Rise of Bunyoro-Kitara. Kintu			Period of early progress in mechanical invention in Europe, which now takes over from China and the Arabs the leadership in these fields of

firmly established in central Kenya.

		Spanish conquests in Caribbean and Central America. Beginning of Trans-Atlantic slave trade.	
1505	Portuguese sack Kilwa and Mombasa. They extend their domination along the coast, but concentrate their trade at Kilwa, Mombasa and Malindi.	Malawi peoples form a strong confederation under separate chieftainships of Undi, Karonga, Mwase and others. These will be strong enough to keep the Portuguese at arm's length.	
		Ottoman Turks conquer Egypt (1517) and move rapidly westward to Tunisia and Algeria.	
1520	Chronicle of Kilwa written in Arabic (approximate date).	Rise of Luba states (in region of Katanga) after about 1500. Soon followed by extension of government of Luba forms of government to Lunda peoples of central Congo grasslands.	Mahmud Kati of Timbuktu begins writing his famous history, the *Tarikh al-Fattash* (1519).
			Copernicus of Poland discovers the planetary system, and describes it in a revolutionary book (1543).

	EAST AFRICA	CENTRAL AFRICA	ELSEWHERE IN AFRICA	OUTSIDE AFRICA
1585	Swahili towns revolt against Portuguese overlordship in alliance with Turkish adventurer Ali Bey.	Portuguese move inland up the Zambezi, and penetrate the (later) empire of Mwanamutapa in northern part of country. They found settlements on the Middle Zambezi at Sena and Tete, and use these increasingly as bases from which to interfere in affairs of Mwanamutapa.	Moroccans invade and ruin empire of Songhay (1591).	Spanish Armada, 1588.
	'Zimba' wreck Kilwa (1587).		Kanem-Bornu at height of its power under Mai (king) Idris Alooma.	Dutch, English and French compete with Portuguese and Spanish for overseas loot, trade, and conquest.
			Bitter wars by Portuguese against Angolan kingdom of Ndongo. Gradual ruin of this kingdom.	Continued expansion of early scientific and mechanical knowledge in Europe.
1593	Portuguese have regained control. They begin building Fort Jesus at Mombasa.			
1607	Dutch attack Portuguese on Mozambique Island.		Continued fighting between Moroccan invaders and soldiers of Songhay.	

defeat army of Mwana-
mutapa (1628–9). They
put their own nominee on
the throne. Beginning of
ruin of (later) empire of
Mwanamutapa. From this
time the Portuguese inter-
fere more and more, and
with increasingly disas-
trous consequences.

1631 Mombasa, under Yusuf
bin Hasan, rebels against
Portuguese control.

Kamba now trading regu-
larly with Mombasa.

Further spread of *ntemi*
kingships in eastern and
north-eastern Tanzania.

Bunyoro at height of its
power.

Rise of Buganda.

English civil wars.

	EAST AFRICA	CENTRAL AFRICA	ELSEWHERE IN AFRICA	OUTSIDE AFRICA
1652	First Omani expedition against Portuguese along Swahili coast.	Many new states in Congo grasslands. Incoming ancestors of Lozi and Bemba enter Zambia at about this time. Angolan kingdoms of Kongo and Ndongo are thoroughly ruined by Portuguese invasions and the Atlantic slave trade.	Dutch found small settlement at Cape of Good Hope (1652). Rise of Bambara on middle Niger, and of Yoruba of Oyo in south-western Nigeria.	Omani Arabs recapture Muscat from Portuguese (1650) and begin to build a new empire based on strength at sea in the Indian Ocean. British fight Dutch for supremacy at sea (1653–74).
1684	Portuguese gradually lose all their positions on the coasts of Kenya and Tanzania, but remain along the coast of Mozambique.	Mambo Changamire Dombo of Urozwi acts against Portuguese in his domains. In 1693 he evicts them altogether from Urozwi. They are never able to return. His capital at Great Zimbabwe is by now an imposing stone structure, such as it may be seen today.	Rise of new states in West Africa, including Akwamu (after 1650), Asante (after 1690) and Dahomey (after 1700).	Huge expansion of sugar and tobacco growing on Caribbean islands, and in mainland of Americas, by colonists of European stock. This calls for great increase in slave labor; and Atlantic slave trade enters its main period. In 1713 Britain becomes the biggest buyer of Africans for enslavement. Great

1696	Omani besiege Mombasa and take it from Portuguese after two years. The Omani commander is a Mazrui, the first of his family to appear on the coast.	Deepening chaos in empire of the (later) Mwanamutapa, mainly because of Portuguese interference and aggression.			profits are made, which help to make possible the British Industrial Revolution.
1728	Earliest known writing of Swahili: the *Utendi wa Tambuka*.		Asante is now a powerful state.		
1750	Coastal cities partially recover from Portuguese ravages of 17th century, but the Indian Ocean trade remains much smaller than in earlier times.	Bemba and Lozi have established themselves firmly in Zambia.	Muslim revival movement in Western Sudan. Rise of new Muslim states.	Boer (Afrikaner) farmers gradually penetrate northwards from Cape of Good Hope.	In Britain, Kay invents the mechanical weaving shuttle (1733); Pearl invents the mechanical spinning roller (1728); Hargreaves invents the 'spinning jenny' by which one worker could operate many spindles at the same time (1768); Watt invents the mechanical pump (1776). In 1803 Trevithick builds the first
1763	Kabaka Kyabuga comes to power in Buganda, opens trade with East Coast, dies in 1780.	Western Angola now reduced by the Portuguese to little more than a reservoir of slaves for Bra-	Yoruba empire of Oyo at height of its power.		

	EAST AFRICA	CENTRAL AFRICA	ELSEWHERE IN AFRICA	OUTSIDE AFRICA
	Rise of overseas slave trade along the coast in this period. Growth of slave-worked plantations in French islands of Mauritius and Bourbon.	zil. But Portuguese unable to penetrate the inland country of Angola, because of African opposition.		steam locomotive to run on iron rails. American Revolution.
1776	French make contact with Kilwa for purposes of overseas slave trade.			
1784	New conflicts between Swahili cities and the Omani.		Foundation of Freetown (Sierra Leone) in 1791.	French Revolution. Sayyid Said of Oman signs treaty of trade and friendship with the British East India Company, by which he makes them his ally (1798).
1804	Sayyid Said becomes	Gradual expansion of	Sierra Leone becomes a	Britain ends her own

ruler of Oman and embarks on new policy of expansion along East African Coast. Makes his main base on Zanzibar, where clove-planting is introduced in 1818.	ivory trade with inland countries. Little by little, this now begins to give way to the slave and fire-arm trades as well.	British colony (1807).	slave trade (1807) and begins trying to persuade other European powers to end theirs. This does not fully happen for more than 70 years.
Supremacy of Nyamwezi as inland traders in central Tanzania.			End of First French Empire. Battle of Waterloo (1815).
1818		Shaka of the Zulu defeats the Ndwandwe. Beginning of the Wars of Wandering (1818).	
1820 Britain now the greatest naval power. Increasing British interest in East African Coast, partly stimulated by drive to end the slave trade.	Expansion of Bemba power under Chitimukulu and other chieftainships. These form a confederacy but do not yet unite into a single government under one ruler.	Ottoman viceroy of Egypt, Muhamad Ali, sends army to invade the Sudan (1820). Beginning of Egyptian southward penetration.	British continue to build a large empire in India.
		Foundation of Liberia (1821).	

	EAST AFRICA	CENTRAL AFRICA	ELSEWHERE IN AFRICA	OUTSIDE AFRICA
1831		Kololo under Sebituane conquer Lozi and settle in Bulozi (1831), defending it successfully against attacks by the Ngoni Ndebele (Matabele) in 1837 and after.	Many more Boer farmers settle in interior of South Africa. Foundations of Orange Free State, Transvaal, and Natal.	
			Foundation of Basutoland by Mosheshwe (after 1825).	
1840	Chaga strong under Horombo. Buganda at height of its power under Kabaka Suna (1856). Karagwe strong under King Ndagara (1832–55).	Strongest states in Congo grasslands are those of Mwata Yamvo in Kasai river region, and Kazembe in Katanga. Kazembe trades with East Coast through Nyamwezi and Swahili merchants. Early Ngoni states in Malawi.	Ndebele (Matabele) established in country of Urozwi and exercising overlordship over neighbors, who suffer much from this. Former Urozwi state totally destroyed.	Revolutions of 1848. In England Chartist Movement fails to win a democratic parliament but lays the basis for the trade union and Labour movement.

1856	Mutesa follows Suna as Kabaka (king) of Buganda. First contacts with British explorers. Majid succeeds Said as ruler of Zanzibar (dies in 1870).	Growth of Yao power in Malawi and southern Tanzania.	Portuguese continue large-scale export of captives from Angola and Mozambique to Brazil.	Crimean War (1853–6). Indian Mutiny (1857–8).
1865	Bunyoro makes comeback under Mukamas (kings) Kamurasi (died 1869) and Kabarega. These ally themselves with agents of Egypt while Kabaka Mutesa prepares to do the same with those of Britain. Rindi rules the Chaga (1860s).	Confusion sown by slave trade, and by increasing use of guns in raids and warfare, continues to spread through western Tanzania, and up the lower Zambezi, into Central African lands. New Ngoni states in Malawi.	Rise of European imperialist ambitions in Africa. At first hesitant and limited to a few coastal areas, the 'scramble for Africa', develops mainly as a rivalry between Britain and France, the two strongest European powers at that time. This rivalry draws in other European powers, including Germany, Italy, King Leopold of Belgium, Spain and Portugal. Eventually they decide to share out Africa amongst themselves.	Western Europe now far ahead of all other parts of the world in science, machinery, and military power.

1876   Mirambo of Unyamwezi,
        in western Tanzania, is at
        height of his power.

1884–5 Congress of Berlin on the European partition of Af-
        rica. British and German action against East Africa
        soon afterwards. British movement into Central Africa
        leads to a renewal of effort by the Portuguese to assert
        their 'rights' in Mozambique. Beginning of the colo-
        nial period.

        Armed penetration of Eu-
        ropeans into every region
        of the continent.

BRIEF GUIDE TO
FURTHER READING

The following is an introductory list of books and papers, all of them relatively easy to obtain, which bear on the history of central and eastern Africa. Most of them have long and specialised bibliographies.

ORIGINS

J. D. Clark, *The Prehistory of Southern Africa*, 1959.

G. Clarke, *The Stone Age Hunters*, 1967.

S. Cole, *The Prehistory of East Africa*, 1954.

B. M. Fagan (ed.), *A Short History of Zambia*, 1961 (early chs.). *Southern Africa during the Iron Age*, 1965 (early chs.).

M. Posnansky, (ed.), *Prelude to East African History*, 1966.

Tarikh (Journal of Nigerian History Society), series of articles in no. 3 of 1966: *Man in Africa from the Earliest Beginnings to the Coming of Metal*.

UP TO AD 1500

EAST AFRICA

N. Chittick, "The 'Shirazi' Colonisation of East Africa," *Journal of African History* 3 of 1965.
"Kilwa: A Preliminary Report," *Azania*, 1966.

B. Davidson, *The Lost Cities of Africa*, (repr.) 1965, chs. 5–7.

J. Gray, *History of Zanzibar*, 1962, early chs.

B. A. Ogot, *History of the Southern Luo*, 1967, early chs.

R. A. Oliver and G. Mathew, *History of East Africa*, 1963, vol. 1: relevant chapters.

R. C. Soper, "Kwale: an Early Iron Age Site in South-Eastern Kenya," *Azania*, 1967.

J. E. G. Sutton, "The Archaeology and Early Peoples of the

Highlands of Kenya and Northern Tanzania," *Azania,*
1966.

CENTRAL/SOUTHERN AFRICA

B. M. Fagan, 1961 and 1965, middle chs.

L. Fouché, *Mapungubwe,* 1937.

R. A. Oliver, "The Problem of the Bantu Expansion," *Journal
of African History* 3 of 1966.

M. Posnansky, "Bantu Genesis—Archaeological Reflexions,"
Journal of African History 1 of 1968.

AD 1500–1870

EAST AFRICA

E. Alpers, "A Revised Chronology of the Sultans of Kilwa etc,"
Azania, 1967.

R. Coupland, *East Africa and Its Invaders,* (repr.) 1956, later
chs.

B. Davidson, *Black Mother: The African Slave Trade,* 1961,
ch. 5 and elsewhere.

G. S. P. Freeman-Grenville, *The East African Coast: Select
Documents,* 1962.

J. Gray, *History of Zanzibar,* later chs.

L. Harries, *Swahili Poetry,* 1962.

K. Oberg, "The Kingdom in Ankole," in *African Political Systems,* ed. by M. Fortes and E. E. Evans-Pritchard (repr.),
1958.

B. A. Ogot, *op. cit.,* later chs.

R. A. Oliver and G. Mathew, *op. cit.,* later chs.

CENTRAL/SOUTHERN AFRICA

D. Birmingham, *Trade and Conflict in Angola, 1483–1790,*
1966.

J. Duffy, *Portuguese Africa,* 1959, relevant chs.

Fagan, 1965, later chs.

C. W. de Kiewiet, *A History of South Africa* (repr.), 1950,
chs. 1–3.

J. D. Omer-Cooper, *The Zulu Aftermath,* 1966.

T. O. Ranger, *Revolt in Southern Rhodesia 1896–97,* 1967.

E. Stokes and R. Brown (ed.), *The Zambesian Past: Studies in Central African History.*

J. Vansina, *Kingdoms of the Savanna,* 1966.

Finally, as further reading for chapters 21 and 22, here are a few cultural studies which, with their detailed bibliographies, will take the reader into the complex but rewarding field of cultural history:

W. Allan, *The African Husbandman,* 1967.

P. Bohannan, *African Outline,* 1964.

B. Davidson, *The African Genius: An Introduction to African Cultural History,* 1969.

M. Fortes and E. E. Evans-Pritchard (ed.), *African Political Systems,* (repr.) 1958.

D. Forde (ed.), *African Worlds: Studies in Ideas and Social Values,* 1954.

M. Fortes and G. Dieterlen (ed.), *African Systems of Thought,* 1965.

T. O. Elias, *The Nature of African Customary Law,* 1956.

J. Middleton and D. Tait (ed.), *Tribes Without Rulers: Studies in African Segmentary Systems,* 1958.

INDEX